# A READING
# OF PROUST

WALLACE FOWLIE is Professor of French at the University of Colorado and Foreign Editor of *Poetry* magazine. He received the A.B., A.M., and Ph.D. degrees from Harvard University and has taught at Bennington College. His books of criticism include *Rimbaud, A Guide to Contemporary French Literature, Dionysus in Paris: A Guide to Contemporary French Theatre, Paul Claudel,* and *Mallarmé.* Among his many translations are: *Cocteau Journals,* Saint-John Perse's *Seamarks,* Claudel's *Two Dramas,* and, most recently, François Mauriac's *What I Believe.* Professor Fowlie's critical studies have appeared in *Kenyon Review, Partisan Review, Modern Philology, The New Republic, Commonweal, Sewanee Review, Poetry* and in French language periodicals in the United States and France.

·

# A READING
# OF PROUST

·

**WALLACE FOWLIE**

·

GLOUCESTER, MASS.

PETER SMITH

1969

·

The Anchor Books edition
is the first publication of
A READING OF PROUST

·

Anchor Books edition: 1964

·

to Ben Belitt

# Preface

For this study, which is limited to Proust's novel, *A la recherche du temps perdu*, I have used the Pléiade edition in three volumes, and included, when it seemed advisable, my own translation of the passages quoted. In keeping with the text, I have used the French titles in small letters: duc, duchesse, prince, princesse, oncle, tante, baron, baronne; and, to simplify matters, I have used several French words which by now have entered the English language: matinée, milieu, salon, coterie, soirée, concierge, chez, bourgeoisie.

The richness of Proust's novel is discouraging for a commentator, and this present study is an effort to understand the structure of the novel and the meaning of the seven parts in their chronological order as established by the novelist. The number of monographs on Proust that have appeared since his death in 1922 and especially during the past fifteen years is a testimonial to the place he occupies in our consciousness. It would be impossible to acknowledge all that I owe previous commentators. Their names and works appear in the bibliography.

Mr. Eugene Eoyang, the Doubleday editor, has played so great a part in the preparation of this manuscript, that I wish to record here my gratitude for his patience and help.

For the writing of this book, I have received aid from the following foundations:

The Newberry Library, Chicago
The John Simon Guggenheim Foundation
The Yaddo Corporation, Saratoga
La Napoule Art Foundation, France

W.F.

# Contents

## III.   Conclusion

# A READING
# OF PROUST

# I. INTRODUCTION

# 1. Proust and the French novel

The history of the French novel stretches back over seven centuries to the mediaeval fables and romances where enchanted forests were inhabited by unicorns and monsters. Yet despite this long evolution, the French still speak of the novel as the youngest of all literary forms, the genre most susceptible to progress and change. And the French novel has, throughout its history, ceaselessly transformed itself, modeling its transformations on the ever-changing structure of society. The expansiveness, the encyclopaedic details, and even the coarseness of Rabelais' *Gargantua* parallel the resurgence of vitality and inquiry of the Renaissance humanists. The close psychological analysis in *La Princesse de Clèves* by Mme de La Fayette reflects the preoccupations of the moralists and dramatists of the age of Louis XIV. The eighteenth was not a great century for the novel in France, but Abbé Prévost's study of *Manon Lescaut* is a significant document on the society of the Regency, and Voltaire's so-called philosophical novels helped to alter public opinion and institute the social changes he advocated. In the nineteenth and twentieth centuries the novel has dominated all other literary forms in France.

In the twentieth century the novel came to be defined, particularly with the example of Proust's work, as the expression of an agreement between man and himself, and between man and the world. But within the novel this agreement is constantly challenged by existence. If we were to define the novel as the search for what is real, granted that such a search may take on many different

forms, we would be in agreement with Proust. Whether
Cervantes or Balzac, the novelist seeks to place man faithfully in the context of life, at the same time that he attempts to show him moving beyond the illusions of life.
Within this double human reality, the particularized universe of the hero and the transformed picture of his universe, the novelist constructs his work. The customary daily
object—a goblet in the story of Tristan, a bride's bouquet
in *Madame Bovary*, a madeleine cake in *Du Côté de chez
Swann*,—is so transcribed and utilized as to become miraculous.

Two worlds, then, are fused in the art of the novelist:
a real world always to some degree familiar to us and recognizable—Dickens' London, Kafka's Prague, Proust's Paris
—and an unreal or possible world, strange to us, but which
attracts us and which, in the case of Proust, grows so forcibly that it ends by dominating our own world. A great
novel is the realm of grace in which there is no unimportant detail, where chance is abolished because it is always
turned into something meaningful, where the characters
understand all the parts of their world and where the novelist succeeds in establishing man's consent to the things
of his world, whether they prolong his happiness or his
misery. Most of the seemingly insignificant events of our
real life remain insignificant and disappear from our memory. The novelist, if he is Proust, resurrects the insignificant, conjures them up with their full setting, and discovers
for them their real meaning.

Today the French do not seem to believe in a purely
French tradition or in a disciplined school of the novel, but
they do believe that the fate of the novel is one of constant
assimilation and metamorphosis. It represents the same destiny as that of French painting, namely of being a creation
in which a particular harmony or fusion takes place between an individual and his world, between the heart and
the mind, between tradition and innovation. This law is as
true of *La Princesse de Clèves* in the seventeenth century,
as of *Le Bal du Comte d'Orgel* in the twentieth, as true
of *Manon Lescaut* as of *A la recherche du temps perdu*.

In French literature particularly, the writer's permanent problem has always been how to transform what he feels into what he wants felt. The mediocre writer in France is often defined as one unaware of his public and of both its limitations and profundities. Many French novelists give utterance to the experience of passion, to the suffering and cries of passion, but they have always believed in the need to submit the experience to the organizing power, to the domain of language. The human experience related by a Laclos or a Stendhal or a Colette is illuminated and controlled by intelligence to an extraordinary degree. This does not mean necessarily strictness of form and composition, which is something else and which has at times been neglected by French novelists.

The intelligence with which a French artist considers his universe or his subject matter is part of his creativeness and his inspiration. It lends both a sense of economy and a sense of monotony to his work. It forces him back again and again to his own subject, as to his one obsession: the cult of energy in Stendhal, the necessary and heroic asceticism of the artist in Proust. This constancy of theme in a French novel reflects the constancy of the writer's soul, his dedicated will. It explains to some extent the permanent shibboleth of all of French art—its classicism, whether it be the classicism of Racine, or the classicism of the Romantics, or that of André Gide. The term "classicism" implies a sacrifice of human time and pleasure, as well as of all the extraneous elements in the work of art. It also implies the worship and practice of intelligence, and the belief that art is at the basis of civilization and of a given code of human behavior. The concept of classicism does not exclude a degree of stubbornness in the French artist, a will to return doggedly to the same problem, the same situation, the same work. A highly developed belief in the efficacy of human creativity lies behind a Gothic cathedral and the *Comédie Humaine* of Honoré de Balzac.

What is looked upon today as a specifically contemporary problem or crisis in the novel has in some form or other always existed in France, a land not so much of nov-

elists as of theorists and critics, orators, and moralists. It
is something of a miracle that the French genius, basically
anti-poetic and anti-fictional, has, in the nineteenth and
twentieth centuries, expressed itself in creative realms and
taken an eminent, if not primary, place, with its trinity of
poets: Baudelaire, Rimbaud, and Mallarmé, and its trinity
of novelists: Balzac, Stendhal, and Proust. These six poets
and novelists never relinquished their right, during their
literary careers, to criticize their own art and to expound
its theory. They were creative artists and aestheticians at
the same time. Often, in fact, they married theory to art.
Some of Mallarmé's poems are about the writing of poetry
and the significance of symbols. One of the principal
themes in Proust's novels is the story of a writer's vocation.

Most critics agree that there is no more totally subjective
novel than Proust's. His claim that the subject matter of the
novelist is his own vision of the world allowed him to con-
cur with the belief, so often expressed, that the novel is the
freest and most adaptable of all literary forms. Everything
depends upon the whim or the taste of the individual novelist; he may introduce what he wishes: a scene of frivolity,
a passage of technical information, an episode of satire, or
a page of lyricism. Many styles and degrees of characterization exist in novels which are looked upon as successful.
Rabelais' *Pantagruel*, Stendhal's *La Chartreuse de Parme*
and Cocteau's *Les Enfants terribles* are all classified as novels, but what do they have in common? In other forms, in
tragedy, for example, the art of Shakespeare and the art of
Racine differ widely in many ways, but such works as *Mac-
beth* and *Britannicus* demonstrate a fundamentally similar
art in that they both affect their audiences in a theatre
emotionally and intellectually by their representation of an
action. It would be difficult to find a similar arbitrary re-
quirement in *Candide, Les Liaisons dangereuses* and Sartre's *La Nausée*. We might, if we insist upon trying to discover a common denominator for such different works,
return to Proust's formula and state that a novel is that
literary form which most fully reveals the temperament of

the artist. Not always directly, it is true; but, by implication and by indirection, at times.

The paradox of all creation is dramatically clear in the case of the novel. There is the reality the novelist proposes: a provincial town called Combray (*Du Côté de chez Swann*), a "pension de famille" in Paris (*Le Père Goriot*), a seminary in Paris (*Manon Lescaut*). But there is also the novelist who, no matter how rigorous his intentions may be, as soon as he puts pen to paper, will intervene in his own plan. A novel can never be a simple reproduction of reality. It is always, to some degree, an interpretation of some instance of reality. Emma Bovary may be modeled after one woman, or she may be a synthesis of two or three women who really existed, but she is also, according to the novelist's famous confession, Flaubert himself. Likewise, Julien Sorel is both the criminal Berthet and the writer Henri Beyle. Critics have tried to explain Charles Swann by his possible models, Charles Haas and Charles Ephrussi, but they have had to conclude that he is also Marcel Proust.

At the time of Emile Zola, at the end of the nineteenth century, the writer's notebook was looked upon as indispensable for his craft. In it he copied down exactly what he heard and observed. It was the "case history," the "human document" that served as the basis for his novel. It would be false to say that the novelists of the twentieth century observe less than the realists. But they are not so naïve as to create their work from the recordings of their notebooks. They claim that the faculty of imagination is the principal instrument of their writing. A literary work is not a copy of life, but the development and the deepening of an original intuition. The permanent law of all art is the necessity of choosing. Even novelists as elaborate as Proust and Dostoievsky and Henry James impose the principle of a rigorous choice on their subject matter. Whatever details they elect to incorporate must have significance. Often details that would appear insignificant in the routine of daily life, are admitted in the art of the novelist because they enhance the impression of truth and the integrity of the

novel. The observations of realist art lack the order and the
symmetry that only the combined powers of the artist's
imagination and intelligence can create. Each novelist has
a source of information coming from outside himself, and
another source coming from his temperament, his sensibility, and from the endless decisions he himself has to make
concerning the inclusions and the omissions of each detail
in his work.

The examples of the major novelists of the twentieth
century have given credence to the theory that a novel is
a creation, and to some degree or other manifests a relationship between the mode of existence of the novelist and
the lives of the characters created by him. If a novel is
looked upon as a creation (and this seems justified in its
most successful realizations: *Wuthering Heights, Les Faux-
Monnayeurs, The Brothers Karamazov*), it will inevitably
call to mind the analogy with the Creation of the world.
Theology teaches that the world was created by an act of
love. This would lead us to the thought that the creatures
of a novelist have been given life by him because of some
connection with them, because of some degree of love he
feels for them, even the monsters of his creation. Those
writers who have created the largest number of characters:
Dante, Shakespeare, Molière, Balzac, and Proust, have
castigated and even damned some of their characters:
Dante's Farinata, Shakespeare's Iago, Proust's Charlus, are
reproved for their evil, but there is little or no trace of
scorn or mockery on the part of their creators. As the most
willfully wicked man maintains some vestige of his relationship with God, so the most deliberately fictional character maintains something of his creator, and hence of his
divine origin. Between Balzac and the criminal Vautrin,
between Mauriac and the monstrous mothers in his books,
there is a secret but all-powerful and vitalizing connivance.
The key to the problem of the novel throughout its long
history, to its permanence, its crises, its survival today in the
*nouveau roman,* as well as in the continuing art of a Julien
Green, is probably in this fundamental, though often hidden, love of the creator for his creature.

One of the haughtiest indictments against the art of the novel came, in the twentieth century, from the pen of Paul Valéry, who claimed that he could never submit to the basic condition of a story and write such a sentence as: *La marquise sortit à cinq heures pour aller prendre le thé.* (Claude Mauriac, one of the "new" novelists in France, gave answer to Valéry by entitling a recent novel: *La marquise sortit à cinq heures.*) The fundamental condition of story-telling does seem to be the capacity to create a situation, to describe a scene at a given moment in time under a specific kind of lighting. We often remember a novel in terms of a scene or scenes which struck us: Meursault, in Camus' *L'Etranger*, intoxicated with sunlight and killing an Arab on the flaming beach; young Marcel watching a performance of *Phèdre* when the theatre takes on for him the appearance of an aquarium. Valéry forgot that such a sentence as he invented to express his scorn for the genre of the novel might, with the skill of a novelist, take on exceptional importance and move the reader of a novel as much as a single line of a poem might move the reader of a poem. In a well-written novel there is no such thing as a flat or useless sentence. Stendhal has often been pointed out as the supreme example of the courage of writing with absolute simplicity.

The French novelist tends to restrict himself to a well-defined, limited setting, to a few carefully delineated characters, to an application of intelligence rather than inspiration. Balzac and Proust seem today, in our perspective of the entire history of the French novel, the two novelists responsible for the greatest innovation in form, and both of them, despite the familiar tags of "realism," attached to Balzac, and "psychologism," attached to Proust, assume the proportions of visionaries—of novelists whose particular view of reality places them in the category of spiritual prophets. Proust's search for truth lies in the reality he discovers behind the appearance of such objects as the church spires of Martinville, the trees of Hudimesnil, and the paintings of Vermeer. Balzac and Proust helped to make the novel into much more than a story—into an instrument

to communicate a vision and wisdom. Some of the most
memorable scenes in French novels are meditations on
French civilization. They are comparable to historical moments of hope and despair: Julien Sorel watching the
circling of a hawk in the sky and comparing his own destiny to the achievement of Napoleon; the first meeting
between Des Grieux and Manon; the games of the girls on
the beach at Balbec.

The name of Balzac evokes a gigantic and powerful
image. In the space of twenty years (1829–48), he was
able to create a literary work of unusual proportions which,
as it developed, fell into the loosely organized scheme of
*La Comédie Humaine*. The ambition of this enterprise—to
present the picture of an entire generation of French society—was almost equalled by Balzac's powers of observation and his prodigious capacity for work. He announced
one hundred and thirty-seven subjects. He completed
ninety-one novels and novellas before his death in 1850.
The history of the European novel can be studied as that
literary form with certain characteristics before Balzac and
which evolved differently after him. Since 1850, there has
been only one novelist who achieved anything comparable
to the structure and intensity of his work: Marcel Proust.

Balzac defined his vocation as that of writing the drama
of three to four thousand characters presented by a given
society. His method of observation and documentation has
been the subject of controversy. Some scholars look upon
him as the research man, the reader of files and notebooks.
Others view him as the diviner and prophet, the intuitive
visionary who had little need of factual documentation.
Between the theory that everything in Balzac was observed and the theory that he reached every fact intuitively,
there are various compromise theories. In an early letter to
Mme Hanska, Balzac writes that memory registers clearly
only what is sorrow. (*La mémoire n'enregistre bien que ce
qui est douleur.*) He was fully conscious that he was un-
dermining his health and sacrificing much of his life in
order to construct his work. To bring to life such characters
as Rastignac, Vautrin, and Valérie Marneffe, Balzac re-

duced many moral and spiritual values in his own life. He failed to acknowledge his own children. He was not a very good son to his mother and father. He was an unscrupulous debtor, a snob, a spurious nobleman. His own life created for him many moral dramas which often gave him the feeling that he was losing his mind. There were few signs of natural goodness and charity in his human relationships. And yet as a novelist, in keeping with one of the profound mysteries of literary creation, he was able to animate characters totally unlike himself. In grace, subtlety, and nobility, Balzac was often surpassed by his own characters. He never ceased meditating on this paradox, on the bewildering contradictions in a human life. He once wrote that no one would ever know the really important events in his life. (*Jamais rien de ce qui m'arrive ne sera connu.*)

The fate of the master creators, of artists such as Balzac, Shakespeare, Dante, Proust, is to provoke an infinite number of studies, monographs, and theses which attempt to explain their work, or some part of their work. The fundamental mystery in Balzac is still intact. The personal alchemy out of which his work came is unknown. He is as inaccessible as Shakespeare.

There are scattered indications throughout his writings and correspondence that Balzac believed the life of the imagination (that is, the life of the creative artist) to be far more destructive than, for example, a life of human passion. To reach the heights of creativity in each night's work was equivalent to some degree of self-destruction: a literary triumph has to be paid for in human life.

The Balzac creation is of such magnetism that it draws even the unsuspecting reader into its center. This phenomenal power is related to the attraction of Balzac's vitality, and his feverish intensity for life. For Balzac's craving to know all and to express all is, finally, the creative principle on which his work rests. When the thought first came to him, in the summer of 1833, that he could fuse all the parts of his work into one system, he became as exalted as Pascal or Descartes or Rousseau when each saw the vision of his life work. He never compared himself to other writers, but rather to Napoleon who had dreamed of uniting all of Europe, and to Cuvier who, in founding comparative anatomy and palaeontology, thought in terms of the globe. Balzac claimed that he bore a whole society within his brain.

After he had used the device of letting characters reappear in novels, and after he had divided his novels in groups, he began to fit his early books into the general plan. Some of his critics have called this system an afterthought, based upon a false unity. Marcel Proust, the most Balzacian of all novelists since Balzac, has argued that precisely because the system of unity was originally a subconscious thought, it has all the more vitality.

Fifty years ago the general critical view of Balzac was different from that held today. The leading factor in this change of attitude was the publication and success of Proust's *A la recherche du temps perdu*, which brought about a revised judgment of the novel as a literary genre. The critic Albert Thibaudet, in 1936, judged Balzac in the light of Proust. Whereas Flaubert's conception of the novel has diminished in prestige and importance during the past quarter of a century, the affinities of Proust's art with Balzac's have turned readers back to *La Comédie Humaine* and to a new evaluation in their assessment of the French novel.

*A la recherche du temps perdu* stands today as one of the most elaborately conceived of all novels and the one that explores most profoundly the conventions of the form. It is a solid reconstruction of a real world: Paris during the first years of the century, a small provincial town in the Ile-de-France, called Combray, and a Norman beach resort, called Balbec. It describes every class of French society, especially the aristocracy and the rich bourgeoisie who undergo very significant changes during the course of the novel. But the book is also the story of a novelist's career, or rather a study of an artist's mission. In one of the opening scenes of the novel, where we see the protagonist as a young boy suffering for fear his mother will not come into his room to say good night to him, we are watching the earliest drama in Proust's literary career, the one in which his will triumphs over the will of his parents. From that evening, when his small frail figure, standing at the head of the stairs, so touches his father that he sends his wife in to comfort him, he dates the decline of his health, a decline which will end by making him into the recluse who uses his days and his solitude to write a long novel. The sickly, highly sensitive child grows up and passes through every phase of development in a life exceptionally privileged in family affection, in wealth, in social connections, in friendships, in literary and artistic relationships. The miracle is that Marcel Proust did not remain simply the historian of the idle rich, an aesthete and disciple of Ruskin, a contributor to *Le Figaro*. His true vocation was latent and disguised during his early years.

The revelation that came to Proust slowly as he wrote his early articles and stories, and became clear to him as he wrote his early novel, *Jean Santeuil,* was the belief that so-called "realistic" art gave only the outlines of existence, the surface of things. True reality, which the true artist must uncover, resides in the objects and within the characters "realistically" described. Objects are signs whose meaning may be discovered by the artist. The artist's perception of the material world and human experience is far different from the perceptions of the ordinary man. For Proust, the artist is one who constantly asks himself, "What is our true life?" From time to time life brings us by chance a kind of happiness which is a memory of the past. Our conscious intelligence envelops our daily life with so many clichés, with so many mechanical responses that for the most part we are completely oblivious to our own real life. Under these clichés and behind these usual responses, real life goes on, and that life Proust took upon himself to explore and illuminate.

Within the space of a mere quarter of a century, Proust has come to represent a new classicism in the history of French letters. He is a classic writer at least in the sense that he is an established writer, one whose name has become synonymous with a certain style and with a certain phi-

losophy concerning the nature of reality. A work of such
dimensions, accompanied by such success in establishing
for itself a place in a long tradition of letters, must inevitably come from the tradition it epitomizes. More and more
the work of Proust is looked upon as the supreme inventory
of romanticism and symbolism. It recaptures, in its extreme
introspectiveness, in its meditations on nature, and in its
analyses of the artistic creations of man, the experiences,
both conscious and subconscious, that we associate with
the romantic and the symbolist movements.

Before the time of Proust, the novel of psychological
analysis had occupied a place of primary significance in
France. But Proust explored much farther than his prede-
cessors the secret meaning of actions man carries out
mechanically. Proust's almost clinical psychology is, however, at all times related to the long tradition of French
moralistic writers: Montaigne, La Rochefoucauld, Mme de
Sévigné, Saint-Simon. This moral-psychological aspect of
Proust's novel, which perhaps comes first to mind when his
name is mentioned today, would not be sufficient to explain his eminence. The other aspect of his writing, always
present but infinitely more difficult to define, is the poetry
he discovers at every moment in life, in the humblest
flowers of nature, in the commonest expression of a mediocre character, in the way a monocle is worn, in the face of a
young girl at a railroad station who holds up to the traveler
a bowl of *café-au-lait*, in the sculptured angels in a bas-
relief of the small village church of Saint-André-des-
Champs.

The major recent French attacks against the novel as a
literary form: by Valéry (who speaks of its uselessness),
by André Breton (who emphasizes the boredom of its inevitable plots), and by Roger Caillois (who points out the
social harm which the novel creates in imposing a triteness
of style and sentiment), are offset by the major achievements of the novel: in the work of Dostoievsky, Kafka,
Proust, Joyce. Each of these novelists has deepened the
use and function of the novel, and explored the conception
of reality. The flexibility of the genre, the absence of fixed

rules, the dangerous freedom of the novelist, have stimulated in France, as well as in other countries, debates and
controversies on the very concept of the novel. The novel
seems to be in a constant state of flux. Perhaps for its very
survival it has to move in one direction or another, toward
the story or the symbol, toward the essay, the sociological
debate, the dialogue, or the poem.

The theory has been circulated—it is discussed in certain
scenes of Gide's *Les Faux-Monnayeurs*—that to make daily
life the subject matter of a novel is to admit defeat, is a
sign of the artist's degradation. Proust's achievement was
to assign to the imagination the initial burden of the work.
*A la recherche du temps perdu* fuses the two indispensable
elements in a work of fiction: the exterior world and society
borrowed by the novelist, and the novelist's own world.
The artist does not rival the universe, he is a universe unto
himself. Like a force of nature, he confers life on what does
not have life, on what has ceased to live.

Proust belongs to that lineage of artists who bear within
themselves an entire world: Dante, Shakespeare, Balzac,
Joyce. Their work has a *largesse,* a prodigality, a part of
their nature which is inscribed on their pages as forcefully
as the nature of their characters. Each one of these artists
is invisibly present in his work. Every detail in the work
designates something about the artist, but nothing reveals
him in an absolute sense. Flaubert's doctrine of the artist's
impersonality is an illusion. In the major instances of the
novel, a fictional world risks the reader's boredom and dis-
satisfaction. It is a world shaped and formed to satisfy the
reader's desires.

The creation of the novelist, according to one of Marcel
Proust's most cherished beliefs, is more "real" than life.
To some degree, this belief is always held by the creative
artist. Balzac used to say: "Let us come back to reality and
speak of Eugénie Grandet." Proust did not create a new
form, but he extended and deepened the form of *La Comédie Humaine*. During the 1950s, the "new" novelists, Alain
Robbe-Grillet, Michel Butor, Nathalie Sarraute, deliberately turned away from the traditional form with its psy-

chological, political, and sociological preoccupations, and
used the novel as an inventory of objects. Yet their for-
malistic changes and even their conception of man do not
seem today, in the 1960s, as revolutionary as they claimed.
The art of Michel Butor and Samuel Beckett presupposes
the method of Joyce, and to some degree, the method of
Proust.

What joins so many different kinds of writers is their will
to make of the novel a climate, so common and so recognizable that a host of readers can breathe and live in it. It
is quite possible to look upon the novel as a formless monster, as a literary genre that has no barriers, no rules. But
it does have to represent, to some degree or other, a meeting place between the novelist and the reader, a conjunction of artist and spectator with the commonplaces of life.
The novelist is fated to draw upon the common experiences
of his reader, and the reader, as he loses himself in the
fictional world of the novelist, feels his own world diminish
in intensity and meaning. The novelist creates by stealing
from the world common to all men, and the reader enters
into the experience of the novel to the detriment of his own
life.

The psychological emphasis in *La Princesse de Clèves*
(1678) did affect and modify to an extraordinary degree
the fate of the novel in France. This fact is recorded in all
the manuals on French literature. The psychological richness of *A la recherche du temps perdu* in the twentieth century represents both a proliferation of this fictional mode
and its culmination. The endless secret world of the subconscious has been added to the consciousness of the characters. But the survival of the novel is not due solely to the
psychological introspection in Proust or the stream of consciousness (*le monologue intérieur*) as used by Joyce.
Especially in the case of Marcel Proust, his major contribu-
tions to the history of this literary form are in the realm of
poetic and moral meaning.

The novel is not only an art form: in such exemplary
cases as that of Proust, it becomes a spiritual exercise, a
form which may be read on more than one level, an esoteric

art reserved for initiates or specialists, and in this sense, the novelist Marcel Proust is also the uncoverer of secrets. In terms of society, love, politics, morality, he is disillusioned, almost totally pessimistic, but he is, nevertheless, a joyous celebrant in his invention of a literary means of depicting the mortality of man's actions and hopes, a style which triumphs over this mortality.

## 2. Marcel Proust the man

The house in which Marcel Proust was born no longer exists. The address: 96, rue La Fontaine in Auteuil, a house owned by his great-uncle, Louis Weil. A large garden, containing a few linden trees, surrounded the property. His mother, Jeanne Weil, came from a Jewish family of Metz in Lorraine. Throughout his life Proust was to remain in close contact with his mother's family and often visited the graves of his Jewish ancestors in the cemetery on the rue du Repos.

His father, Dr. Adrien Proust, who would ultimately become a professor, came from a Catholic family long established in Illiers, a small town near Chartres in the region called la Beauce. Since the seventeenth century this family of merchants and farmers had maintained close ties with the Church. Proust's grandfather was a maker of wax candles and tapers in Illiers. His daughter married Jules Amiot, an important business man in Illiers. She became Proust's *tante Amiot* (who would become *tante Léonie* in the novel). Her house on the rue du Saint-Esprit, with its front door opening on to the street, and the back door on to a small garden is today a museum, administered by the very learned and helpful M. Larcher, secretary-general of the "Société des Amis de Marcel Proust." There, one can visit the kitchen of Françoise and the dining room, mount the famous stairway at the top of which the young boy waited for his mother, enter the bedroom of Marcel, and that of tante Léonie, and walk in the garden where the family, in the novel, used to listen for the ringing of the bell which announced Swann's arrival.

Adrien Proust was the first of his family to leave la Beauce. His father had hoped he would become a priest, but his vocation was medicine, and he became a well-known physician, a director of a clinic and a hygienist honored and respected by his country. In 1870, he met and married Jeanne Weil. Their first child was born on July 10, 1871, just after the momentous days of the Commune, the siege of Paris, and the disasters of Sedan and Metz. At baptism the child was given the names: Valentin, Louis, Georges, Eugène, and Marcel. It was feared at first he would not live. As he grew up he was precociously intelligent and sensitive, but his health remained, and was to remain, precarious. At the age of nine, on returning from a walk in the Bois de Boulogne, he was overcome with an attack of asthma so violent that his father feared he might suffocate. Asthma was destined to play an all-important role in his life, to impose many limitations on his activity and at the same time to permit him, in accord with a strange compensatory law, to deepen his sensibility, to withdraw from the world, and to compose in his long seclusion the major novel of his age.

Marcel Proust was so obviously the product of two very different families and backgrounds and races that it is a temptation to explain his genius by his rich varied heredity. Such a theory is difficult and perhaps impossible to substantiate. The Beauceron background of his father and his paternal ancestors seems to have bequeathed him the gift of builder and architect, the skill of the type of artist able to work within a vast structure, as elaborate and complex as the cathedral of Chartres. From his mother and the age-long tradition of Israel, Proust seems to have inherited a certain kind of sensibility, a keen awareness of everything around him, a tendency to hyperbole and exaggeration, a lyric quality in his writing which often suggests a lament, a sorrowing estrangement from reality, a threnody which has at times a prophetic, even apocalyptic, tone.

Marcel was baptized in the Catholic faith and made his

first communion at the age of twelve. He affirmed at various moments throughout his life that he was a Catholic, although he practiced no religion and was unconcerned with
religious problems. His love for churches and cathedrals
was something else. He informed himself on churches, on
the beauty and details of steeples, towers, stained glass
windows, rose windows, porches, and statues, with the
same fervor that he contemplated and studied flowers
(hawthorns, roses, buttercups, water lilies) and the intricate manners of society, of human behavior, of vices and
virtues.

Unlike some, Proust himself placed credence in the belief that the family determines a writer's vocation. According to him, the immediate influences count as well as the
distant, atavistic forces of ancestry. Proust's belief was
neither the strict determinism of Taine, nor the sentimental
attachment to the chosen myths of Barrès (the land, the
dead, etc.). But he believed that a work of art is not the
creation of a single artist. A man writes from the accumulation of memories that reach far back in time, far beyond
his own life. And when he writes, he is not free in facing
the work to be written. An artist expresses not only himself, but hundreds of ancestors, the dead who find their
spokesman in him.

The garden of Combray in the novel was two gardens
in Proust's background: the small garden of Illiers which
belonged to his uncle Amiot, and the larger garden in
Auteuil belonging to the Weils, who had come from Alsace-
Lorraine at the beginning of the nineteenth century and
settled in Paris. Behind the Combray garden were two
kinds of ancestors: the Prousts of Illiers and Jules Amiot
who owned a large store on the Place du Marché, and the
Weils of Paris, including Proust's grandfather Nathée Weil
who lived in Paris eighty-five years without leaving the
city for even one day.

Dr. Adrien Proust and his younger son Robert, who was
to follow the same profession and become a surgeon in
Paris, were similar in temperament, serious in the accomplishments of their work and duties, scientifically minded,

devoted to that kind of routine and work which made their lives useful and respected. There were strong affinities between Marcel and his mother. Emotional and sensitive, each resembled, even when Marcel was young, the type of human being he was to call *les grands nerveux*, the race of highly sensitive beings, glorious and pitiful at the same time, who have accomplished much in the service of mankind, who have founded the religions of the world, and composed the masterpieces of art.

Despite bad health, Marcel regularly attended classes at the lycée Condorcet where he was appreciated by his teachers and well liked by his schoolmates. During his first two years at Condorcet, Mallarmé was a teacher of English there, but Marcel was only thirteen years old when Mallarmé left the lycée, in July 1884, and it is unlikely that he had begun the study of English.

He did his military service in 1889, in Orléans, where he met Gaston de Caillavet and Robert de Billy, and then took courses at the Sorbonne and at the Ecole des Sciences politiques, where he knew Léon Blum. He was temperamentally unsuited to diplomatic service, toward which his father had urged him, and by instinct he moved in the direction of literature. He wrote for *Le Banquet* and *La Revue Blanche*. The friendships he formed with Robert de Flers, Lucien Daudet, Jacques Bizet, and later with Robert de Montesquiou, Emmanuel and Antoine Bibesco, and Reynaldo Hahn opened up for him the Paris art circles and the most sought after salons of the day. He frequented the salons of Madeleine Lemaire (who illustrated his first book, *Les Plaisirs et les Jours*), of princesse Mathilde, and, especially, of Mme Straus (mother of his friend Jacques Bizet) and Mme de Caillavet, where he met Anatole France and Charles Maurras.

He became a favorite in the highest, most brilliant social circles of Paris. But he questioned, more and more seriously as time went on, this dissipation of energy and time, the vanity of social life, and the value of easy successes. He was unquestionably fascinated by the mannerisms and the dramas of society, but he realized—and probably earlier than most of his biographers claim—the disillusionments of that kind of existence, the waste it represents for the artist. Great books are not created out of social activities and conversations, but out of solitude and silence. Proust's illness grew more serious as his convictions about a writer's mode of life became clearer to him. The crucial period in his life was the gradual development of a resolution to live only for the work that was in him and that only he could write. As a member of the social groups in Paris, he wanted to be loved and esteemed and sought after, but he knew that the greatest kind of glory for him would come when, his work achieved, he would be able to unite the lives of countless readers and bring them a remedy for their boredom or despair.

The genesis of Proust's art is nostalgia for childhood, for the happiness of certain moments when, for example, he played with children in the Champs-Elysées, particularly with Marie de Bénardaky, whom he loved when he was twelve, and who later became princesse Radziwill, some of whose traits are unquestionably in Gilberte. The general atmosphere of upper bourgeois culture in Marcel's family marked him and instilled in him the passion for reading. His mother and grandmother (as in the novel) were readers of the classics, of Racine and Mme de Sévigné, and Marcel, under their guidance, developed a strong attachment to such works as George Sand's *François le Champi* (destined to figure prominently in the novel), *The Arabian Nights*, George Eliot's *The Mill on the Floss*, and Dickens' *David Copperfield*. Like most artists, Proust remained a prisoner of his childhood. His lucidity is that of a child sorrowfully conscious of the world.

When the boy became a novelist, many of the names of places changed. Méréglise turned into Méséglise, Illiers into Combray, Beg-Meil into Balbec. But the change of names was minor, compared to the mythological endowment he gave to the gardens of his childhood, to the park of oncle Amiot (Swann's Tansonville), to the water lilies of the Loir, to the church of Illiers. These elements of his childhood became more real to him as the years passed, and as he recreated them.

Marcel Proust was always apart from others, and yet he was also an admirable friend, devoted and attentive. It was easy to interpret these qualities as obsequiousness. As a young man, and even later when he had proved the seriousness of his vocation, he was called a dilettante, a *fumiste*, a flatterer, a fop. His kindness and generosity were so tenacious as to be, on occasion, irritating. His mannerisms and his gifts, the clothes he wore, his endless curiosity about social events and social distinctions caused many to characterize him by his snobbism. Their judgment seemed to be confirmed by his friendship with Count Robert de Montesquiou-Fezensac, a model for the character Des Esseintes in Huysmans' novel *A rebours*, himself the author of *Les Hortensias bleus*, who was often ranked as the leading dandy of the day, and who was enraged to recognize some of his own traits in M. de Charlus.

It was Proust's privilege to know Paris society at all levels of its prestige and power. He was attracted to this experience, not by snobbism (he was fully aware of the perils of worldliness, of the vacuity and the fundamental tediousness of social intercourse), but as the observer of a world which he was to transmute. It was a new age, or rather the end of an old age, parts of which had been painted by the artists: the Opéra scenes of Degas, the Folies-Bergères scenes of Manet, the water lilies and the cathedrals of Monet. After his experiences with this Paris society, Proust was to make the largest fresco and the most complete documentation that exists.

The most exclusive salons he frequented were those of the comtesse Greffulhe and the comtesse de Chevigné, models, to some extent, for the princesse and the duchesse de Guermantes. Princesse Mathilde, niece of Napoleon III, appears in the novel under her own name. She had received in her salon on the rue de Berri, long before Proust's day, such writers as Sainte-Beuve and Musset, Flaubert and Renan, Jules and Edmond de Goncourt, and Mérimée. In the salon of Madeleine Lemaire, the water-colorist (who

created, it is said, the largest number of roses after God),
Proust met the theatre world: Coquelin, Réjane (who appears in the novel under her own name), Mounet-Sully;
the composers Saint-Saëns, Massenet, and Reynaldo Hahn;
and the painters Puvis de Chavannes and Forain.

Because of his friendship with her son Jacques Bizet,
Proust was a frequent visitor at the home of Mme Straus.
This salon, one of the most interesting in the upper bourgeois echelon, is used in several ways in *A la recherche du
temps perdu*. Mme Straus was Geneviève Halévy, daughter of the composer of *La Juive*, widow of Georges Bizet,
and, with her beauty and wit, one of the models for Oriane
de Guermantes. It is claimed that an incident in which
Mme Straus figured was the original for the famous episode in the novel of the "red slippers of the duchesse."

Though Proust had great propensities for friendship, he
was not an easy friend. Demanding and jealous, he inspired affection and loyalty in a large number of friends
who were vastly different in temperament and social class.
Hyperbolic in his expression, obsequious according to several observers, he seemed worldly to a perilous degree and
avid to know every stratum of society, every social type.
Despite all the privileges that were his, despite the many
friendships from which he derived satisfaction and happiness, despite his freedom from economic worry, Proust was
a solitary figure, anguished over his health and the gradually increasing threat of death, tormented by his ambition
to be a writer and unsure for many years of exactly what
work would best represent him and his talents.

The publication of Proust's first book *Les Plaisirs et les
Jours*, in 1896, did not alter existing opinion of his character and his talent. These stories and sketches, lavishly
presented in a costly book, with a preface by Anatole
France, illustrations by Madeleine Lemaire, and even musical texts by Reynaldo Hahn, seemed to the first readers the
product of an overprecious temperament, an example of
the *fin de siècle* decadence. "Too coquettish and too
pretty," said Léon Blum. André Gide was one of the first
to point out that almost all the themes of the novel are

here in the early work, and this judgment holds today. In such an episode as "Confession d'une jeune fille," the theme of the mother, and the sense of sin, guilt, and profanation are present.

It is highly probable that during the next three years, 1896–99, Proust wrote most of the work first published in 1952 under the title *Jean Santeuil*. This first sketch of the novel comprises more than one thousand pages which were discovered by Bernard de Fallois in a hat box among the papers that Dr. Robert Proust found at the death of his brother in November 1922 and gave to his daughter, Mme Gérard Mante. In 1962, Mme Mante-Proust sold to the Bibliothèque Nationale the unpublished *carnets* and *cahiers* as well as the manuscripts and corrected proofs of her uncle. Precisely during those years when Proust was being accused by friends and family of wasting his time, of indolence and social preoccupations, he was writing *Jean Santeuil*. In the light of what has been discovered in recent years, Proust was not, during the five or six years which preceded his father's death in 1903, the amateur, the dilettante, and the spoiled child. Rather he was the writer in search of the laws of the universe and the principles and the themes of his art.

Proust discovered the writings of John Ruskin in 1899, and during the next five years he devoted much of his time to the study of Ruskin, a translation of two books, *The Bible of Amiens* (*La Bible d'Amiens*, 1904) and *Sesame and Lilies* (*Sésame et les Lys*, 1905). This work was far more than a discipline in literary effort and precision and scholarship. It was the discovery of a study of aesthetic beliefs which confirmed ideas and principles he had already reached. In the labor of translation, he was helped by his mother and especially by a friend, Marie Nordlinger, a cousin of Reynaldo Hahn. The prefaces and notes in his two translations form an important part of Proust's aesthetics. The study of Ruskin partially revealed to Proust the meaning of mediaeval religious art and the beauty of French churches and cathedrals: Bayeux, Beauvais, Chartres, Bourges, Coutances, Rouen, Saint-Lô.

In his personal life, Proust was deeply affected by the death of his father and of his mother two years later in 1905. At the age of thirty-four, he became an "orphan" and, more rigorously than heretofore, consigned to a life of solitude which was to deepen tragically with the continuing and increasing symptoms of asthmatic disorders until his death in 1922. His life changed quite radically after the death of his mother. The bereavement and the new form of solitude bewildered Proust, although he had by this time accepted the idea that solitude is necessary for the writer. He believed that a clarity of vision could be reached only under circumstances of solitude; that ideas —goddesses of an intransigent nature—would appear only to the man who had cut himself off from the normal attachments of existence.

The year following his mother's death, Proust moved to 102, boulevard Haussmann and occupied an apartment there until June 1919. Free now of any parental advice, he arranged the apartment as he wished and created the room that is the real unity of place for *A la recherche du temps perdu*. He had the walls lined with cork, the door covered with heavy tapestry, and the windows closed so that no noise and no odors from the street below would reach him. The room where he wrote and slept was a kind of catacomb where constant fumigations made the air almost impossible to breathe for friends who called, usually late at night, in accordance with Proust's wishes.

This cork-lined room is as famous now in the history of French literature as residences of other self-imposed exiles in solitude: Montaigne's tower room where the *Essais* were written, Vigny's castle in Le Maine-Giraud which Sainte-Beuve dubbed "the ivory tower," Hugo's island posts on Jersey and Guernsey, Flaubert's retreat at Le Croisset.

The maximum span of time for the writing of Proust's novel would be seventeen years: from the death of his mother in 1905 to his own death in 1922. The first six

years in the apartment on boulevard Haussmann (1906–
12) were devoted to the plan and draft of the work and
the writing of *Du Côté de chez Swann*. From the publication of this first part, in 1913, to 1922, he ceaselessly ex-
panded and amplified the novel; corrected proof; corresponded with publishers and critics: and until the end of
his life, carried on the careful defense and justification of
his work as well as the verification and alteration of details
in the already written work.

In June 1919, he moved briefly to an apartment at 8 bis,
rue Laurent-Pichat, and in October to his final address,
44, rue Hamelin, where he occupied an apartment on the
sixth floor (*cinquième étage*). It was there, in a room not
cork-lined, that he died on November 18, 1922. In 1913,
Céleste Albaret became his housekeeper and remained
with him for the last ten years of his life. Céleste was a
tall handsome woman, whose husband, Odilon Albaret, a
taxi driver in Paris, kept his cab always ready for Proust's
use.

With Céleste, and her sister Marie Gineste (both of
whom appear in the novel under their own names) Albaret
formed a kind of family for the recluse. Céleste in particular was devoted to Proust and served him faithfully.
She adapted her days and nights to his strange regimen,
and gradually, as the years went by, ruled his life in a
mildly dictatorial way, protecting him from intruders and
keeping visitors waiting if necessary. She accepted his ex-
travagances and demands in the knowledge that he was a
great man. Her long cohabitation with him and her sympathetic understanding marked Céleste in many ways, in
manners of speech, in habits of observation, in a spirit of
tolerance. Proust treated her as a confidante. He dictated
passages of the novel to her, he transposed some of her
traits to the character Françoise, he used her as an intermediary between himself and the outside world.

During the past ten or fifteen years, in the small hotel
she owned, on the rue des Canettes, Céleste Albaret has
spoken to many admirers of Proust and conveyed to them,
in whatever detail she has judged appropriate, the man-

ners and traits and the anecdotes of her master. She has
now left the hotel, but her testimonials and, one can almost
say, her interpretations have been recorded and form important material in any study of the life of Marcel Proust.

The article on Sainte-Beuve, begun in 1908, and which
grew into a three-hundred-page book, *Contre Sainte-Beuve*,
published in 1954, is one of the original sketches for *A la
recherche du temps perdu*. To the critical reflections on
the method of Sainte-Beuve, Proust added personal memories, portraits of friends, and impressions of various au-
thors and books. These chapters were part of the early
draft of the long work. When *Du Côté de chez Swann*
was ready for publication, Proust encountered many difficulties with publishers. One by one, they declined: *La
Nouvelle Revue Française* (Gide was a reader and gave
an unfavorable report which he was later to call his most
serious literary blunder), *Le Mercure de France*, Ollen-
dorff. Finally Grasset agreed to publish it when Proust
consented to pay the cost of publication. The work appeared on November 8, 1913. *La Nouvelle Revue Française* reconsidered and published the second part of the
novel, *A l'ombre des jeunes filles en fleurs*, in November
1918. The following year the book was awarded, thanks in
part to the enthusiasm of Léon Daudet, the Prix Goncourt.
Thereafter the publication proceeded regularly: *Le Côté de
Guermantes* in 1920, *Sodome et Gomorrhe* in 1921 and
1922, *La Prisonnière* in 1923, *Albertine disparue* (now
called *La Fugitive*) in 1925, and *Le Temps retrouvé* in
1927. The Pléiade edition in three volumes (1955) is a
carefully corrected edition, based upon proofs and manuscripts corrected by Proust before his death.

At the time of the Goncourt Prize and the publication
of *A l'ombre des jeunes filles en fleurs*, Proust was an almost
legendary figure. The countless anecdotes about his way
of life and his behavior partially distorted the truth about
the man, but this was the moment when serious readers
especially in France and England began discussing his
novel, long before the secret plan of the work could be
fully understood, long before the final scene of *Le Temps*

*retrouvé* was published. For fifteen years, between the ages of thirty-six and fifty-one, Proust struggled to complete his novel. He fought against the usual demands of daily living, against physical and moral suffering, against the many disillusionments that tormented his last years and that are reflected in the writing. He was deeply upset by the war and the heavy loss of lives his country suffered.

Most readers preferred the novels of Anatole France, of Paul Bourget and Maurice Barrès. Younger writers were attracted to Proust and deeply intrigued by him. Some of them were among his last visitors: Cocteau, Léon-Paul Fargue, Mauriac, Ramon Fernandez, for example, all of whom have described Proust in his final cloistered life as resembling a night bird, a strange being hovering between life and death. His closest friends, men like Lucien Daudet and Reynaldo Hahn, found him more embittered, more difficult in his human relations. Proust himself acknowledged this to be true. He had changed considerably since the earlier years when he was described by the princesse Bibesco as a young Persian prince, or when Jacques-Emile Blanche painted his portrait as a youthful dandy.

Work on his novel dominated the last days of Proust's life, overshadowing his unrelenting illness, his social ties, even the profound moral anxiety of his personal life. The motivations behind Proust's novel are to be found in a proper understanding of his life and temperament. Henri Massis suggests the thesis that the novel is Proust's disguised confession, prompted by a personal moral crisis. But there are as many good reasons to support a purely aesthetic explanation.

Proust unquestionably felt guilt on many counts: for immorality, and for lesser reasons: dissipation of energies, waste of time, worldliness. But in his case worldliness is so closely allied with his writing that one cannot be considered without the other. He followed an order which is clearly visible in the career of many writers (all of whom bear resemblances with Proust): Montaigne, Saint-Simon and even Pascal, who dissipated their energies in worldliness, then concentrated their energies in their work.

Much more has been written about Proust's sexual inversion than the known facts warrant. The degree to which it affected his moral and spiritual life, in terms of remorse and shame, can never be ascertained. The theme of inversion in the novel is of major importance, but the narrator is not a pervert. A famous passage in Gide's *Journal* on the problem of what Gide considered Proust's hypocrisy and dissembling has influenced critics and scholars to alter the novel and make it fit what is known and surmised about Proust's personal life. The novel does not support this, particularly in its depiction of Albertine and of Charlus as a study in moral degradation. Homosexuality is never condoned in *A la recherche du temps perdu;* it is always treated tragically and with a sense of the Biblical injunction.

That Proust was strongly attached to the young man Agostinelli is part of his biography which cannot be denied. In the summer of 1907, in Normandy, Proust employed Agostinelli as a chauffeur. Later, in Paris, in 1912, he named him his secretary. The intimacy of their relationship was not unknown to Agostinelli's wife. In May 1914, Agostinelli was killed in a plane accident near Antibes. As a student pilot, he was using the name of Marcel Swann! Proust himself acknowledged that the passage in his novel which describes Marcel's admiration of three church spires on a drive through the countryside was in fact the description of an incident when Agostinelli drove him by the steeples of Caen.

During the last years of Proust's life, when he had less need to conceal his sexual proclivities, he employed as a confidant and procurer a man destined to serve as the leading model for the character Jupien. Albert Le Cuziat, born in Tréguier, in Brittany, in 1881, came to Paris as a young man where he served as a valet in the homes of several noble families: prince Radziwill, prince d'Esslering, comtesse Greffulhe, duc de Rohan. His admiration for titled nobility and his discretion made him a valued servant, and, in time, more than a servant, a confidant, an adviser. He became an authority on social protocol and etiquette, and

Proust, when he met him, realized the extensive knowledge this young man had of the ways of society and of the secret stories of moral turpitude in the higher classes. Proust consulted and befriended Albert, as he was called. His name suggested "Albertine" to Proust, although Albert himself never claimed to be one of Proust's lovers. He later became rich, and purchased the small Hôtel Marigny on the rue de l'Arcade in Paris. In 1917, the hotel was investigated by the police and condemned as being, in part, a house of male prostitution. Certain scenes in *Sodome et Gomorrhe* and *Le Temps retrouvé* are doubtless modeled on Albert's Hôtel Marigny and other establishments which he was to own: hotels, baths, a *bal musette* on the rue de Lappe. At his death, in the late thirties, Albert had in his possession a large number of letters from Proust which now seem to have disappeared. His death was announced in an issue of *La Nouvelle Revue Française* where the account, in deliberately veiled terms, spoke of "the death of a man whose name had been given to one of the most famous heroines of French literature."

During the last two years of his life, Proust left his apartment on the rue Hamelin only on rare occasions, and usually on an errand which would serve in the writing of the book. Fifteen months before his death, he visited the Jeu de Paume in order to see an exhibition of Dutch paintings and especially the *Vue de Delft* of Vermeer. He was taken ill at the exhibit; this incident he used, in a fairly literal way, for the entire episode of Bergotte's death scene. One of the Proust legends that is impossible to substantiate describes his retouching the scene on the day before his death and quite literally using his own experience of death for the documentation in the fictional scene.

About this same time, in May 1921, the English novelist Stephen Hudson invited James Joyce to a party he was giving for Stravinsky and Diaghilev. Hudson (whose real name was Sidney Schiff), one of the early English admirers of the French novelist, had told Proust of the gathering but had hesitated to invite him because he felt that Proust would not be willing to come. But he did come to the party, quite late, and there he met Joyce. This meeting has been related in many varying ways. William Carlos Williams, in his *Autobiography*, reports that in the brief conversation between the two men, Joyce complained of headaches and trouble with his eyes, and Proust complained of his poor stomach. Both men left the party soon after arriving. This meeting of the two greatest contemporary literary figures was a disappointment to all the guests present who had counted on hearing one of the illuminating discussions of the day. Joyce himself, reporting on it later, said that their talk consisted solely of the word "no." Proust asked Joyce if he knew the duc de so-and-so, and the answer was "no." Then Joyce asked Proust if he had read such and such a passage of *Ulysses*, and he replied "no."

The last two years of his life were for Proust a race against death. He worked with the passion and the suffering of a man watching himself die. As he corrected proof, he doubled and tripled the length of some of the passages, and these additions forced him to change and amplify passages in the manuscript of the last sections of the work not in print. In the last month of his life, November 1922, when his illness became acute, he demanded promises from Céleste that she would not allow the doctors to overrule his own directions. In the final stage, she was unable to keep this promise. Proust's surgeon-brother Robert took charge with other physicians, but it was too late to administer new treatments.

On the seventeenth, he felt slightly better and even gave some dictation to Céleste. On the eighteenth, at four in the afternoon, he died peacefully. Céleste closed his eyes and prepared him for burial. In her account of Proust's last days, she claims that he wanted Abbé Mugnier to come, after his death, and recite the prayers of the dead, and that Céleste was to place in his hands the rosary which Mme Lucie Félix-Faure Goyau brought to him from Jerusalem. Proust's death mask, drawn by Dunoyer de Segonzac, shows an El Greco face of clear serenity.

At the time of his death the really fervent admirers of

Proust were few. And the most discerning among them were unable to see to what degree his work was going to change the perspectives of fiction. John Middleton Murry was soon to hail *A la recherche du temps perdu* as the most minute dissection of the modern conscience, but for approximately two decades most of the critical estimates of Proust were efforts not to disturb the standards of fiction and to point out the resemblance between Proust and other writers. He was then (as now) compared to everyone—Saint-Simon, Racine, James, Thomas De Quincey, Dickens—as if his work were simply an example of *déjà vu*.

It has taken many years for the contemporary reader to understand the many facets of Proust's genius, to acknowledge him not only as a peer of Balzac, but also as the skilled technician of introspection who completes the method of Montaigne, and, finally, as a creator of metaphor who continues the tradition of Baudelaire and Mallarmé. Proust celebrated the beauty of the Creation as few writers have been able to do, and in this regard it is not difficult to remember that he was a faithful reader of *The Imitation of Jesus Christ*. If, in a strictly theological sense, Marcel Proust was an agnostic, he demonstrated throughout his life a courage that comes from the spiritual strength of conviction. He believed that his life's accomplishment, if such a thing existed, would be the creation of his work. If Proust had lived longer, his work would have changed in a formal sense, but it would not have changed in the philosophical sense that *A la recherche du temps perdu* represents the search for the absolute within a duration of time.

## 3. The literary and social background of the novel

During the twenty years which followed the Franco-Prussian War, 1870–90, and which corresponded exactly to the first twenty years of the life of Marcel Proust, France as a nation lived through a period of comparative isolation. The invasion of 1870 and the defeat in 1871 brought an inevitable sense of shame and disillusionment for the French. Gradually, and at times painfully, a recovery was made and national prestige was regained. These goals had been more or less achieved by 1890, and the entire decade of the nineties marked a change in French spirit and energy and attitudes. A sense of youthfulness and hope began to prevail in the arts and in public life. Symbolism as a poetic school had reached the moment of self-realization. Its public was not only Parisian, it was becoming international. French socialism, with the example of Jean Jaurès, was rejuvenated and strengthened. Catholicism was entering upon an era of ardent reinvigoration that was to prepare many conversions and reconversions among intellectuals: Léon Bloy, Charles Péguy, Jacques Maritain, Ernest Psichari.

The fullest development of symbolism came in the final decade of the century when it fathered the early works of those writers destined to play the key roles in twentieth-century French literature: *Le Traité du Narcisse*, for example, of André Gide; the first poems (*Album de vers anciens*) of Paul Valéry; the first versions of *Tête d'Or* and *La Ville* of Paul Claudel; certain themes in *Les*

*Plaisirs et les Jours* of Marcel Proust which were to crystallize and deepen in *A la recherche du temps perdu*. Just
as romanticism, after its exuberant decade of 1830–40,
found its fullest expression in the writings of Nerval and
Baudelaire, symbolism, after its active period of 1880–90,
was to discover in the final works of Mallarmé (*Un coup
de dés jamais n'abolira le hasard*) and in the novel of
Proust, some of its most spectacular achievements.

Marcel Proust turned twenty in 1891, which happened
to be the year called by the historians of the symbolist
movement, "the happy year of symbolism," when it too
was twenty years old! It had by then installed itself in
Paris, with banquets, manifestoes and with its own magazine *La Plume*. It had even taken over, to some extent,
the more traditional *Mercure de France*. The Tuesday evening meetings in the home of Mallarmé (*les mardis*) had
been going on for ten years. They were famous by 1891—
internationally famous, as foreign writers and artists were
now attending the gatherings. The young French writers
—Gide, Valéry, Claudel, and Proust—were coming under
the influence of Mallarmé in his apartment on the rue de
Rome. All four were in their early twenties and heard
some of Mallarmé's last conversations, and his arguments
for the superiority of the Book (*Le Livre*) over other
forms of art. His argument is summed up in the now famous sentence which appears in his collected essays
*Divagations* (in the article *Le Livre*): "Everything in the
world exists in order to end in a book" (. . . *tout au monde
existe pour aboutir à un livre*).

Proust was sensitive to Mallarmé's example of devoting
thirty years of his life to the writing of a small number of
poems. He was never to forget Mallarmé's lessons—expressed in quasi-mystical language—concerning the Book,
its power to suggest the very structure and to provide an
Orphic explanation of the world. The Book was, for Sté-
phane Mallarmé, and would become for Proust, the fruit
of a ceaseless struggle, of the slow conquering of chance
by the word (. . . *le hasard vaincu par le mot*). The
Book ends by becoming, in the language of the poet, an

instrument of the spirit (*instrument spirituel*) in which the smallest detail has some meaning.

During these years, the realists among the French writers—Flaubert, Maupassant, the Goncourts, Zola—were turning toward what they called "life," toward the exterior world and the observable patterns of human behavior. The symbolists, guided by Baudelaire's example and his compelling theories, turned toward the inner life of man, toward what they called "inner reality." In major controversy over the subject matter of art, Marcel Proust, together with the young French philosopher Henri Bergson whose early teaching and publications immediately preceded the major writings of Proust, justified and clarified the symbolist attitude.

During his last years at the lycée Condorcet, 1888–89, *l'année de philosophie,* Proust and most of his classmates had been profoundly stimulated by Professor Darlu and in particular by his discussions on the reality of the exterior world. Many of his ideas on the unreality of the world as perceived by the senses, on memory, and on time appeared more than twenty years later transformed within the pages of the novel. But it is the philosophy of Bergson that represents the metaphysical point of view closest to the philosophy of Proust's work.

In their personal relations there was little agreement between the two men. Proust never acknowledged any direct influence of Bergson on his writing, and Bergson seems to have ascribed little or no importance to *A la recherche du temps perdu.* Yet, by his marriage to Mlle Neuburger in 1891 Bergson became one of Marcel Proust's cousins.

What, in France, is referred to as "bergsonisme" and looked upon as a major revolt against a purely scientific explanation of the world is explored in the two books Bergson published during Proust's early manhood: *Les Données immédiates de la conscience* of 1889 and *Matière et mémoire* of 1896. In acknowledging and restoring the place of spirituality in human nature, Bergson allied himself with symbolism, although he looked upon the symbol itself as an object that conceals the deeper part of the self from man's consciousness. Bergson is suspicious of the tricks and ruses of language, of the inevitable and frustrating obstacles language creates in the very act of articulating the "data of consciousness."

But when Bergson writes of *intuition*, of the sources of knowledge residing in the deepest part of the self, of the immediate communication between things and man that may be brought about by intuition, he places himself in, or near, the center of the great tradition of idealism (in the Vedanta, in Plato, and modern romanticism) and announces a conviction of metaphysical truth easily decipherable in *A la recherche du temps perdu*. Bergson's distinction between man's two egos, the social ego (*le moi social*) with its discursive knowledge, formed by the multiple demands of daily living, and the real ego (*le moi profond*) which is intuitive and continuous, residing below the social self, will be brilliantly illustrated in Proustian psychology.

From Mallarmé (or the school of symbolism) and from Bergson (or the philosophy of memory and intuition), Marcel Proust inherited—it is impossible to use any more precise word—the use of the metaphor as a more reliable transcription of reality than direct expression, and introspection as the surest means of bridging the gap between commonplace reality and authentic reality, of reaching a form of ecstasy.

It is quite true that in one of his early essays, "Contre l'obscurité" in *La Revue Blanche*, July 15, 1896, Proust seemed to attack the art of the symbolists, or rather the symbolist mode of expression. However, the novel itself contradicts these oppositions or reticences on the part of Proust the man, by the multiple examples of metaphor and analogy and by the five or six examples of involuntary memory as described by Proust the artist. Proust subscribes to the Mallarméan principle that the "truth" of an object is not in itself, but in its higher or analogical and anagogical meaning. And he subscribes to the Bergsonian principle that the "truth" of an object, its power to stimulate a sensation and evoke a memory of the same sensation,

resides not in the object but in man himself. A purely philosophical interpretation of ·Proust could justifiably claim
that by exercising his creativity, he sought to uncover his
soul and to liberate it from the constraints of time and
existence. Many of the leading passages of the novel are
analyses of the impenetrability of the soul, of the difficulty
of knowing the soul. The writer, the artist, is he who tries
to plumb the soul, to illuminate dark reaches of the soul.
These very terms are, in some way, mystical, but Proust
does not hesitate to use them, especially at the end of the
novel when the exploration of the soul coincides with the
act of writing, the act of artistic creation.

In Proust's novel, there are a few direct references to
Mallarmé and quotations from two sonnets. There are
many more references to Baudelaire and many more direct
uses of his poems. The question of literary influences is
fundamentally insoluble in the case of such a writer as
Proust, because his art, drawing upon multiple sources,
transformed them by a very personal style and by a sensibility which altered and deepened every theme and every
detail. There is little doubt that Proust looked upon Vigny
and Baudelaire as the two greatest poets of the nineteenth
century. He seems to have admired in particular the six
*Pièces Condamnées* ("Lesbos," "Femmes Damnées," etc.)
and yet the specific poems referred to or quoted in *A la
recherche du temps perdu* are not the Sapphic pieces but
such poems as "L'Imprévu," "Chant d'automne," "L'Alba-
tros," "Le Balcon," "La Chevelure," "Parfum exotique."

M. Galand, in his succinct article (see Bibliography) on
this problem of influences, wisely stresses not the borrowing
of aesthetic views and theories but the striking affinities of
temperament and character between Proust and Baudelaire. Both writers came from the same kind of family in
the wealthy bourgeoisie. Paris, in its multifold cultural
aspects, was important both in their personal lives and in
their work. Maternal love counted excessively for both,
not only in childhood, but throughout most of their lives.
Critics have tended to overstress, especially in the case of
Baudelaire, the sexual component in the writers' love for

their mothers. Intensity of feeling is too easily branded as abnormality.

Beyond these resemblances, which have their relative importance, it is dangerous to speak with conviction. It is futile, for example, to equate Baudelaire's love for Jeanne Duval with Proust's preoccupation with inversion; futile also to equate the significance of syphilis in Baudelaire's life story with asthma in Proust's. In fact, the similarities between the two men are somewhat offset and weakened by the great difference between them in their religious experience. The religious anguish, of both guilt and acedia, reflected in the life and the writings of the poet, did not plague Proust. In fact there is no trace in Proust of any religious crises.

Beyond doubt, both Baudelaire and Proust belong to that category of artists who are called *les nerveux* by Proust, and who give to the world, each time one appears, a new sense of greatness and nobility. They are endowed with deeper powers of perceptiveness than other men. They are prophets, the founders of religions, the artists who discover for the world a new meaning of existence.

Very few of the great French writers are what might be designated universal writers—universal in their appeal to other countries and cultures, universal in the significance they have for nations other than France. Baudelaire is—even more than Hugo today—the most universal French writer of the nineteenth century, and Proust is unquestionably the most widely read and admired French writer of the twentieth. Molière has a place among this very small number of widely recognized French writers, and possibly Rabelais, Voltaire, and Jean-Paul Sartre. Ronsard and Chateaubriand enjoyed during their lifetimes an exceptional degree of fame abroad, but today they resemble the more typical French writer who demands from his non-French reader a vital interest in the culture of France, and a more than casual understanding of French customs, attitudes, and art.

In this perhaps vain attempt to characterize Marcel Proust, it should be pointed out that neither Baudelaire

nor Proust founded, in any real sense, a literary movement
or school. And yet, in the work of each, all the literary
schools are present in an unusual kind of synthesis of both
poet and novelist. In the art of Baudelaire it is possible to
see psychological attitudes of romanticism, practices and
theories of parnassian and symbolist poetry, influences of
Swedenborg, Poe, Wagner, Delacroix, Constantin Guys,
Joseph de Maistre. In the art of Proust, forms that may be
designated as romantic and symbolist occur in close proximity with themes or preoccupations or artistic effects
that recall Mme de Sévigné, Saint-Saëns, Racine, La Rochefoucauld, Baudelaire, Balzac, Nerval, Meredith, Bergson,
Mallarmé. In each case, the list of influences is endless,
and in each case, the art is an achievement far beyond the
influences, superior to any combination of influences in
its originality and universality, and totally mysterious in
its ultimate uniqueness.

The phenomena of memory, so minutely analyzed by
Proust, and even the power of certain privileged moments
in the past which return unexpectedly in exceptional vivid-
ness, are also to be found in the writing of Baudelaire, as
well as in such works as *Sylvie* of Nerval and *Mémoires
d'outre-tombe* of Chateaubriand. Baudelaire transformed
his experience of evil (*mal*) into flowers (*fleurs*), and
Proust resurrected his past life (*temps perdu*) and recon-
structed it in a novel (*temps retrouvé*). Baudelaire and
Proust were both deeply and persistently conscious of the
vanity of man's ambitions, of most of his achievements and
even of his very existence, and yet their work retains and
consecrates the poetry, the magic and the beauty of certain moments of life. *Les Fleurs du mal* and *A la recherche
du temps* are two works in which a marriage takes place
between the disarmingly courageous lucidity of man's intelligence and the triumphant creativity of his imagination.
Between the parallel forces of their intelligence and their
sensibility Baudelaire and Proust created an extraordinary
harmony.

In his novel Proust relates the story of one man's life, one
man's conscience to an entire historical era. The effective

conjugation of these themes, the reinforcing support that one gives the other, is the source of Proust's originality. And here his real forerunner is Balzac. Both novelists were more than observers, they were witnesses to their eras, and Proust, by the simple fact of chronology, a witness to what the living can still call our own age.

*La Comédie Humaine* and *A la recherche* are two *summas*, in the mediaeval sense of encyclopaedic, exhaustive, gigantic. The mediaeval ambition of putting everything into one work, whether it be a Gothic cathedral or the *Summa Theologica* or *La Divina Commedia* is evident in the life work of Balzac. But where the parts of Balzac's work are only loosely connected, in Proust, the seven-part novel is constructed so that the parts are interrelated and securely intertwined.

And still more important than its size and encyclopaedic content in this mediaeval analogy is the coexistence in Proust's novel (and to a lesser degree in *La Comédie Humaine*) of an exoteric and an esoteric meaning. As in Dante's *Divine Comedy*, the sermons of Saint Bernard on the *Song of Songs*, the work of the mediaeval sculptors, there is in Proust's novel an exoteric aspect, easily comprehended, in the pure narrative, in the documentary details, in the "literal" story. But there is also, as in the mediaeval works, an esoteric aspect, a doctrine more difficult to elucidate, a secret interpretation reserved for the initiates. This is the symbolic meaning of a work, as opposed to the literal meaning. By the writer's use of words and by mythological allusions, a modern work may even go beyond the consciously intended symbolic meaning.

The decade and a half during which Proust composed *A la recherche du temps perdu* (1905–22) was a period when other writers and thinkers were concerned with the same explorations of the subconscious and with the same study of the esoteric meaning of myths and symbols: Freud and Jung, with their discoveries in the domain of psychology and religious symbolism; James Joyce in his use of free association, stream of consciousness, and semantics; and, to a lesser degree, Pirandello and D. H. Lawrence in

their psychological innovations. All of these writers agree
on the importance of the practice of introspection, the
analysis of the subconscious, and the power of inherited
symbols and inherited mythic patterns.

There are, of course, great divergences in their styles and
in the emphases, but all of them approach, by different
paths, the same subject. A very general definition of this
subject might be: a study of what is permanent in the
present state of consciousness of a living man. All of them,
but perhaps especially Proust, Joyce, and Jung, tried to
discover in what way the eternal story of man is visible in
his day-by-day life, how a life as it is being lived recapitulates all lives that have been lived.

Proust's own life would seem parochial and limited. He
went outside of France only four or five times, and each
time briefly: to Venice, to Bad Kreuznach in Germany, to
Engadine in Switzerland, and to Holland. But he succeeded in making Paris the microcosm of the world. He
celebrates in the novel principally one section of Paris, the
Faubourg Saint-Germain, and a provincial town in the
Ile-de-France, a Norman beach resort, a garrison town,
and Venice. Despite this circumscribed geography and
despite a marked emphasis on two social classes (the
upper bourgeoisie and the aristocracy), the novel is un-
accountably international and cosmopolitan. Out of a detailed analysis of French traits in two social classes and a
few portraits of servants and members of the lower classes,
Proust created a recognizable humanity with the abiding
features of goodness and wickedness. In accord with Montaigne, who believed that each man represents all of mankind and bears within himself the total picture of the
human condition, Proust, limiting himself to little more
than a decade of French history and to a very particularized world within the society of that period, composed a
work in which a moment of French civilization is painstak-
ingly portrayed, and in which most of the perennial problems of civilized man are sympathetically analyzed.

Proust's generation was that of symbolism, impressionism, and the Dreyfus Affair. All three subjects are referred

to at many points throughout the novel. There are specific references in the text to Manet, Monet, and Renoir, to Mallarmé, Rimbaud, and Francis Jammes. It was also the generation of Charles Péguy and *Les Cahiers de la Quinzaine*, but neither he nor the periodical is named in Proust's novel. He is silent on the meaning of religious experience and this serious omission in Proust's picture of French civilization is doubtless explained by the absence of this experience in Proust's own life.

The most significant social change that took place during Proust's life was the collapse of the old aristocracy when the highest caste gradually disappeared as it was infiltrated by the bourgeoisie and, to some extent, American and Jewish families. The prewar years (1900–14) were the end of the old world and the beginning of a new. This social change is one of the most dramatic themes in the novel, and one of the most assiduously pursued. The great mutations demand the entire length of the work. The character Odette, for example, we see first as "the lady in pink," a friend of the narrator's oncle Adolphe; then as Odette de Crécy in the Verdurin circle where she is wooed by Swann; then as Mme Swann; and finally in a still higher echelon of the aristocracy, as Mme de Forcheville. This metamorphosis is paralleled by that of Odette's daughter, Gilberte, who marries a Guermantes and becomes the marquise de Saint-Loup. The most overwhelming and the most unexpected of all social changes is that of Mme Verdurin herself into the princesse de Guermantes at the end of the work.

Proust is not only the chronicler of his age: he is its poet as well. In a sense, while drawing upon a very real subject, he so transforms it as to make it a fresh creation, unique, and at the same time soundly based upon historical reality. Each of his major characters is a synthesis of several persons whom Proust knew or knew of: Swann, for example, is composed of traits drawn from Charles Haas, Charles Ephrussi, Louis Weil, and Marcel Proust. In Bergotte are characteristics and features of Anatole France, Henri Bergson, Maurice Barrès, and Ernest Renan. The fictional towns in the novel (Combray, Doncières, Balbec) and the churches (the "old" church of Combray and the "Persian" church of Balbec) are created in this same way, by borrowings from many sources and deft, patient, artistic reconstruction.

Proust resembles in many ways his great ancestor in French letters, Michel de Montaigne: in his Jewish-Catholic family background, in the need to cloister himself to work, in his fascination with social gatherings, in his detailed observing of mores and manners, in his deliberate will to welcome and see everything that transpires within him and outside of him, in his fanatical, alert curiosity. Together with a similar kind of tolerance Montaigne and Proust shared a fundamental honesty and hatred for dissimulation (despite all that Gide has written on the subject of Proust's dissimulation). The subject matter of the *Essais* and of *A la recherche du temps perdu* is the writer himself: the objects of his affections and worries, his dreams and sicknesses. The ability to imitate others, encountered in social intercourse—Montaigne called it *la condition singeresse et imitative*—is strong in both men. And both had the inclination and the capacity, in the art of writing, to evince excitement over an idea and follow it, through associations, along many bypaths. Both were deeply affected by the inevitable and cruel changes brought about by the passage of time.

Montaigne, sedentary in the library of the tower on his estate outside of Bordeaux, and Proust, immobilized in his cork-lined room on the boulevard Haussmann in Paris, were writers essentially concerned with the activity of life, with the slow never-ending process of modification in human lives and human societies. It was never sufficient for them to describe the genesis of an idea. They were more interested in tracing its elaborations. They tracked ideas and beings through their progress in time, through evolutions and revolutions of time, through the gentle tide which pushes man into dreams of ambitions and death.

Students of French literature today tend to look upon Montaigne as the dominating figure of the second half of the sixteenth century. The *Essais* are a summation of their age as well as a work whose wisdom seems ageless. In a similar way, Proust's novel both represents and transcends its age because it has as its principal theme the subtle and abiding conflict in all men of all ages between appearance and reality—the most persistent theme in literary art. Proust's greatness depends not on the themes or the subject matter of his novel, but on the method by which these themes are explored, and the depth of his analyses.

The first generation of the twentieth century does not live as vibrantly, as completely in the work of Gide, Valéry, or Claudel, as it does in Proust. Together, these four writers, born approximately the same year, made of their age one of the most brilliant, if not the most brilliant, in the history of French letters. The novel enabled Proust, as the essay Montaigne, to achieve a work of art more complete, more unified, and more profoundly conceived than any single work of Gide, Valéry, or Claudel. To assign a quantitative value to works of art is futile, but in this case it seems to be related to the quality of Proust's achievement, to the "tonic" effect the work still has on readers who have come to it after his age has ended. Gide's *Journal* and *Les Faux-Monnayeurs*, Valéry's *La Jeune Parque*, Claudel's *Le Soulier de satin*, are all masterpieces of the same age, and each one unique in its form and in the understanding it brings to the spirit of man. And yet no one of these works makes the world of the artist so objective and the inner world of his sensibility so real as does Proust's novel. Already, in the years that have elapsed since the immediate initial international effect of Proust's novel, that is, since 1930, the documentary aspect of the work seems remote. It has become a classic, with that central power of a classic when it has grouped around itself cliché judgments, often rehearsed explanations, climates of opinion. The fearful static moment in the life of a work of art when its initial impact dissipates is perhaps now coming to an end for *A la recherche du temps perdu* and for *Ulysses*. Even as an historical character changes his meaning for posterity, without any change taking place in the documented facts of

his existence, so a novel changes, when there is no change
in its form—changes in terms of its meaning, its relatedness
with subsequent, newer works, in its social and historical
context.

It becomes clearer, in the proliferating monographs and
studies of Proust comparing him with other writers, that
his greatness does not depend on "originality." This word,
one of the most perilous in characterizing the work of an
artist, no longer seems to apply to *A la recherche du temps
perdu*. As a psychologist, for example, Proust has very few
original thoughts. His leading psychological concepts can
be found, for example, in Laclos' *Les Liaisons dangereuses*,
in La Bruyère's portraits, in La Rochefoucauld's aphorisms,
in the pages of Pascal where he describes the constant
change human beings undergo. Proust's principal ideas concerning art, if they are not in the writings of Ruskin, can
be found in *Curiosités esthétiques* and *L'Art romantique*
of Baudelaire. The theory itself, with illustrations, is to be
found in Chateaubriand (in the passage, for example, on
the song of the thrush in *Mémoires d'outre-tombe*), in
Nerval (the opening of *Sylvie* presages the opening of
*Du Côté de chez Swann*), and in many passages of Baudelaire.

Proust's originality (here the word may be justified)
lies in the richness, in the extraordinary elaboration of his
analyses. His is an originality of form and style. His writing
has a vast repertory of tones and moods. His sentence may
be above all expository in its detail and exhaustiveness. Or
it may be essentially descriptive where comparisons and
metaphors dominate and create a poetic effect. The Proustian metaphor was often denounced by early critics, by
Albert Feuillerat, for example, who described it as an
"artificial Gongorism." But today we tend to ascribe to the
wealth and brilliance of Proust's metaphors one of his
major accomplishments as a writer. When in the restaurant of Rivebelle, in the last part of *A l'ombre des jeunes
filles en fleurs*, the waiters, as they move swiftly from table
to table, are compared to large parrots of South America
(aras), beings who circulate with vertiginous speed and

establish, like angels, an almost supernatural harmony (I, pp. 810–11), when the tables are seen to be planets, astral tables, and the two lady cashiers hunched over their book, as magicians making astrological calculations—the entire scene of the dining room takes on a power and a clarity that are, quite simply, "Proustian."

At the beginning of the twentieth century, the word "sincerity" was used almost as a battle cry for the new literature. Léon Bloy in his *Lettres à sa fiancée* said that a new epoch had begun in which the writer was to hide nothing (*Nous touchons à une époque du monde où tout doit être dit*). The example of André Gide has been used more than any other to point out this new "sincerity," this effort on the part of the writer to reach an innocence, a frankness of confession, a state of mind that would antedate the establishment of moral laws and therefore the engendering of inhibitions. Convention was looked upon as the fecund purveyor of lies and the explanation for the several roles each man is called upon to play in society. It is true that Gide preached a mobility of spirit and attitude, a *disponibilité* which would allow man to remain youthful and uninhibited and sincere. But today Proust even more than Gide seems to be the great liberator from convention by his faithful and relentless depiction of it. More boldly than Gide, Proust raised the question of what man's real life is, and with greater fullness than Gide provided, he answered it.

## II.  THE NOVEL

## 4. Du Côté de chez Swann.
## (Swann's Way)
### A. The method of writing

The first of the seven parts of Proust's novel, *Du Côté de chez Swann,* serves as an introduction to the long work, but it is far more than that. It is itself a novel, with a beginning, a middle, and an end. It is true that these three demarcations, as they occur in *Du Côté de chez Swann,* are not typical of the usual novel. The beginning of the book, *Combray,* is the introduction to characters and the announcement of themes to be continued throughout the entire work. The themes of *Combray* will be explored with the ever-deepening sensibility of the protagonist, and the characters will evolve and change with the passing of time. The ending of *Du Côté de chez Swann,* which is given the special title: *Noms de Pays: le Nom (Place Names),* is both an end and a rebeginning, a recapitulation of *Combray,* the child's world which constantly returns in that circular movement we call memory with no absolute beginning and no absolute ending. The middle section, *Un Amour de Swann (Swann in love),* is a flashback, but so elaborate and so unified a flashback, that it is a novel in itself, a love story, the first of a series of love stories. But it is also quite literally the middle of *Du Côté de chez Swann,* because it initiates the boy of *Combray* to the world. It is Marcel's introduction to the world in a general sense, that is, to everything that is not his parents' home, as well as to the three specific worlds or experiences that form the substance of *A la recherche du temps perdu:* the world of passion, the world of society, and the world of art.

With the very first word of the novel, *Longtemps* (which
will reappear capitalized, as if it had become one of the
characters, as the very last word of the novel: *dans le
Temps*), Proust offers the key to his work. It is the phenomenon of the time during which the novel was written,
because of which the novel was conceived, and which the
novelist hopes to defeat in the successful completion of the
novel.

A preoccupation with time and its irrevocability is a familiar human experience. With Marcel Proust it became a
veritable obsession. The changes brought about in nature,
in human beings, in society, by the passing of time are
sung by him almost as a lament. Time is the relentless force
that attacks the beauty of the human body, the stability of
human personality, the freshness and the completeness of
works of art—a painting, for example, or a cathedral.
Proust grew to look upon life itself as a constant struggle
against time. Much of the so-called pessimism of his book
comes from the hopelessness of this struggle, from the inevitable failure of life to preserve itself intact from the
encroachments of time.

He analyzes one after the other those major experiences
of life that are the most hallowed efforts of man to reach
some absolute within time, some stable value that will
oppose the flow of time: the loyalty of friendship, for example, the passions of love, the steadfastness of convictions,
either theological or philosophical or political. Proust the
novelist discovers that even such experiences, which, when
they are real, seem absolute, are, in time, subjected to
change and even oblivion. The human self, immersed in
time, is never exactly the same two days in succession. All
the elements of personality are constantly being affected
by time: they are either being weakened or strengthened.
They are receding or in the ascendant. Even the self which
is in love, deeply, jealously and passionately, will change,
according to Proust, and become disillusioned.

The self is never one but a succession of selves. If this is
true—and the substance of the book as well as the method

of writing are based upon this Bergsonian assumption—
what happens to the selves we once were? Do these selves,
which were once real, sink into oblivion? Proust answers
this question with a vigorous no! They are not lost. They do
not disappear. They are in us, in that part of us that is often
called the subconscious. They live in our dreams and indeed at times in our states of consciousness. The opening
theme of Proust's novel is the protagonist's literal awakening. This is a familiar experience for everyone every morning when we leave the state of sleep for the state of consciousness. Proust looks upon this emergence as an effort
to recover our identity, to find out who we are, where we
are, and what particular self we are inhabiting.

A short and important sentence in the opening pages
of *Du Côté de chez Swann,* those eight or nine pages
often referred to as the prelude to the entire work, states
the great power a man in sleep has over the past, over the
selves he was and the relationship he had once established
with the world: *Un homme qui dort tient en cercle autour
de lui le fil des heures, l'ordre des années et des mondes*
(I, p. 5). The powers of sleep mount in an alarming cre-
scendo, for they are powers held over the *hours,* the *years,*
and the *astral bodies* controlling our destinies. In emerging
from sleep, the protagonist tries first to realize what room
he is in, and in that effort evokes several of the rooms in
which he has lived. The memories associated with these
various rooms form the start of his search, and he actually
names the five places in which the action of the novel will
take place: Combray, a provincial town of the Ile-de-
France; Balbec, the Norman seaside resort; Paris; Doncières, the garrison town; and Venice, which he will visit
with his mother. Proust's geography embraces two real
cities: Paris and Venice; and three fictional towns all of
which correspond to very real places: Combray, a faintly
transposed Illiers; Balbec, patterned after Dieppe, Cabourg, Trouville; and Doncières, strongly reminiscent of
Orléans.

When the impetus is given to his memory, by his moving out from the state of sleep into the state of full con-

sciousness, these are the places that come to the mind of
the protagonist, with the evocation of the rooms in which
he had slept. Throughout the novel, the recall of memory
will be closely associated with sleep, where the boundaries
and the limitations of consciousness melt away, where the
past returns to the mind in a fullness, within a detailed
accuracy, which the conscious mind cannot remember.

These opening themes: the erosions brought about by
time, the limitlessness of sleep, the rooms in which the
narrator has slept, indicate to what degree this novel of
search (à la recherche de) is related to an experience of
alienation. The transition between sleep and consciousness
is a moment in which the self is alienated. He is leaving
the world of sleep with its complexity, its phantasmagorical
clarity, its extraordinary disclosures, and he is returning to
the objective world we call reality. During this moment of
alienation, when the self belongs to neither world, he inevitably makes an effort of adaptation. The mind and the
physical body, in its supine position, in its relationship to
the objects in the room, have to be orientated toward a
finite world.

These opening pages on alienation stress the protagonist's
effort to adapt himself to reality and hence to understand
reality. This is the first step, kept in view throughout the
novel, in the "search" which is announced in the general
title. The French phrase, à la recherche de, chosen by
Proust as the definitive title, after he had discarded other
possible titles (Sodome et Gomorrhe, Intermittences du
Coeur), is a common everyday locution. But the very fa-
miliarity of the phrase, à la recherche de, undoubtedly
conceals an esoteric meaning. This search is a quest. The
protagonist Marcel is another Galahad engaged in a quest
for the absolute, or for what he will designate as the absolute. This search, taking place in contemporary France
and, briefly, in Italy, will involve all the dangers and disillusionments and defeats associated with the ancient traditional "quest." An entire life has to be lived before the
vision can be seen. Proust's novel is the life and the vision,
the life that unfolds with intermittent hope for the vision,

and the vision at the end that explains the existence of the
work that has been read.

Initially in the opening pages, and even in the form of a
quasi-initiation, the principle becomes clear to the narrator
that the past which seems lost because it is time elapsed is
not lost. It is within us, and ready, under the appropriate
circumstances and the appropriate stimuli to return as the
present. In each of us the past is something permanent
and unchangeable. Time is constantly destroying the present. But memory is able to restore the past, because memory, and capacious registers, are unaffected by time.

Proust explains early in his novel that there are for him
two ways in particular by which the past can be recalled.
The first, on which he will rely a great deal, and which
he acknowledges to be, of the two, less sure and less sound,
is the willful memory of the intelligence. *La mémoire
volontaire*, as he calls it, seems to be the rationalistic, the
deductive method which is based on documents, testimonials, and ratiocination. When Marcel evokes a typical
summer evening at Combray, when the family spends the
last hours of daylight in the garden, we have a good example of willful memory. Habitual acts are easy to recall: his
grandmother's walk among the flowers (even when it
rains); the ringing of the gate bell which invariably announces the arrival of M. Swann, a neighbor never accompanied by his wife; the gratuitous speculation as to who is
at the gate, although everyone knows it is Swann; the boy's
nightly departure from the family circle when he goes
upstairs to his room; and his waiting there, ready for bed,
for his mother's good night kiss.

Then, after describing the evening scenes at Combray,
the narrator evokes one in particular: the traumatic evening that marked an important change in his life and
which will be recalled at intervals throughout the narrative.
It was an evening when Swann dined with Marcel's family,
and his mother had said she would not be free to kiss him
good night. Unable to accept this privation, the boy, almost
ill with grief, sends a message by Françoise, the housekeeper, to his mother at table. But she refuses to come. He

waits until he hears Swann leave the house, and then he posts himself at the top of the stairway, to catch his mother's attention. Unexpectedly, his father, who is generally quite severe, takes pity on the child and suggests to his wife that she spend the night with the boy to console him. In this way, and at this particular moment, the familiar rules of family discipline are broken. The mother gives Marcel a birthday present, anticipating his birthday: a copy of *François le Champi* by George Sand, which his grandmother had chosen for him, and from which his mother now reads to him. In thus winning far more attention and affection than he had hoped, he worries that he will never again know such contentment.

This famous scene was to be understood later by Marcel as the first incident in which the family indulged his excessive nervousness and tenseness. The incident signals the decline of his health and will power, and sets him aside as someone to whom the normal rules of conduct could not apply. On that night when his mother read to him from the red-bound volume of *François le Champi*, the will of his parents weakened.

The narrator, in the ensuing theoretical discussion, indicates the limitations of *la mémoire volontaire*. He realizes that this kind of memory is able to recall only a small part of his past, and he asks whether all the rest of Combray has been forgotten. The answer again is no. Another kind of memory—involuntary—*la mémoire involontaire* is able to evoke the real past. But the operation of this kind of memory depends on chance. To illustrate, the narrator now relates the episode of the madeleine cake, *la petite madeleine*. Once when dipping a madeleine into a cup of tea, he remembers his tante Léonie at Combray who used to give him a madeleine and a cup of linden tea (*tilleul*). Through the sensation of taste, he recalls, without effort, a similar experience (of *déjà vu*), and the complete picture of the past returns to him: his aunt, his room in her house, the garden, the town, the square where the church is, the streets and the paths. All of Combray, in fact, as if by magic, came out of his cup of tea. *Tout Combray et ses environs, tout cela qui prend forme et solidité, est sorti, ville et jardins, de ma tasse de thé* (I, p. 48).

Thus a sensation in the present is able to recall not only a similar sensation of the past, but all the elements attached to it. The past returns, as it were, with a completeness that cannot be recalled with voluntary memory. The sensation and the sentiment accompanying it are extraordinary. For Marcel, the entire experience is strongly mystical because it is the return of a past he thought dead. He is momentarily released from the truncated vision of things which time gives, and a great happiness pervades his being. *Un plaisir délicieux m'avait envahi* (I, p. 45).

In a sense, Proust has conquered eternity. If such an experience can be translated into art, the past will be preserved against the erosion of time. The episode of the madeleine is not only a significant experience in the life story of the narrator, it demonstrates a basic principle in the method used in composing the novel.

Recollected experiences, even the most sacred, are dominated by time and change. Destined to fall into the void of oblivion, they nevertheless belong to the world of "becoming," as Bergson would say. Yet, in the good night kiss episode, even at the moment of greatest happiness, Marcel feels the premonition of finality. He feels the happiness already sinking into the past, and he senses the anguish of loneliness, which had so upset him, returning. *Je savais qu'une telle nuit ne pourrait se renouveler. . . . Demain mes angoisses reprendraient* (I, p. 43).

After the announcement of the two principles of voluntary and involuntary memory, the narrator describes the past he associates with Combray. The real name of this town, where Marcel Proust the boy and his family spent their summers, is Illiers, near Chartres, in the region called la Beauce. The Proust family had lived there for generations, under the shadow of the famous cathedral. The reconstruction of Illiers into Combray is so accurately done that today Illiers, for the pilgrims who go there, is Combray.

In Illiers where the elements of Combray are recogniz-

able—the house, the garden, the streets, the steeples, the
Vivonne, the park, the hawthorns, the fields—it is not difficult to imagine there the characters to whom we are introduced in the narrative: Léonie herself who, from her bed,
follows so intimately all the events of the town; her faithful Françoise; Eulalie who brings much of the gossip; the
kitchen girl; and the other, more distant characters: oncle
Adolphe, the lady in pink, Bergotte, Bloch, Gilberte.

Marcel's life in Combray was very much related to two
walks he describes after the transitional passage. After
the brief analysis of past time, and the possibilities of
bringing it back, he reconstructs the past by means of another dimension: space. Swann's Way (le côté de chez
Swann), or, as it is sometimes called, Méséglise, is a long
walk that leads past the park of Tansonville, the estate of
M. Swann. Guermantes' Way (le côté de Guermantes) is
an even longer walk which leads in the direction of the
Guermantes', the aristocratic family that resides at least
part of the year at Combray. This walk goes along the
Vivonne, the small stream with water lilies.

Marcel takes these walks at first with members of his
family, and then alone. Without his consciously realizing
their meaning, the walks are detours that will lead him
away from his family into the distant worlds of love and
society and art.

After Swann's marriage, Marcel's family tended to avoid
Swann's Way for fear of encountering Mme Swann. But
one day Marcel and his father walk along the hawthorn
hedge bordering the park of Tansonville when on the
other side of the hedge they see Mme Swann, her daughter
Gilberte, and, behind them, a portly gentleman. Marcel
associates this walk with the mysteriousness of Mme Swann
and Gilberte, with the two steeples of the church of Saint-
André-des-Champs, with flowering apple trees, with hawthorns and finally with Montjouvain where the obscure
composer M. Vinteuil lives with his daughter. On one occasion when the weather was bad, Marcel took shelter in
some bushes near Vinteuil's house, and from there witnessed, through the open window, lesbian actions involving

the daughter of M. Vinteuil and her friend. It was a shocking scene of profanation and even sadism, of anger against
the absent father. On some of his walks alone, Marcel experienced a deep lyrical exaltation in his contemplation of
nature. No one was present, but his feelings were amorous
and he longed to hold a young peasant girl in his arms.

Guermantes' Way is associated with the prestige of nobility, with the wholly inaccessible duchesse de Guermantes. Marcel's best chance of seeing the Guermantes is
in the parish church of Saint Hilaire. Once, at the nuptial
mass of the daughter of the local physician, Dr. Percepied,
Marcel sees the duchesse de Guermantes. He associates
her with the stained glass windows of the church, their
blue in particular, and when she looks at him in the church
with a sovereign lady's blue eyes, he feels himself falling
in love with her. This impossible love is, in its intensity,
like Marcel's ambition to become a writer, and his constant
self-examinations toward discovering whether he has any
real talent, or real disposition for literature. At Combray
his conclusions are invariably negative on this subject.

To Marcel, both Swann's Way and Guermantes', are
remote. Both represent a vague geographical distance.
Swann's Way is far off, a point somewhere on the horizon.
Guermantes' Way is even farther off, and more removed
from reality. It has the remote unreality of the equator,
or the North Pole, or the Orient. Each "way" is related
to an aspect of Marcel's initiation to life. Méséglise (or
Swann's Way) is the hawthorn-lined park of Tansonville
where he first sees Gilberte and hears someone call her
name. It is also the way to Montjouvain where he observes
the scandalous scene of sexuality. Swann's Way is Marcel's introduction to pure and impure love. Guermantes'
Way, from which he can see the water lilies of the Vivonne
and the steeples of Martinville, is associated not only with
all the Guermantes' prestige, but also with Marcel's concern with his own literary talent and his vocation.

The two ways lead Marcel away from his family and
initiate him into the three orders of experience which are
to dominate his life: love, society and art. At Combray

the two ways seemed to the boy to lead in opposite directions, toward opposite goals, totally cut off one from the other. But one of the principal actions of the entire novel is to demonstrate that time, in its fluidity and its power to effect metamorphosis, will join the two ways and fuse them in an extraordinary fashion.

*Combray* is not only the introductory section of *Du Côté de chez Swann*, in a sense, it is the entire novel, the premonition of all that is going to be lived. The nightly anguish Marcel describes, as he waits for his mother's good night kiss, will be repeated and deepened in his later experiences of love for Gilberte and Albertine. The two ways along which he walked as a boy are fixed in his mind as two routes of exploring the world outside the family, the two tests of reality he will undergo in terms of himself as a social human being and as an artist. Three episodes in particular announce a condition, a method and a theme each to be developed throughout the work.

The "condition," on which much of the novel rests, is the episode of the good night kiss. It is called by Proust the abdication of the parents in favor of the will of the child. It is significant in the sense that it determines the kind of life the protagonist will lead. Their discipline is weakened by this scene, and Marcel willfully takes on the role of a child whose health and temperament will permit him to make special demands. George Sand's *François le Champi*, from which his mother reads to him, depicts symbolically a moral collapse. This same book in its red binding will play an important part in the culminating scene of the work.

From symbolism, and especially Mallarmé, Proust acquired some of his fervor for introspection—no ordinary introspection or day-dreaming, but the kind capable of leading the artist into a form of ecstasy where he has access to intuitions of reality. Proust explained on several occasions, notably in the final chapter of his novel, that his work came from a revelation, a profound intuition.

He explains this revelation first in his famous account of the madeleine dipped in tea. In the pleasure of that experience, he became a man who ceased to feel "mediocre, accidental, mortal." (*J'avais cessé de me sentir médiocre, contingent, mortel*. I, p. 45.) His usual personality, so subjugated by time and the disparate sensations and illusions, was replaced, in this experience, by another personality that seemed more fundamental, more active and more real.

The "method," announced in the madeleine passage, is the first of the six or seven examples of involuntary memory that are used at intervals in the novel for recollecting and understanding the past. The eclectic experience of memory, accompanied by a sense of joy, is the result of feeling released from the oppressiveness and constriction of time. It resembles a psychic triumph over time, and it leads Marcel quite naturally to thoughts about his possible literary vocation. The experience of recall is so rich he feels compelled to transcribe it. It is a sign for him that his vocation may become a reality.

The scene of Montjouvain is shocking to young Marcel. Despite his age (although it is impossible to estimate his exact age at any point in the novel), he understands he is observing immoral acts which combine sadism and profanation. It was hard for many of the first readers of Proust to accept this scene, to understand its purpose and to excuse its vulgarity. Proust himself defended it and called it the cornerstone (*la pierre angulaire*) of his work. This scene is the origin and the explanation of a certain kind of jealousy, associated with sexual inversion, which is to torment the protagonist during a long section of the novel.

*Combray* has a structure that is not always apparent on a first reading: its careful pattern is a good example of Proust's method and style. The actual physical awakening analyzed in the opening pages is followed by a psychic awakening which, though not the awakening from sleep, yet resembles such an awakening in its involuntary and unconscious nature. As he tastes the tea-dipped madeleine, the essence of life already lived returns to him, almost as a miraculous gift. Proust looks upon the normal everyday life of which there are countless scenes in the novel, as another kind of sleep. The first time we live a scene—a

garden party, a dinner, a soirée, or a conversation with a
friend—it is an incomplete experience, with vague outlines,
where speech is only half articulated and half heard. Only
in the second kind of psychic awakening, such as the experience initiated by the taste of a madeleine, will moments of the lived past, return integrated: unchaotic and
whole.

The quasi-magical return of part of the past, which permits us to see a good deal of Marcel's life as a child at
Combray, also permits him as narrator to introduce several of the important themes of the work. His grandmother
is for him an example of goodness and spirituality. In his
efforts to recapture her in his mind, he remembers the
way she looked at the steeple of the Combray church,
Saint Hilaire. In that architectural ornament dominating
the center of the town, she found an absence of vulgarity
and falseness and meanness. Her life, in its full sense of
responsibility, seemed to be affirmed by the steeple. It
is the theme of human goodness, reserved for very few in
the novel—for his grandmother and his mother in particular—that he analyzes briefly at the beginning, in terms of
the solidity of Saint Hilaire.

Our introduction to the characters of Legrandin and
Bloch permits Proust to make his first analysis of the psychology of *snobisme*. Legrandin is seen as a haughty figure, a sometime writer, a man envious of the aristocratic
Guermantes and their impregnable world of social privilege. Bloch is the very cultivated, intellectual young Jew,
an aspiring writer and a social climber. The *snobisme* of
these two characters is related to the anomalies of passion that will be analyzed in later portions of the novel.
Legrandin and Bloch are comparable to Marcel in many
respects, but they will not be fulfilled in their vocation as
Marcel is. An obsession with the world and vice impede
their spiritual development.

In the prefatory note to his translation of Ruskin's *Bible
of Amiens*, Marcel Proust designates as the supreme task
of the critic the reconstruction of the particular individu-

alized spiritual life of the artist with whom he is concerned. Proust's work is so complicated and elaborate that
it is almost impossible to think of it as one work, to find a
formula or an abstraction that would embrace it in its
multiple entirety. And yet we know today the design of the
whole was clear to Proust at the beginning, that he was
fully conscious of the goal he was seeking to reach in the
composition. "The last page of my book was written several years ago," he writes in a letter to J. Boulenger in
January 1920. In another letter, he calls his work the story
of a vocation, and this important clue he repeats and develops in the final volume, *Le Temps retrouvé*.

Marcel, however, does not represent the artist's vocation in *Du Côté de chez Swann*, nor in any of the volumes
until the last. Vinteuil is the authentic artist in *Du Côté de
chez Swann*, the composer who "appears" very briefly,
whose life is referred to in elliptical terms, but whose
sonata will take on for Swann very great importance. If
the man Vinteuil is obscure, his daughter is sharply out-
lined by her viciousness. The sonata, in a sense, is another
offspring who represents Vinteuil and who becomes a background theme in Swann's love for Odette. Although the
reader may at first be mistaken about him, Vinteuil, and
not Legrandin or Bloch, is the real artist, the real creator
destined to posthumous glory.

Freud explains the act of writing about one's past as an
effort on the part of the writer to exorcise himself of whatever he is suffering from. This formula would seem too
facile to apply to Proust; for him—and on this point he
would appear to be in agreement with Bergson—all reality
is subjective or psychological. In *Du Côté de chez Swann*,
he tells us that "the places we have known do not belong
solely to the world of space." (*Les lieux que nous avons
connus n'appartiennent pas qu'au monde de l'espace.* I,
p. 427.) When—by a sudden illumination—the places that
Proust had known reappear before him in so vivid a form
that his intelligence understands and sees them as it had
never understood and seen when first it experienced them,
he realizes that he has before him the subject matter of his

work. Proust never denied the importance of experience, what might be called living our life or participating in the social activity of a given moment, but he claimed, and his novel is the justification of his claim, that we understand any given experience only much later in time. We are unable, when the experience is first lived, to extract the important from the trivial. Only later, when the experience, through memory, impinges on our minds and our psyches, can we comprehend its significance or, in a word, its reality. Whatever feeling of beauty we have grows in intensity and profundity when it is remembered, recalled fortuitously by unexpected sense-experience. It is with this basic theory that Marcel Proust stresses the superiority of the inner or contemplative life. The great illuminations he speaks of in his book, occur as infrequently as they do for the saints and the mystics. But they are followed by long intensive meditation in which the task of the writer is to reproduce the past in as much detail as he can remember.

Today it is difficult for us· to remember that the early critics of Proust accused him of describing only *salonnards* in his book, of being interested only in social snobs or members of the aristocracy. *Combray* itself contradicts this suggestion because it introduces us not only to the local aristocracy of the little town, but to the humdrum manners and prejudices and habits of the inhabitants from all classes: Eulalie's church gossip, Léonie's hypochondria, Legrandin's rhetorical eloquence, Abbé Perdreau's far-fetched etymologies, Théodore's grocer-boy simplicity, the sinful women of Montjouvain. The humanity of Combray is varied and typical. This tiny center in the Ile-de-France is the microcosm of the world for Marcel in his three roles of protagonist and narrator and novelist.

We see Combray through the eyes of the boy Marcel who is to grow up and undergo a series of initiations to life. The narrative of the novel describes his life, from boyhood to middle age. The character who grows up, to whom life makes various revelations, is, as in a tragedy, the protagonist on whom the action is felt. But there is also the narrator apart from Marcel who tells us about Combray, who is omniscient about Marcel's entire life before he lives it, and who is, strictly speaking, the protagonist in the far more detached role of narrator. There is also the novelist Marcel Proust, the creator, the very special type of artist into whom the boy Marcel will grow. He is not merely the witness to the events, as the narrator is. He is the aesthetician who discovers, at the end of the narrative, the vocation of a writer because he has discovered also many things concerning the reality of art.*

In this trinity, the novelist is the one who learns the importance of describing the banal daily occurrences of Combray. The novelist tells us at various points throughout the novel that something more than the town of Combray has been formed through the centuries, something that explains the town and all the lives it has protected. He calls this the *esprit de Combray*, which he acknowledges as difficult to define. It is a kind of code, never written down, familiar to everyone in the town, which is exemplified in Françoise's attitudes and actions, referred to by Marcel's mother and by Charlus. The *esprit de Combray* seems to refer to rules of politeness learned instinctively, to an acknowledgment of hierarchy, of class distinctions, of a feudal viewpoint that still persists in modern France.

By tradition, this *esprit* centers around the small church of Saint-André-des-Champs. The grocer boy Théodore may reveal instincts and acts of naughtiness, but he is also capable of demonstrating a deep sense of respect. His face resembles the faces of small angels in the bas-relief of the church. These faces, sculptured in the thirteenth century, are visible today in all classes of French society: nobles, bourgeois, and peasants. Marcel recognizes them in Théodore's face, and, later, in Albertine's. When Saint-Loup, a Guermantes, makes every effort to get to the front in the war, he represents a greatness of spirit in the tradition of Saint-André-des-Champs, and Théodore, as he helps to lift

---

* Louis-Martin Chauffier finds not three but four interpretations for the "I" in Proust's novel. See Bibliography.

tante Léonie from her bed, shows on his face traits of zeal
and innocence carved in stone on the church.

Proust's method, apparent in this opening section of
*Combray*, is the threefold presentation of reality, by the
protagonist who grows up, by the narrator who knows
what has happened and therefore knows what to relate
from the life of the protagonist, and by the novelist who
has chosen the novel as his mode of transcription, in his
effort to recover the past.

5. *Du Côté de chez Swann.*
B.   The initiation to love

*Un Amour de Swann,* the second section of *Du Côté de chez Swann,* has been often looked upon as a separate novel that interrupts the life story of the protagonist. In reality, this episode has innumerable bonds with all parts of the work, and the significance of Swann's role becomes more evident the closer we read the novel.

The importance of Charles Swann, at least in the three divisions of *Du Côté de chez Swann,* is clear. In *Combray* he is the refined and rather mysterious friend who visits the boy's parents. We are made aware of his intelligence, his erudition, his elegance of manner and dress. We even learn some things about him that Marcel's family does not know: his cordial relations with the highest society, with the aristocratic Guermantes, even with the Prince of Wales. For the boy Marcel, M. Swann is a gentleman of sympathetic kindness, endowed with great prestige, who stands out as an almost godlike figure in Combray. In the second division, *Un Amour de Swann,* Swann is the protagonist and the story is centered on his love for Odette: the origin of his love, the experience of suffering and jealousy, and love's end. In the third division, *Noms de Pays: le Nom,* Swann plays a more effaced, a more subtle role. Marcel's dreams about Balbec and Italy have been somewhat induced by Swann's conversations and allusions. The boy's dreams about Gilberte, and his love for her in the Champs-Elysées scenes, are also dreams about the name of Swann and the strong attraction the boy feels for the glamorous

Mme Swann. One always feels behind the sentimental boy-
ish love of Marcel for Gilberte, the stronger, more violent
and more deeply analyzed love of Swann for Odette.

*Un Amour de Swann* is far more than a separate mono-
graph on passion. Swann, as Marcel's precursor, is related
to the two "ways"; his own way, first, which leads us to
Odette, and the Verdurin clan where Swann sees Odette,
and to Elstir (or rather, M. Biche), the painter, and the
work of the composer Vinteuil. But Swann is also a close
friend of Oriane, duchesse de Guermantes, and of the baron
de Charlus, both of whom represent Guermantes' Way.
Swann's daughter, Gilberte, will finally marry a Guermantes, Robert de Saint-Loup. With this marriage, at the
end of the novel, in Mlle de Saint-Loup, the two ways are
joined. Thus, *Un Amour de Swann* is the indirect but indispensable prelude to the great social upheaval which
will be described in *Le Temps retrouvé*.

Swann's introduction to Odette presents Proust with the
opportunity to describe the Verdurins and their little group.
All the details of the opening scenes—the unity of the clan
(*le petit noyau*), the only partly disguised dictatorial habits of Mme Verdurin (who calls everyone outside her group
*les ennuyeux*), the good music they listen to, the dinners,
the expeditions to the country on holidays, the demands of
fidelity that are made on new and old members of the
clan—form brilliant social satire in its close analysis of an
upper bourgeois group, neither quite as elevated as the
worldly, aristocratically elegant groups, nor as solidly artistic as the company of intense intellectuals. But this first
social world of the Verdurins involves other worlds, with
secret and not so secret correspondences with one another.
The miracle of Proust's novel is the relationships established
between every character, every scene, every theme, within
the entire work.

The seemingly isolated episode, *Un Amour de Swann*, is
in reality, then, as indispensable as *Combray* is to the meaning of the novel. *Combray* covers childhood when a boy
has to submit to the affectionate tyranny of grown-ups,
when he is mystified and tormented by the mysterious

bonds of affection and sentiment and the painful yearnings of an ill-defined vocation. *Un Amour de Swann* concerns adulthood, when a man is overpowered by the tyrannical suffering of passion, when he is mystified and tormented by the inability to communicate his thoughts or to know the thoughts of the woman he loves, when he is harassed by an incapacity to fulfill his vocation.

Finally the two stories of Combray and Swann's love are resumed in Marcel's obsession with names, with his dreams of Balbec and Venice—two escapes from the beloved but overfamiliar Combray, and with Gilberte, who is a Swann, and therefore distant and unapproachable, who yet draws him dangerously outside of the charmed circle of family, outside the absolutely secure and undoubted love of his mother and grandmother.

Swann is first introduced to Odette de Crécy at the theatre. He has heard of her beauty and knows her reputation as a *demi-mondaine* or *cocotte*. At this first meeting he is indifferent to her special kind of beauty and feels no desire for her. Odette becomes attached to Swann and asks to see his art collection. She introduces Swann to the Verdurins. Against the two backgrounds of the Verdurin salon and Odette's apartment on the rue la Pérouse, with its Chinese art objects and vases of chrysanthemums and cattleyas, her favorite flowers, Swann's mild interest in her grows into a passion and jealous suffering which abates and then completely disappears. At this point Swann marries Odette de Crécy.

At first Swann was amused at her mania for using English words in her conversation, flattered by her attentions and her seeming eagerness to know about the essay he was writing on Vermeer de Delft. Early in their relationship he was struck by Odette's resemblance to Zephora, daughter of Jethro, in a Botticelli fresco of the Sistine Chapel. Swann's sexual relationships were usually with chambermaids or common women but in his relationships with other women (such as Odette or the duchesses he knew), he elevated the relationship to an aesthetic plane. The character of Swann is denigrated only by *muflerie*, a word

difficult to translate, which seems to suggest a form of cad-
dishness, a callous insensitivity. On most occasions Swann
demonstrates marked delicacy of feeling, but he has his
moments of loutishness.

One evening at the Verdurins, while a pianist is playing,
Swann hears a phrase from a work for piano and violin he
heard the year before, which he very much liked, but
which he had not been able to identify. Now, in the Verdurin salon he learns it is the andante movement from
Vinteuil's sonata for piano and violin. He asks about Vinteuil's life and work. This musical phrase, described as
ethereal and sweet-smelling (*aérienne et odorante*), Swann
associates with his love for Odette. With this theme, which
will grow in importance throughout the novel, Proust states
the problem of the relationship between love and suffering,
between happiness and art. It will explain, to some degree,
Swann's incomprehensible choice of Odette. The Botticelli
painting and the *petite phrase* of Vinteuil's sonata reveal
the aesthetic basis of his love for Odette.

Like all love affairs, Swann's love for Odette is composed
of rites which have special meanings only for them: the
face of Zephora in a painting, a high sustained note in a
sonata, the cattleyas which Swann arranges in Odette's
corsage and which is the reminder of love-making, since
he did this for the first time on the night he possessed her.
Swann sacrifices more interesting social relations for the
privilege of attending the Verdurins' salon where he can
see Odette. The Verdurins will finally turn against him and
ostracize him in favor of a new admirer of Odette, a titled
gentleman named de Forcheville, but not before he has
fallen deeply in love with Odette.

Swann suffers the full impact of his realization of losing
Odette, when one evening he does not find her at the Verdurins. He looks for her in the restaurants in Paris where
he thinks she might be. Impelled by the full force of suffering (*cette agitation douloureuse.* I, p. 295), he comes
to know that his love is now real by the measure of her
absence.

Swann's last elaborately narrated encounter with his love occurs at a musical soirée at the marquise de Saint-Euverte's, a lower echelon member of the Guermantes family. Much care is given to the description of Oriane, the princesse des Laumes, the future duchesse de Guermantes. Oriane is not as kind to Mme de Saint-Euverte and to her cousin Mme Gallardon as to her friend Swann. Swann is deeply attached to Oriane, for she reminds him of Combray. (Because of his love for Odette he now has no desire to return to Combray.) That evening Odette recognizes sympathetically Swann's suffering over love. In the midst of these many complex social relationships, Swann hears Vinteuil's sonata being performed, and when the little phrase is played, his suffering becomes so acute that he raises his hand to his heart. Before he can distract his mind, all his memories of happiness with Odette overwhelm him: the chrysanthemum petals she threw at him, her handwriting on a letter, the exact line of her eyebrows when once she asked him not to be too long in coming back to her.

For the first time that evening, as he listens to the little phrase of the sonata, Swann feels sympathy and love for Vinteuil, the obscure gifted composer whose work must come from suffering. Vinteuil becomes his partner in suffering, as his little phrase becomes identified with Swann's love for Odette. Vinteuil's music evokes in Swann memories of an entire part of the past just as drinking a cup of tea in tante Léonie's room had for Marcel. The parallel is striking in these first two sections of the novel where Marcel and Swann learn the first great principle Proust the novelist wants to demonstrate: that the soul is not an impenetrable and forbidding void, but the container of a great richness: with explicit reminders for Marcel of happiness, and for Swann of love.

The experience of that evening marks a turning point in Swann's love. He knows then that Odette's love for him, as she once had expressed and felt it, will never return. He resumes his work on Vermeer, while Odette leaves for a visit to Egypt, with Forcheville. Through an anonymous

letter, Swann suspects Odette of lesbian relationships, and
during their scenes together after her return, he plagues
her relentlessly until she confesses. He begins to believe
that love is a succession of loves and jealousy a succession
of jealousies. His suffering diminishes, and his *muflerie* returns intermittently. The last sentence of *Un Amour de
Swann*, one of the most disillusioning statements in the
novel, is Swann's claim that he has wasted years of his life
and felt his greatest love for a woman whom he did not
really love, who was not his type of woman. *"Dire que j'ai
gâché des années de ma vie, que j'ai voulu mourir, que
j'ai eu mon plus grand amour, pour une femme qui ne me
plaisait pas, qui n'était pas mon genre!"* (I, p. 382.)

Swann's liaison with Odette before their marriage is the
first full illustration in the novel—prelude to the rest—of the
dual experience with which man is involved every moment
of life, consciously or unconsciously: the duality of destruction and preservation. Time is the force that slowly and
inexorably destroys everything. But memory is time's only
deterrent, the one staying factor, the one force for permanence. The scene where by chance Swann hears again Vinteuil's sonata at Mme de Saint-Euverte's concert is Swann's
most exalted moment. At this point in the liaison, he senses
that Odette is unfaithful and has become Forcheville's mistress. But before the scene closes, he relives the past: he
recaptures what is lost to time. The musical phrase of the
sonata, which his sentimentality identified with Odette,
forces him, without his willing it, to feel once again the
sensations and the gestures and the loving kindnesses that
he shared with Odette. These memories are so precisely
real as to be almost intolerable. This moment of total recall
transcends the mere story of the liaison: its slow beginning,
its passion, and its decline.

This intuitive theory of time contrasted as memory's de-
stroyer and preserver was already adumbrated in the madeleine-tea passage of *Combray*. But the story of Swann's
love is its first full application. The story becomes then not
an interruption in Marcel's life story, but a necessary prologue which will attach Marcel to the man who has the

mysteriousness and power of a god for him as a boy. Swann's love is compounded of pathos and triviality, of disastrous characteristics of equivocation allied in Proust's mind with the word "love." We follow Swann's love in considerable detail as it develops in its temporal aspect. It is chronologically the history of a love. We are present at its inception. We follow its slow development and we witness Swann's anguish when he rushes from restaurant to restaurant in search of Odette and when he acknowledges that his love is comparable to a bodily sickness that is no longer operable. We are made to feel love's diminution and death. . . . When Odette becomes Mme Swann, we are in another section of the novel where the focus is back on Marcel.

Swann's love for Odette is a clearly circumscribed, isolated episode in his life. There are references to love affairs before and after Odette, but they seem to be superficial attachments, where sexual attraction was strong and no intellectual or spiritual affinity existed. With Odette, Swann's not knowing her life, her thoughts, her sexual adventures creates in him intense suffering. She was always the mistress pursued, and she always appeared as unapproachable, elusive, and somehow ineffable. This is the persistent pattern of all the love affairs in Proust: of forbidden pursuit. The lover is hunter; and the beloved, harassed and tormented, a beast of prey, a being which the hunter is forbidden to hunt. *Combray* once again offers the prelude to the entire theme of love in the very faintly sketched liaison of oncle Adolphe with the "lady in pink." The boy Marcel, when he meets the attractive *dame en rose* in his uncle's apartment, feels embarrassment, while he begins to understand why his parents had not wished him to meet the lady in pink and why they disapproved of Adolphe. This liaison of a wealthy bachelor and beautiful mistress is the first adumbration of *Un Amour de Swann* and indeed of all the love episodes in the novel. *La dame en rose* is none other than Odette de Crécy, destined to become Mme Swann. In the story of Swann's love, the element of pursuit is very pronounced, and the element of the forbidden is also present. In order to preserve her clan, Mme Verdurin will play

even the role of an *entremetteuse*, by encouraging Odette's
liaison with Swann; when she tires of Swann, she performs
the same function for Odette and Forcheville.

The elements that accrue around the love stories, as they
succeed one another in the novel, grow increasingly con-
taminated with a labyrinthine search for what it is wrong
to hunt and what is unseizable to begin with. The elements
of anguish and suspicion and prevarication in Swann's love
grow to hallucinatory proportions in subsequent episodes
of the novel.

*Un Amour de Swann* provides one of the clearest analyses of the genesis of what may be called Proustian love.
The drama of this love, with its obsessiveness, immorality,
and inevitable end are more fully narrated in other parts
of the novel, but Swann's love is the source.

Dante once called love a mental thing (*una cosa mentale*), which is an apt description for Swann's experience.
Before Odette becomes a real person for him, she is the
Botticelli face of Zephora. She is juxtaposed with a painting that had once stimulated his aesthetic sense. Later she
is associated with a musical phrase from Vinteuil's sonata
that allows him to enjoy her in an atmosphere of peace,
beauty and imagination where emotions one more delecta-
ble than the other can be conjured up. Odette is for Swann
an eidolon created by his own mind through its sensitivity
to painting and music. There she is safe: beautiful, totally
possessed. But there is another Odette, a living woman,
completely outside of his images of her. Swann is destined
to suffer because he cannot join this woman with the mental picture he has created. As time goes on, the abyss separating the two widens. Odette's appearance is so different
from her image in Swann's mind that his love becomes the
story of an impossibility, and a continual frustration. His
despair is caused by the collapse of a myth.

This myth and its collapse are beautifully described on
the two occasions that Swann hears Vinteuil's sonata. The
first time is at the Verdurins, when the music touches
Swann's heart with its promise of happiness, and the love
it inspires in him not only for Odette but for life itself. He

calls the little phrase the "national anthem of their love" (*l'air national de leur amour.* I, p. 218), a testimonial or memory that isolates them from the world. The second time Swann hears the sonata is in the salon of Mme de Saint-Euverte, but this time the memories are painful because they bring to mind a lost happiness (*ce bonheur perdu.* I, p. 345). This time the notes of the *petite phrase* reanimate all the moments of suffering he has lived through because of Odette. When the music ends, there are tears in his eyes. He weeps pityingly, as if for another, then realizes that he pities himself. Swann does not fully understand this experience, but Swann's love for Odette provides a prelude to Marcel's love for Albertine, where a fuller understanding of love will be reached.

In the third section of *Du Côté de chez Swann, Noms de Pays: le Nom*, we leave Swann's world of passion and disillusionment, and return to Marcel and a boy's world of mystery. It is not Combray now but Paris. And throughout the meditations on names (Balbec, Venice, Florence especially, and the towns through which the train passes: Bayeux, Coutances, Vitré, Lannion, Lamballe, Pont-Aven), and on the afternoons spent in the Champs-Elysées where Gilberte, known at first only as a cipher, comes to life, and in the Bois de Boulogne, where Mme Swann passes in her carriage along the Avenue des Acacias, the theme of love is never lost: it is only momentarily subdued in Marcel's thoughts of Balbec and La Berma. (His doctor has forbidden him the voyage to Balbec and the excitement of attending a performance of La Berma.) For in the excitement and frustration and bewilderment of Marcel's obsession with Gilberte, the theme of love rises to a high pitch. He learns many of the classic impediments to happiness in love: the seeming indifference of the beloved, the uncooperative weather which limits her appearances in the Champs-Elysées, the final despairing realization (despite the cherished acts of kindness: the agate marble, the booklet by Bergotte on Racine, the permission to call her by her first name: *vous pouvez m'appeler Gilberte*). In all these amorous adventures it seems to him that he is the only one who loves. Finally, the romantic frustration is reiterated in the Bois de Boulogne scene, where Marcel is the worshipful lover and Mme Swann the distant unapproachable goddess.

One of the traditional clichés in the criticism of Proust's art is the observation that it is static, that it has no action, that it never progresses. A close reading would easily prove that the contrary is true, that it is an art of perpetual movement, in which concepts, sensations, and characters are constantly undergoing change. It is true that violent action is not stressed, but the entire work describes the phasing of things and places and people into darkness, and then out of the darkness into light, only to relapse again into obscurity.

This unceasing movement is demonstrated in the contrast between Marcel of Combray at the beginning of *Du Côté de chez Swann*—where the world is exciting and beautiful for the boy: the walks he takes with his parents and those he takes alone, the churches he studies and admires, the flowers, the readings, the ever-present affection and attentiveness of his mother and grandmother—and the Marcel of Paris, in the last section of the same book. In Combray satisfactory answers had been given to the boy's questions about life and the world about him. In Paris alone and in doubt, life contains the dimension of mystery in everything he feels and sees. He is perturbed by the relationship between a word and what it designates, between a word and the reality to which the word corresponds. The mystery in names will become part of every major theme in the novel: with love, pre-eminently, as in his obsession with the name of Gilberte; with social hierarchy, as in the fascination and magic Marcel finds in the name of Guermantes; with time, measured by the days and the years it takes the narrator to fuse the spell created by a name when only a name, and the disillusioning experience of reality when he encounters what the name designates.

A possible definition of Marcel's life story would be a search for the meaning behind the mysterious names which obsessed him: Balbec, La Berma, Bergotte, Gilberte, Guermantes, Mme Swann, Venice. The action of the novel is Marcel's encounter with the realities corresponding to these names.

Balbec, one of the most important sites in the novel, is carefully described and meticulously introduced long before the action of the story shifts there. One of the rooms that comes to mind during Marcel's nights of insomnia, early in *Combray*, was the room he occupied at the Grand Hôtel de la Plage in Balbec. Before living in that room, Marcel associated the name Balbec with shipwrecks and storms at sea. Françoise, in the afternoons spent in the Champs-Elysées had often referred to such catastrophes narrated in the newspapers, and Marcel longed to observe, without the intervention of the written and the oral word, a great storm at sea.

Once M. Legrandin, their Combray neighbor, had mentioned the name of Balbec as a beach quite close to the tragic coastline (presumably of Brittany) celebrated for countless shipwrecks. Legrandin's florid style is beautifully illustrated in the passage (which Marcel quotes) where he calls this spot on the coast the farthest point of the ancient land of France and Europe, "the last encampment of fishermen who since the world began, live facing the eternal kingdom of sea fog and shadows" (*le dernier campement de pêcheurs, pareils à tous les pêcheurs qui ont vécu depuis le commencement du monde, en face du royaume éternel des brouillards de la mer et des ombres. I, p. 384*). It is a passage apt to fire the imagination of a boy who is to remember it so vividly that one day, at Combray, he asks M. Swann about Balbec. Swann speaks not of storms or of the seacoast, but of the church of Balbec, half Romanesque from the twelfth century and half Norman-Gothic from the thirteenth. The architecture is so unusual, according to Swann, that it seems almost Persian. These two allusions are fused in the boy's mind. His desire to see the Gothic architecture of the church and a storm over the ocean stimulates him to board the 1:22 train from Paris that would take him there. The real Balbec, when he does go there, seems vastly different from the imagined

Balbec, which was a composite of impressions of Legrandin and Swann.

This propensity of the protagonist of associating a name
(of a place or of a person) with elements of poetry, history,
geography, fictive allusions; thereby creating a highly
charged, highly poeticized picture in the imagination was
characteristic of Marcel Proust the man. Among Proust's
personal friends, the young aristocrat Bertrand de Fénelon,
by his very name with its strong literary resonance, by his
blue eyes and relaxed graceful manners, served as one of
the elements used in the creation of Robert de Saint-Loup.

A long repertory of names is passed in review at the
beginning of the section, *Noms de Pays: le Nom,* and they
culminate, in terms of the narrative itself, in the name of
Gilberte. The chance beginning of what develops into an
experience in love for Marcel occurs in the simple sentence
he hears one girl say to another in the Champs-Elysées:
"Good-by, Gilberte, I'm going home. . . . Don't forget
that we're coming to your house tonight after dinner"
(*Adieu, Gilberte, je rentre, n'oublie pas que nous venons
ce soir chez toi après dîner.* I, p. 394). Marcel once heard
this name "Gilberte" as he walked along the narrow path
in Combray. He knew this red-headed girl to be the daughter of M. Swann. In the Champs-Elysées, where he hears
the name again, he is deeply affected by the mystery surrounding Gilberte; and he is gnawed by the thought of
friends approaching her so casually when he himself cannot reach her. He imagines all aspects of Mlle Swann's life,
and is again reminded of all the things that separate his
life from hers. Even when he comes to know her and participates in games with her and her friends, he ruminates
endlessly on all he does not know about her, and which
keep her from coming every day to the Champs-Elysées.

Marcel's love for Gilberte deepens the mystery surrounding her life, and gradually the mystery surrounding
her mother and her father. The better he knows her, the
more there is to learn about her, because she inadvertently
reveals the existence of further unsuspected mysteries. Her
very name becomes the talisman by which Marcel evokes

an imaginary world. He writes her name and her address over and over again in his school notebooks and thereby calls up images of her in a purely magical way. He speaks to her of his desire to see La Berma in a classical play, and asks if by chance she owns the small book on Racine by Bergotte. The next day she brings him this brochure as a gift. Marcel, in the manner of the courtly lover, learns to live from day to day for the next time when he might see Gilberte, when there is the chance of adding one experience however slight, one more detail, to this chaste fervent adulation.

This section of the novel, which completes *Du Côté de chez Swann*, returns to Marcel's principal narrative by its allusion to the moment back at Combray when he had first heard the name of Gilberte in the garden of Tansonville. The first elaboration of the major philosophical theme of the disparity between the imagination and reality, the section is also an analysis of an initial phase in Proustian love, which will be more lengthily treated in the case of Marcel than in the case of Swann.

Marcel's love for Gilberte has little or nothing to do with the satisfaction of the senses (which was of vital importance in Swann's love for Odette). It is predominantly the proliferation of the lover's imagination. Marcel forms an elaborate mental world in which Gilberte is the center. Exalted by the slightest attention she manifests, he is equally depressed by her slightest indifference. The fits of despondency are forms of suffering which have the strange perverse power of attaching Marcel to Gilberte even more firmly than in moments of happiness.

The tone of the courtly romance (*roman courtois*) is stressed as the episode moves toward its end. Marcel becomes more and more clearly the lover entranced within a world controlled by supernatural forces. When M. Swann appears in the Champs-Elysées to fetch his daughter, he is compared by Marcel to a god who exerts the prerogatives of a god over Gilberte (*comme il convenait à des dieux tout-puissants sur elle.* I, p. 407). This figure is no longer the Swann of Combray whom Marcel once knew; he

is the father of Gilberte, a new personage in his godlike
mysteriousness and power.

One day Gilberte casually announces to Marcel that she
will be absent from the Champs-Elysées for some time:
she must visit with her family, take a trip, etc. Marcel's
disguised despair and stifled sobs contrast cruelly with
Gilberte's elation. During her absence, he cherishes the
few objects which remind him of her: the little book of
Bergotte on Racine, the agate marble, which he kisses
fervently in the solitude of his room. But Marcel is not
only the love-sick knight who indulges in sentimental
reverie. He faces the reality of the situation when he acknowledges to himself that Gilberte is indifferent to him and
that he alone loves (*c'est moi seul qui aimais.* I, p. 412).

This realization initiates a new phase when Marcel's
attention shifts from Gilberte to her parents. In his relationship with M. and Mme Swann, Marcel appears even
more knightly in his silent devotion (*une sorte de fidélité
chevaleresque.* I, p. 413). His great satisfaction comes
from hearing the name of Swann pronounced, and with his
own parents he contrives to bring this about. The two
families have strained relationships. Marcel's parents are
fond of Swann, but they do not wish to meet Mme Swann.
The conversation about the Swanns is evasive and equivo-
cal, but Marcel's private pleasure comes when he merely
hears the name of Swann mentioned. On the days when
Gilberte is absent, Marcel forces Françoise to walk with
him in front of her house and repeat to him what she has
heard of Mme Swann's superstitious beliefs. The boy is
constantly excited by a "supernatural apparition" (*apparition surnaturelle.* I, p. 417)—his phrase for the possibility
of encountering M. Swann.

This passage uses the mediaeval word *merveilleux* (miraculous) to designate the appearance of M. Swann in the
real world of Paris. The word introduces the longer passage on the Bois de Boulogne, called the Garden of Women,
where, especially in the Allée des Acacias, Mme Swann
could be seen walking. There Marcel used to wait in order
to see her pass, and he feels more veneration for her than

for Gilberte. When walking, Mme Swann was dressed quite simply but with incomparable "chic," wearing violets and appearing always to be in a hurry. In her victoria, her bearing was that of a queen and Marcel thought of drawings of Constantin Guys, which showed the elegant fashions of Baudelaire's day. Her smile was ambiguous because it seemed to be the smile of a royal personage (*une Majesté*. I, p. 419) and the provocative smile of a courtesan (*cocotte*). She was recognized by many, and the boy, as he watched her pass, could hear references to Odette de Crécy and Mme Swann. But she did not even know his name, and he compared himself to one of the ducks in the lake to which she might throw a piece of bread. He was, at this point in the narrative, removed, unnoticed, a still uninvolved observer, but he was already an ardent votary.

A pause in the text separates this moment in the experience of Marcel from the last six pages of *Du Côté de chez Swann*, which form a finale movement, a coda, an elaborate orchestration of the principal theme of time, in which the narrator intervenes as an adult of several years later.

It is November. The rain has stopped. The narrator returns on foot to see the Bois. Some of the trees are already bare, while others are crowned with an "incombustible candelabra" of yellowed leaves flaming in the sunlight. He goes to the Allée des Acacias, as if returning to boyhood. He wants to see again what he had once loved. But the graceful carriages, such as the one Mme Swann had appeared in, have now been replaced by automobiles driven by chauffeurs with mustaches. The hats and the dresses of the ladies in the automobiles are not as beautiful as those worn by Mme Swann. The new fashions seem common and trivial. The loss of the beauty in the Bois de Boulogne on this November morning seems to the narrator comparable to a loss of faith, though he knows that when this occurs we still have the power to reanimate the past. Proust uses in this passage the key word "fetish" (*un attachement fétichiste*. I, p. 425). A seemingly innocuous new object can have the power of recalling the past. The gods reside in objects rather than in us.

The narrator's consolation is the past, and he goes back farther than his own past, farther than the Bois de Boulogne, to the groves celebrated by Virgil, to the Elysian garden of beautiful women, to the Druidic crown of the oak trees. He finds himself, on this sunlit November morning of his adulthood, in an empty unused forest. Where has the past, the past which he once lived on this very spot, gone? The last lines have the solemnity of a partial revelation. He knows that his past is not here in the Bois de Boulogne. The reality he had once known is over. *La réalité que j'avais connue n'existait plus* (I, p. 427). The places we have known in the past do not belong solely to the world of space. *Les lieux que nous avons connus n'appartiennent pas qu'au monde de l'espace* (I, p. 427). The desolation of the November scene and the sadness of the narrator form an experience in his life as a man. The reader does not fully realize at this point that the work he is reading is the only possible remedy to the desolation and the sadness. The narrator observes that houses and roads are as fleeting as the years. *Les maisons, les routes, les avenues, sont fugitives, hélas! comme les années* (I, p. 427). Without using the word *time* in these final sentences, Proust focuses our attention on the passing of time, the intangibility of the past, and its elusiveness.

## 6. A l'ombre des jeunes filles en fleurs.
### (Within a Budding Grove)
### A. The magic of names

Marcel's age is left vague at every point in the narrative, and yet the novel, for the most part, follows a chronological order. Roughly speaking we can call *Du Côté de chez Swann*, in its first and third sections, the boyhood of Marcel. *A l'ombre des jeunes filles en fleurs*, the second part of the novel, which is longer and more complicated, corresponds to Marcel's adolescence. In *Le Côté de Guermantes* he appears as a young man.

*A l'ombre des jeunes filles en fleurs* is divided into two long chapters of unequal length. The first (and shorter) is *Autour de Mme Swann*, which is largely concerned with Marcel's entrance and reception in the Swanns' Paris apartment. This is his first escape from home, tante Léonie's house in Combray, and his parents' apartment in Paris, and it is the realization, on one level, of Swann's Way, the first of the two walks in Combray. Marcel's first visit to Balbec, carefully prepared for in *Du Côté de chez Swann* by all the meanings he has attached to the name Balbec, occupies the second chapter, *Noms de Pays: le Pays*. In Balbec, Marcel will meet three members of the Guermantes family: Mme de Villeparisis, Robert de Saint-Loup, and the baron de Charlus. Balbec is his second escape from home, bolder and more exotic than the escape represented by the Swann apartment, and in his first encounters and friendships at Balbec, he recognizes the Guermantes' Way, the second of the walks at Combray.

After a boyhood dominated by his parents and Fran-
coise, when he had very little desire to move outside of
the family circle, Marcel's adolescence is characterized by
an extension of the social horizon. Eagerly and gratefully,
he becomes a familiar visitor to M. Swann's apartment and
Mme Swann's salon, and at Balbec he drives through the
countryside in Mme de Villeparisis' carriage as a youthful
and very much appreciated companion of a Guermantes.
After these two experiences—initiatory steps toward the
world outside of his family—Marcel will enter, now with
even more enthusiasm and with greater self-assurance, the
Faubourg Saint-Germain and the highest circles of the
Guermantes.

*A l'ombre des jeunes filles en fleurs,* then, is first Marcel's
adolescent search for meaning in the two ways of Combray.
He defines them as two ways of life which are destined to
evolve and change, in accordance with the greater laws of
change in societies and civilizations. The explicit example,
in Proust's art, is always used to explain much more than
itself. The understanding of these changes, both personal
and social, comes slowly to Marcel. The life of the novel is
their gradually revealed meanings. A lifetime is required
to understand life.

Three names in *A l'ombre des jeunes filles en fleurs* are
to change from their imagined to their real significance for
Marcel. In the first chapter, Gilberte, the imagined heroine
of the boy's dreams, becomes the real Gilberte when he
sees her leaning on her father's shoulder in the Swann
apartment. And Bergotte, the novelist and writer, surrounded by an aura of glory and fame, becomes the real
Bergotte when Marcel meets him at Mme Swann's luncheon
party and learns some of the basic concepts for the word
"genius." In the second chapter, the Balbec of Marcel's
imagination, as influenced by the words of Legrandin and
Swann, is realized: a beach, a large hotel, and the many
lives encountered during the relaxed moments of a summer vacation. The three names—Gilberte, Bergotte, and
Balbec—in the radical change they undergo during the
narrative of *A l'ombre des jeunes filles en fleurs* comprise

three exercises on the startling disparity that exists between one's imagination and reality.

The theme of disparity and change is a subtle minor development of the major theme of time in the novel. At the very beginning of the first chapter of *A l'ombre*, we learned of two changes in names which served as preludes to more significant changes. The first, already slightly adumbrated in the first book, is the change in M. Swann. For Marcel he has now become Odette's husband. One would not have suspected this change from the M. Swann of Combray who used to call after dinner on the family in tante Léonie's garden. The second change, of somewhat slighter consequence, is the transformation of Dr. Cottard, or simply Cottard, an habitué of Mme Verdurin's salon, into le professeur Cottard. The honors of the medical profession have come to Cottard. He is a famous diagnostician, a character who bears little resemblance to the almost illiterately bad punster of the Verdurin clan whom Swann sees when he sits there in order to be close to Odette.

The first fully developed episode centers about the marquis de Norpois, the ambassador friend of Marcel's father. But the episode involves many more themes than the dinner for M. de Norpois. It is related to the scruples he feels about disobedience, even in a slight degree; to his parents; to Françoise's culinary art—Françoise excited over preparing dinner for so eminent a gourmet as Norpois; to the matinée performance of La Berma in two acts of *Phèdre*, and Marcel's reactions to Norpois' analysis of La Berma's art; to his praise of Françoise's *daube de boeuf;* to the architecture of the church of Balbec; to the social position of Swann since his marriage with Odette de Crécy; to a discussion of the literary art of Bergotte; to Marcel's renewed conviction that he is without talent for writing; to Marcel's request that Norpois speak of him to Mme Swann so that he may one day meet her.

It is a long repertory of themes and characters, of intertwining relationships and preoccupations. The unity of place is the dining room in the apartment of Marcel's par-

ents, but this site serves for the rehearsal and development
of new and old themes. La Berma is a new subject, a new
dimension in Marcel's life story. Swann, whose life and
character is a familiar subject, is now presented from a new
viewpoint. The episode that begins on page 434 with the
sentence *Disons pour finir qui était le marquis de Norpois*
("finally let us say a word about le marquis de Norpois")
and ends on page 480 with the line *Quand M. de Norpois
fut parti* ("When M. de Norpois had gone") is a brilliant
example of Proust's art of recapitulation as it mirrors the
subtle changes constantly taking place simultaneously in
human relationships and in the understanding that we
bring to situations and to people.

The episode seems focused on M. de Norpois, on his
past career of ambassador-diplomat, its influence on his
character and his speech, on his judgments and comments.
But, in reality, the episode is actually concerned with
Marcel. The fifty pages describe a moment in the evolution of Marcel's character, in his search, not initially for
lost time, but for that knowledge of himself in relationship
to people and society and art that will lead him ultimately
to the search for lost time.

Marcel is still in a state of almost total dependence, a
state of fundamental contentment because the protection
of his parents provides him still with a logical assurance
concerning almost every subject. His father and mother are
still omnipotent and godlike. His father is the true head of
the household. If his mother is not fully convinced of M.
de Norpois' greatness, she wants quite sincerely to believe
in it in order to please her husband who is flattered by
the presence of such a widely traveled and courteous dip-
lomat at the family table. A word from Norpois is enough
to convince the parents they should allow Marcel to go to
the theatre and see La Berma. Norpois' interest in literature and his friendship with writers and editors changes
the attitude of the parents toward their son's literary gifts.

Although Marcel is still dependent on the family, his
willing acceptance of their protection and their way of life,
he is still stirred by the two interests that will ultimately

lead him away from his parents: love and society. The
theme of Gilberte and amorous intrigue is well established
by this time; so is the theme of excitement over knowing
another family milieu, another mode of life. But these two
major curiosities in Marcel have not yet endangered or even
weakened his obedience to parental law. He is within the
family circle and looking out beyond it. M. de Norpois'
presence brings to the surface many of Marcel's thoughts
about the theatre, love, society, and a literary vocation
which under normal circumstances, during the usual family dinner, he would not have discussed. He is still protected by the family because M. de Norpois, who encourages him in every way to enrich his life by experiences
outside the family, is his parents' honored guest.

Under his parents' surveillance, Marcel plots to enter the
sacred precincts of Mme Swann's salon, and he secures in
the most natural way possible his liberation from his be-
nevolent jailors who themselves do not fully realize what
they are doing. Parental pride intermittently softens earlier
restrictions. M. de Norpois' interest in Marcel's writing
causes his father to see his son as an academician (*mon
père, me voyant déjà académicien* . . . I, p. 453). But if
the patterns of the escape are already conceived, thanks
to the support of the famous ambassador, Marcel at this
stage is still unwilling to take any real risks by changing his
way of life and by doubting the authority of his parents.
However, Gilberte Swann's appearance in the Champs-
Elysées, in the last chapter of *Du Côté de chez Swann*,
is the starting point for Marcel's emergence from the parental fold—the moment when his eyes turn toward the
world as they behold the red-headed girl and someone
calls her name.

For Marcel, the "world" is first polarized in Gilberte. His
curiosity and his ambitions are subsumed in his strong attraction for her. The slight yet overwhelming obstacles only
exacerbate his love. There is a scene, briefly narrated, of a
physical struggle with Gilberte, half playful, half erotic,
which does, for Marcel, reach an erotic climax, afterwards
reminding him of the cool smell of the trellised room of

oncle Adolphe in Combray. His desire to see and know Gilberte is the propelling force that will carry him into the social world of the Swanns. When his love for Gilberte ends, he will remain a spoiled and favorite member of the Swann world. His acquaintance with Gilberte is the major step toward entering the world of the Guermantes.

Though the salon of Mme Swann is an initial phase, it resembles in many ways all the other phases of Marcel's social conquests. Proust treats each level of society as a spectacle, and there are countless variations in the many social scenes of the novel with descriptions of the beauty, the intelligence, the elegance of Mme Swann, or the extent of her influence on or attraction for those who attend her court. The social scenes in Proust are not unrelated to scenes in the courtly romances of Chrétien de Troyes in the twelfth century where woman for the first time in the history of French literature presided over her house and inspired fidelity and love in the men of her entourage. They are even more strongly reminiscent of the social scenes at the court of Versailles in the *Mémoires* of Saint-Simon.

The Verdurin salon only pretended to be a stronghold, a world closed off from all boors: Mme Swann's salon is somewhat patterned on the Verdurin circle. It is not the citadel of the Faubourg Saint-Germain and the Guermantes' world. It is more adaptable and far more difficult to characterize than the Verdurin world or the Guermantes' world.

We are first introduced to it at the dinner for M. de Norpois when the ambassador answers questions about the Swanns and offers comments which provide a picture, at times cruel but not at all inaccurate, of this first world Marcel is destined to conquer.

Norpois stresses Mme Swann's beauty but strongly underscores the irregularity of the Swann marriage. M. Swann, once the friend of all the highest social groups, has had to create another world around his wife. He has had to make himself into a kind of *parvenu,* in the words of Norpois, and induce those susceptible of being induced to pay homage to Mme Swann. We learn in one of the many

prophetic passages of the omniscient narrator that Swann's
most cherished desire is to introduce his wife and his
daughter to his great friend, the princesse des Laumes,
who is to become the duchesse de Guermantes. This scene
of presentation remains in Swann's mind, his one major
social ambition. But he will die before it takes place. As a
result of the duchesse's adamant refusals, he is denied his
most cherished dream.

Marcel questions Norpois on Bergotte, whom he knows
to be a frequent visitor at the Swanns. This initiates a
rather lengthy critical discussion of Bergotte that upsets
Marcel. Norpois calls Bergotte a "flute player" (*joueur de
flûte*. I, p. 473) and an overmannered, overaffected stylist
who has had an adverse influence on the piece Marcel had
written and shown to the ambassador. This harsh comment momentarily confirms Marcel's doubts about his own
intellectual capacity and his literary future.

The boy asks about the daughter, Gilberte, and Norpois
half remembers seeing her briefly at the Swanns' and
prophesies she will never attain her mother's beauty. The
conversation provides a picture of Mme Swann's world that
makes Marcel more than ever eager to know it. But such
an attainment demands an initiation, and a series of tests.
The hero first has to be prepared. At the very end of Norpois' visit, Marcel clearly defines his position as an outsider
when he says that he has never been introduced to Mme
Swann: *je ne connais pas Mme Swann et . . . je ne lui ai
jamais été présenté* (I, p. 478).

As soon as the request is formulated, Marcel knows by a
slight expression of displeasure on Norpois' face, that he
will not mention his name to Mme Swann. The easiest and
the most natural way for the boy to be introduced is not
through the intervention of Norpois. The test of society has
begun. Marcel the initiate has encountered his first obstacle.

Later, when he falls ill and has to be absent from the
gatherings in the Champs-Elysées, he receives a letter
from Gilberte, inviting him to a *goûter* (or high tea) at

her house, and encouraging him to come often. His happiness at Gilberte's letter knows no bounds, and he savors it as a *cosa mentale*. Marcel learns that the solution to problems often comes from unexpected sources. Bloch and Dr. Cottard had helped to change the attitudes of Gilberte's parents toward Marcel and had thus facilitated his entering the Swann circle. When he begins to frequent the apartment, he is surprised to find himself welcomed and surprised that Gilberte's parents should arrange for him to be with her. He becomes familiar with many aspects of the family: with the *gâteau au chocolat*, an inevitable treat for the *goûter*; Mme Swann's "day" when she receives her friends; Mme Swann's behavior somewhat resembling Mme Verdurin's pouting despotism; Odette's friend Mme Bontemps, whose famous niece is Albertine.

He participates more and more intimately in the family life, enters the "sanctuary" of M. Swann's library, goes on small trips with the Swanns, listens to Mme Swann play the Vinteuil sonata, part of which Swann had once loved so dearly. He is troubled by the discourtesy Gilberte shows her father one day when she insists on attending a concert on the anniversary of her grandfather's death. These episodes lead up to the scene at Mme Swann's luncheon party for sixteen to which she invites Marcel, and where he meets his idolized Bergotte for the first time.

This meeting has been meticulously prepared by Proust. In *Du Côté de chez Swann,* Bergotte was for Marcel the consecrated author, the man haloed with literary prestige and glory. Part of Marcel's attraction to Gilberte stemmed from her friendship with Bergotte, and the gift of the booklet on Racine was a tangible and perhaps exaggerated testimonial of her affection for him. Marcel did not know that Bergotte was to be present at Mme Swann's luncheon. Suddenly he hears the name Bergotte pronounced, and he is face to face with the man himself. The physical appearance of Bergotte corresponds in no way to the image Marcel had formed in his mind. He is facing a young man, short and thick set, myopic, with a red nose in the form of a snail shell and a black goatee: *un homme jeune, rude, petit, râblé et myope, à nez rouge en forme de coquille de colimaçon et à barbiche noire* (I, p. 547). Marcel is bewildered by the disparity between Bergotte's literary character and physical appearance. His shock deepens as he hears Bergotte speak and learns of the writer's dubiously effective ways of securing admission to the Académie.

Marcel refers to the small book on Racine and tells Bergotte he saw La Berma in two acts of *Phèdre*. Here again, it is difficult for the boy to reconcile Bergotte with his derogatory remarks on the art of La Berma. An effect of green light makes Phèdre resemble a coral branch at the bottom of the sea. He knows this is related to the vengeance of Neptune, but after all, Racine was not telling the love story of sea urchins: *ce que Racine a raconté ce ne sont pas les amours des oursins* (I, p. 561). The tone of Bergotte's speech, the witticisms, are in strong contrast to the noble literary style of the writer.

This first meeting with Bergotte is a vital experience in Marcel's intellectual and aesthetic formation. He is in the presence of a man he has long considered a genius, and his meditation centers for a while on the meaning of the word "genius" as it applies to the writer. As he listens to Bergotte's elocution and conversation, as he perceives moral defects in his god's character, he concludes that genius is derived less from intelligence and social refinement than from the capacity to transpose and transform these elements. When Marcel defines genius as that which allows one to make his personality into a mirror, endowing one with the power of reflecting rather than of conveying the intrinsic quality of what is reflected, he announces aesthetic convictions that will be developed and applied to the other creative artists in the novel—to Elstir the painter and Vinteuil the composer. Traits in Bergotte's style mirrored in some ways the writings of younger men of his day, and his work thus created affinities with other works of his time. Bergotte seemed to owe nothing or very little to other writers, yet Marcel carefully makes the point that Bergotte's way of speaking comes from an old friend, a brilliant speaker who had written only mediocre books.

Bergotte is looked upon as an authentic writer of genius, but his genius comes to very little. He learned from others that he had genius, but this awareness did not seriously affect him or interrupt his egotistic ambitious search for literary recognition and glory. Marcel is quite ready to believe that the great writer has developed in Bergotte at the expense of the mediocre character. He ponders the discrepancy between the nobility of a writer's work and the secret vices of the writer as a man. The encounter initiates difficult moral problems for young Marcel, but he is made to feel that he himself has made something of a conquest. At the end of the visit, Bergotte manifests interest in the boy, inquires about his bad health, and congratulates him on his intelligence and the pleasures he must derive from it. Marcel's answer is surprisingly clear—and negative. He claims that the pleasures of the intellect are of little importance for him, that he does not seek them out and has never really enjoyed them. *Non, monsieur, les plaisirs de l'intelligence sont bien peu de chose pour moi, ce n'est pas eux que je recherche, je ne sais même pas si je les ai jamais goûtés* (I, p. 570). Startling on first reading, this acknowledgment on the part of Marcel is probably one of the most important clues to the character of Marcel Proust and to the art of *A la recherche du temps perdu*.

No scene in Proust ever concentrates for long on one theme. The passage on Bergotte is interrupted at one moment by a portrait of Gilberte whom Marcel watches as she stands between her mother and father, and coyly leans her head on M. Swann's shoulder. There is a striking contrast between the black hair of Odette and her daughter's red hair. Gilberte has her father's ruddy complexion. But Marcel realizes she reflects and exemplifies characteristics of both parents. Her nose, for example, is her mother's, and there are expressions in her eyes that are like both Swann and Odette. Her parents' two natures are in her, as if her body were Mélusine's. This is Proust's first reference to the famous Poitou fairy, half woman, half dragon, who will

reappear at the beginning of *Le Côté de Guermantes.*\* The
fusion of qualities and defects in Gilberte's character and
body is not unlike the analysis of Bergotte in the same
scene, or, for that matter, of any Proust character.

Marcel's meditation on Bergotte's genius, and his musing
on Gilberte, seen as a kind of Mélusine, conclude Marcel's
initiation to the social world of the Swanns. Marcel cannot
imagine at this point in the story any social world more
different from the first social world he had known in Combray. He realizes that his acceptance in the salon of Mme
Swann is his first move toward society (*le monde*), and he
is already sufficiently experienced about such matters to
know that he has not yet reached the mainstream of society but only a backwater. *Ce n'était pas encore la grande
mer, c'était déjà la lagune* (I, p. 572).

The test has been passed; the candidate is received. And
now during the final seventy pages of the chapter, *Autour
de Mme Swann,* we follow the diminution of the very motive that had led Marcel to undertake the perilous journey
from Combray to Swann's Way: his love for Gilberte.

The end is not abrupt. Sentiment in Proust is an elaborate story which survives long after in the memory. It
mingles, during the last part of the chapter on Mme
Swann's salon, with many activities of life, new events,
familiar patterns. Bloch confides to Marcel that women
like to make love and introduces him to a house of prostitution. Out of friendliness for the *patronne*, Marcel gives
the house one of tante Léonie's sofas on which as a boy he
had his first sexual experiences with a girl cousin. The
*patronne* tries to focus Marcel's interest on Rachel, a Jewish
girl, whom Marcel associates, without knowing her, with an
aria from Halévy's *La Juive,* "Rachel, quand du Seigneur."

This episode of the *maison de passe* is one way to dim
his love for Gilberte. Another is an effort to write an article
for *Le Figaro.* After his last visits with Gilberte, the two
continue to correspond. Marcel's suffering turns into senti-

---

\* This reference to Mélusine is not recorded in the index of
names of the Pléiade edition, III, p. 1241.

mental memories. The return of New Year's Day, for example, reminds him of his far more acute suffering the year
before. He realizes that the part of him that loved Gilberte
is committing suicide (*un long et cruel suicide du moi qui
en moi-même aimait Gilberte.* I, p. 610) while the other
part of him, unaffected by Gilberte, grows stronger. He
sells a Chinese vase, given to him by tante Léonie, so that
he can send flowers regularly to Gilberte, but then, from
a cab, he sees her walking with a young man. This chance
encounter in the street allows him to terminate his love
more quickly and more definitively. His visits to Gilberte
become more infrequent and then stop altogether.

In Marcel's mind, his feeling for Gilberte is transferred
to Mme Swann and his courtship of her continues, more
respectful, charged with more poetry and abstractions, because the goal is now merely the empty ritual of courtship,
with no hope, and, ultimately, no real desire, for reward.

It is spring, and Holy Week. Pagan and Christian terms,
related to seasonal changes and adoration, will permeate
the last pages of the chapter. Mme Swann feels the cold of
early spring. Wrapped in ermine, she receives her guests
in her apartment. She is surrounded by white flowers
(*boules de neige*), and Marcel admires the virginal setting, the white flowers and furs. He remembers the per-
fumed path of Tansonville in Combray and measures the
distances between the hawthorns of Combray when Mme
Swann was only a name, a remote figure, and this spring in
Paris where she insists that he continue to see her even if
he will not see her daughter.

On a May Sunday at noon they plan to meet at the Arc
de Triomphe for a walk. She appears walking on the sand
of one of the *allées* so suddenly and with such beauty that
Marcel compares her to a flower opening in the warmth of
noon. Her costume, different each time, is usually dominated by the color of mauve. Her silk parasol is mauve and
matches part of her costume. She appears surrounded by
Swann and four or five club men. This appearance is not
casual. It is a liturgical part of spring for Marcel, a rite,
and he fervently compares Odette's opened parasol to a

miniature sky, warm, sheltering, clement. Odette is the spring and the sun, and she greets him with the English phrase, "Good morning!" Everything designates her as the goddess, the priestess: her beauty, the intricacies of her attire, especially visible when she opens her coat. Even on foot, as she appears on this particular Sunday, when no carriage follows her, she is for Marcel a sovereign lady mingling with the crowd, comparable to the Greek figure of Hypatia.

Even as Odette acknowledges prince Sagan's theatrical bow and as Marcel observes young men hesitant about approaching her for fear M. Swann will not recognize them, she expresses her regret that Marcel has stopped seeing Gilberte and says he must continue to see her. The entire scene, where Odette appears as the incarnation of Woman, is an antidote for the scenes of the past year when Marcel has suffered in his love for Gilberte. And he draws the conclusion that the memory of poetic moments in life, such as this morning scene in May between 12:15 and 1:00, is longer and more tenacious than the memories of suffering. Odette's silk parasol symbolizes the scene with its mauve color, as strongly mauve as if it reflected an arbor of wisteria. The passage ends on the pastel-colored word *glycines*.

In seven pages of long sentences, the allegory is fully developed, richly orchestrated: love in its courtly aspects, spring, the sun rites of spring, and the specific habits and conversations of Parisian strollers on a Sunday morning. It forms one of the great scenes in Proust, a strict parallel to the final page of *Du Côté de chez Swann,* where Woman is incarnated in Odette in the Bois and men are described as satellites moving around her. Odette's second appearance near the Arc de Triomphe, which concludes the first chapter of *A l'ombre des jeunes filles en fleurs,* is far more theatrical and far more important for the protagonist than the appearance of La Berma on the stage in the role of *Phèdre.* Life itself is the drama in Proust, in moments remembered and understood only after the passing of years.

7. *A l'ombre des jeunes filles en fleurs.*
B. The problem of incommunicability

The title of the second and last chapter of *A l'ombre des jeunes filles en fleurs* parallels, with one important change, the title of the last chapter in *Du Côté de chez Swann: Noms de Pays: le Pays.* In the first book, the emphasis was on the magic properties of the name Balbec (*le nom*). Now, in the second book, Marcel discovers the place itself and experiences it directly: *le pays.* More than three hundred pages long, the chapter follows, in its general lines, a chronological order although we are reminded on the very first page that our "real" life is not chronological. Marcel's new indifference to Gilberte is intermittent, and he can return mentally, while still in Balbec, to the Champs-Elysées and Mme Swann's apartment where he had loved his young friend.

The first development of the chapter is the transition from Paris to Marcel's room in the hotel at Balbec. It is composed of many episodes: the Gare Saint-Lazare, the 1:22 train trip to Normandy, the companionship of his grandmother who interrupts her trip to visit a friend, the early morning stop in a station where he sees a girl selling *café-au-lait,* the arrival at Balbec and his disappointment with his impressions of the town and the church, the final lap of the trip to Balbec-Plage, the impressive stairway in the Grand Hôtel, his grandmother's embarrassing discussion with the manager over the terms for the rooms, the elevator, the room, and his grandmother's constant attention. Marcel is in a new room in a new place, but he still

enjoys the protection and the advice of his family, represented by his intelligent, noble-minded, selfless grandmother.

The second development is Marcel's introduction to the
varied world of the hotel: visitors who come to see him or
his grandmother, people who work for the hotel, and tourists. He observes the headwaiter Aimé, a country gentleman and his daughter from Brittany, M. and Mlle de Stermaria, who seem to scorn everyone else, the marquise de
Villeparisis who had gone to school with Marcel's grandmother and who takes him on carriage drives to visit
churches. Mme de Villeparisis turns out to be a member of
the Guermantes family, the first whom Marcel can call a
friend, and she introduces him at Balbec to two other members of her family: Robert de Saint-Loup, a handsome
young man elegantly dressed and mannered, and his uncle
M. de Charlus. Again, through Mme de Villeparisis, Marcel
meets his "first highness," the princesse de Luxembourg.
Bloch, one of Marcel's Paris friends, is also at Balbec, and
Marcel observes some of the Jewish characteristics of
Bloch's family.

Marcel's growing interest in a very attractive group of
young girls he sees on the beach and the sea wall (*digue*)
is the third development in this first visit to Balbec. He
learns some of their names and recognizes among them that
of Albertine Simonet, niece of Mme Bontemps, about whom
he had first heard in Mme Swann's salon. The theme of
*les jeunes filles* is closely related to Marcel's introduction
to the painter Elstir whose studio he visits and with whom
he discusses the art of painting. Albertine is a friend of
Elstir. The painter turns out to be M. Biche, habitué of
Mme Verdurin's clan, who had once used Odette as a
model for his painting entitled "Miss Sacripant."

A possible fourth and final movement of the long chapter is Marcel's awareness that he prefers Albertine to all the
other girls, that he is even beginning to suffer because of
his attraction to her. But at this point the summer season
is over. The first chill of fall settles over Balbec and the

Grand Hôtel de la Plage begins the complex preparations
for closing down.

Despite the presence of Mme Amédée, Marcel's grandmother, his sojourn at Balbec is a far more serious separation from home than his introduction to Mme Swann. By
his gifts of curiosity and sympathy, he is attracted to a
great variety of people: the elevator boy in the hotel,
whom he compares to a squirrel in his cage; Mlle de Stermaria, to all appearances cold, haughty beauty; Mme de
Villeparisis, ceaselessly attentive and thoughtful to both
Marcel and his grandmother; Bloch, whose awkwardness
and social pretensions he describes in an objective fashion;
Robert de Saint-Loup, whose striking appearance, a "gold-
crested bird," and whose mechanical movements of politeness make him first into an inaccessible human being; the
baron de Charlus, whose behavior and conversation are a
complete enigma to Marcel; Elstir, gentle and thoughtful
and already a great artist, who befriends Marcel; Albertine,
the black-haired cyclist, whose polo hat is recognizable at
a distance.

The chapter is a maze of sensations, one of the most intricately presented episodes in the novel, with a constantly
moving, constantly shuttling background of landscape and
beings. It is a development of continuing themes, of new
themes which emerge from familiar names, situations, and
concepts. Balbec and the ocean are always present, even
if they recede from immediate focus. Marcel's excitement
and extraordinary attentiveness are sustained by the novelty of the place for him, by the endless richness in human
types and human dramas, in the architectural revelations
of the churches, in the natural settings of sea and country.

Each of the four arbitrarily chosen "developments" in
the chapter is replete with details, and the four are made to
fuse with one another as if to prohibit any editorial separa-
tions. And yet, in each of these possible developments, one
episode or theme stands out in relief and gives a focused
meaning to the specific moment in the narrative. This is a
recurrent technical device in Proust's art which permits

pause and allows for reconcentration in passages of heavily charged narrative writing.

In the first development, the transition from Paris to the Grand Hôtel, it would seem to be *la chambre*, the theme of Marcel's new room where he will live and sleep, in accord with the pattern of other rooms, where he will savor, in his solitude, the new experiences of the seaside resort. In the second development, as he is introduced to three members of the Guermantes, it is the vision of the three trees of Balbec, seen during the carriage drive with Mme de Villeparisis—a vision which he had, as a young writer, from his childhood, associated with the magic of the name Guermantes. The third development, which occurs outside of the precincts of the hotel, culminates in Elstir's studio when the painter analyzes his art of metamorphosis and gives his young admirer thereby a new understanding of the principles of art. The fourth development is characterized by the genesis of Marcel's love for Albertine. She emerges from the group of *jeunes filles*, and even from the sea itself, as the figure destined to precipitate the longest single theme in *A la recherche du temps perdu*.

These four motifs: the hotel room, the vision of the trees, the art of painting, and Albertine all have to do with the experience of communication, of human understanding, of its possibility and its impossibility. The four motifs illustrate four answers that Marcel Proust gives to the problem of human expression and communication. In Marcel's new room at Balbec, the thoughtfulness of his grandmother seeks to establish communication by a system of tapping on the wall separating her room from his. The room is fundamentally the site of solitude and memory where the boy is, in the experience of sleep and meditation, quite literally cut off from the world. But if he is in need of attention, he can rap on the wall and his grandmother will respond. There is still some sense of security, of family warmth, of a primitive kind of signaling established to relieve the monotony of solitude and the anguish of estrangement. It is not communication in any full verbal sense, because, much later in time, Marcel learns that, in the sum-

mer, he had not understood his grandmother: he had failed
to comprehend her suffering and the pathos of her feelings.
It was a bare communication, a bare signaling of human
presence. We are led to feel also that the grandmother
could not possibly follow all the thoughts of her grandson
or understand the meaning of the experiences he was living
through. This lack of full understanding between the
young man and his grandmother begins in the 1:22 train
from Paris, where he drinks cognac (on the advice of his
doctor) in order to reach a state of euphoria and to alleviate
any suffocating seizures which, if they occurred, would upset her. But her deep dislike of alcohol and her deep mis-
givings at any signs of inebriation in members of her family
are not to be mollified. She tries not to look at Marcel when
he returns from the buffet car, and each remains isolated
from the other in an impossible impasse of stricture, love,
medical expediency, sorrow. A humorous incident, indeed,
but one fraught with all the desperate impossibility of communication between two individuals. From this one incident
in the train, we learn one of Proust's general theses:
that what is communicated between two individuals is at
best fragmentary and usually susceptible of radical misunderstanding.

The importance of the train ride to Balbec and of Marcel's room at the hotel is explained in each case by the
presence of his grandmother. She is both with him, in the
train compartment and the room, and separated from him,
as when she leaves him to complete the trip by himself,
and when she is occupying her own room in the hotel. The
communication between grandson and grandmother is on
the level of mutual assistance, of watchfulness, but it is
interrupted by the grandmother's absence.

When the grandmother joins the boy at the hotel, she
happily resumes her role of servant and protectress, as she
helps him take off his boots and prepare for bed. In the
morning, however, Marcel feels his aloneness in the unfamiliar room, separated from familiar habits. (*Habitude*
is one of the key words in the novel.) As he washes and
tries to find his things in the new setting, he thinks of the

pleasures which the day will bring him. The stiff starched towel, bearing the name of the hotel, will not absorb the moisture on his face and hands. It is a physical evidence of Balbec's strangeness, one of the many obstacles to overcome before Balbec becomes familiar, *une habitude.*

The role played by the grandmother in Marcel's earliest initiation to Balbec is played by Mme de Villeparisis in the wider, more social initiation to the beach resort. This is one of the many instances in the novel when Marcel learns about life and society and art from an older woman. In another way, more sensual and more brief, he is attracted to beautiful young girls (the peasant girl at the railroad station and the *jeunes filles* of the beach), but he is more lengthily described by Proust (except in his love for Albertine) as the admiring young man attracted to older women because of their knowledge of the world and their social charm, and perhaps especially because of the mysteriousness of their past and the way in which it lives in them.

What we learn about the personality of Mme de Villeparisis is a foreshadowing of the significant episode of "the three trees of Balbec." The carriage drives she offers Marcel accommodate both the boy's sickliness and his interest in church architecture. Mme de Villeparisis continues, as far as her social position will allow, the role of nurse, of intellectual guide and stimulator. Not only is she the grandmother's former schoolmate, she is partially the grandmother's substitute as both nurse and mentor. Marcel was born into a world of virtue and honor, and he will end by knowing a world of vice and dishonor, but his introduction to the world is gradual. Between these two extremes revealed in *A la recherche du temps perdu,* the phases leading from one to the other are multiple, overlapping, and subtly interdependent. Mme de Villeparisis has more than a superficial knowledge of churches and church architecture. Marcel notices the precision with which she describes historical monuments. She avoids using technical terms, through a sense of modesty, but she has revealed a rather extensive knowledge of painting, music, and literature. This knowl-

edge is connected with her way of life and the Guermantes'
past. There is, for example, a portrait of one of her ancestors by Titian.

This is the background for the particular carriage drive
with Mme de Villeparisis when the important episode of
the "trees" takes place. *Nous descendîmes sur Hudimesnil*
is the introduction to the passage where Marcel speaks once
again of feeling a deep happiness (I, p. 717) which he has
not experienced since Combray. Before explaining it, he
associates it with what he felt on seeing the steeples of
Martinville. The relationship between the present experience and the earlier experience in the carriage of Dr.
Percepied is swiftly established. As if traveling in orbit,
Marcel returns full circle to a point where a vision initiates
a spiritual experience. Many elements in the two carriage
episodes of Combray and Balbec are similar, but the orbit
is wider (Marcel is older) and the point at which he pauses
is therefore richer in experience and knowledge.

The passage on the "trees of Hudimesnil," which lasts
only three pages (I, 717–20), is a study of the impotence
of voluntary memory. As the carriage passes along the road,
Marcel sees ahead of him a group of three trees at the beginning of a path. They form a design which he remembers having seen somewhere. In his effort to recover the
source of this picture, everything becomes unreal for him:
the carriage, Balbec, and Mme de Villeparisis. He almost
succeeds in recapturing the memory, but to work the miracle he must be alone. He notes the rarity of this experience
as he speaks for a moment as the omniscient narrator.
When an experience is fully recaptured, Marcel's happiness
is intense, as with the cup of tea and the madeleine.

The three trees seem to be moving straight at him as the
carriage approaches. Where has he seen them before, in
real life or in a dream? They assume, during a very brief
moment in time, a mythic appearance. Marcel thinks of
them as friends who have died and who are pleading with
him to bring them back to life. The branches are like arms
gesticulating in a tragic way (*leur gesticulation naïve et
passionnée*). But the carriage has passed the point where

he can see them, and he can no longer retrieve this moment from the void of the past. Marcel accepts the fact that he will never know what the trees meant to him, or be able to comprehend the message which was expressed in the desperate, articulate gesture of the branches. Though it does not specifically refer to the myth of Daphne, the passage does bring it to mind. A tragic tone of impotency pervades the entire passage. Marcel feels guilty in not being able to recall the past moment when he had seen the same design as that created by the trees of Hudimesnil. Powerless to help a phantom friend, as it were, he has also failed to acknowledge a god. Unable to stir from his *strapontin* seat in the carriage, he compares himself to Prometheus chained, who can only listen to the sound of the sea and the cries of the spirits around him.

The experience of *les trois arbres de Balbec* is far more than a minor episode or accidental occasion. It is related to Marcel's reason for writing a novel, to his concern with the entire problem of communication. As a writer, Proust's most deeply felt need was to make intelligible, to recast in the form of concepts and notions, sensorial experience. Marcel's regret at not having the faculty of total recall as his carriage drives past the three trees of Hudimesnil is similar to the writer's experience of impotency when he tries to put into words non-verbal sensory experiences. *A la recherche du temps perdu* is a gigantic record of Proust's multiple hypotheses by which he tried to answer this personal—yet universal—need: the need to recapture the past and communicate one's most deeply felt moments of happiness. The episode of the *trois arbres* illustrates this need.

Unconsciously, inadvertently, Mme de Villeparisis is responsible for this unfulfilled experience. But quite consciously, she introduces Marcel to her young nephew (just a bit older than Marcel), Robert de Saint-Loup, attached to the garrison in the neighboring town of Doncières and a candidate for the military school in Saumur. Robert is an elegant, handsome Guermantes: blond hair, with eyes the color of the sea, athletic, stylishly dressed, virile, passionate. Before meeting him, Marcel had counted upon him as a friend, but at the introduction Robert appears haughty, indifferent, almost insolent. This is one of the many errant first impressions in the novel, because the day after the introduction, Robert expresses an eagerness to become friends with Marcel, and a friendship does develop. The manners of the aristocrat are, however, different from the manners of a young bourgeois—as Marcel learns through his own ineptness. Each Guermantes in the novel seems aloof at first, and devoid of warmth. The *grand seigneur*, in Robert, for example, is always in him, but in contradiction to his affectionate nature and excessive kindness. The way in which the two traits are mingled is carefully analyzed, but the full revelation of this dichotomy comes only in time.

The half-successful communication with the trees is beautifully paralleled in counterpoint (the prevailing technique of Proust's composition) and on the human level in Marcel's introduction to Robert de Saint-Loup, Mme de Villeparisis' young nephew, and to her older nephew, forty-year-old M. de Charlus. The male characters in Proust's novel are far more mysterious than the women. They are more complex because they practice far more drastically than the women the art of dissimulation. They are less satisfied with their social class: they are either looking up to a higher class (Legrandin, Bloch, Morel) or down to a lower class usually for sexual reasons (Robert, Marcel, Charlus). The female social climbers (Odette, Mme Verdurin) in keeping with their distinct characterizations, are clearly depicted. But the male characters in their envy of social classes other than their own and in the many conflicting elements of their temperaments are actors in the human drama, disguised characters who function on more than one level simultaneously. Marcel himself is a complex character, as is Swann also. The higher the social class, the more complex the personality becomes, because the need for dissimulation is greater. The two male members of the Guermantes family, the younger Robert and the older Charlus (or "Palamède" as Robert calls his uncle) are the most subtle, complex, richly fulfilled, and ultimately the most tragic figures in *A la recherche du temps perdu.*

The seeming contradictions in Robert's manner do not puzzle Marcel for long. He is quickly won over to Robert's charm, to his intelligence and goodness. Robert is concerned with Marcel's health, and he is gracious to his grandmother. His infatuation with an actress and his suffering over her indifference to him never affect his impeccable manners and his feelings of friendship. Though Mme de Villeparisis introduces her nephew baron de Charlus to Marcel, it is Robert who describes his uncle to Marcel by stressing his athletic prowess, his masculinity, his amorous conquests. Marcel, however, hesitates to draw any conclusions from his own observations of Charlus' strange behavior. Marcel is both puzzled by Charlus' sudden changes in tone and behavior, and attracted by the man's perceptiveness and intelligence. He often speaks in aphorisms (which Marcel carefully notes) such as the remarks on love in the conversation on Mme de Sévigné and Racine: Charlus claims that the experience of love is far more important than either the lover or the beloved—*l'important dans la vie n'est pas ce qu'on aime, . . . c'est d'aimer* (I, p. 763). It is one of the first statements we hear from Charlus, and an important clue to an understanding of all the love stories in the novel.

In these introductory scenes at Balbec, when Marcel stands just outside the mysterious, privileged Guermantes circle, we feel the drama of incommunicability and of misunderstanding, as we had felt it in a less humanly poignant way in the episode of the trees of Hudimesnil. But if incommunicability is destined to form the dramatic crux in Proust's work and the factor that creates suffering for the protagonist and other characters, its depiction in the novel reflects the wisdom and tolerance of one of the great observers of the human heart. He has learned many things from the love lavished on him by his mother and grandmother, from Swann's love for Odette, from his own infatuation for Gilberte, from the sight of the Martinville steeples and the Balbec trees, from even the taste of a madeleine. He has learned the disparity between the evocative power of a name (Gilberte, Balbec, Guermantes) and the reality which a name designates. All of these lessons, these tests of character, cast in the form of a hero's initiation, form parts of the central Proustian lesson on happiness. *Bonheur* is one of the major words in Proust's vocabulary. It has been used in describing the great sensory recollections of the past, those realized (the incident of the madeleine) and those unrealized (the trees of Balbec), but for the first time it is explicitly alluded to in Marcel's introduction to Robert de Saint-Loup. The friendship he desires with the young aristocrat, a friendship he will have for a long period of time, is more pleasurable in contemplation than in actual involvement.

Marcel has already felt a similar happiness when alone in nature (when contemplating, for example, the hedge of hawthorns in Combray, or walking in the woods and imagining that he was holding a peasant girl in his arms). Alone in most of the major scenes of involuntary memory, when a fragment of the past emerges again in his memory, he is overcome with a deep personal jubilation. And now, in his analysis of friendship, though he speaks of the pleasure he feels in the presence of Robert during their long conversations, he recognizes that his happiness is far greater when he is alone and only thinking of his friendship with Robert.

This important passage (I, p. 736) concerns Marcel's predestined solitude (the solitude, of course, not only of Proust but of every creative artist). It is the acknowledgment of the power and superiority of the imaginative life over "real" or social life. The hours spent willingly and happily with Robert in conversation are always followed by a sense of remorse when Marcel realizes that the time was, in a sense, wasted. He might have spent the time alone and at work. Marcel is making the point that no real communication is possible in any conversation with Robert, nor in any social activity, but only in the creation of a work of art. And such creation demands solitude.

The third episode or development that continues the theme of communication is Marcel's introduction to the stu-

dio of Elstir and his discussions with the painter. As the
vision of the trees of Balbec was prepared by Marcel's
meeting with Mme de Villeparisis and continued in his
meetings with Robert and Charlus, so the meeting with
Elstir and the discussions on aesthetics are prepared by
Marcel's vision of the young girls at Balbec. They excite
his imagination and his senses, and they are described as
groups of statuary, as models for a painter. The entire experience of the *jeunes filles* and Elstir is one step farther in
Marcel's separation from home. In his meeting with the
three Guermantes, he relies on his grandmother's early
friendship with Mme de Villeparisis, but the girls he encounters as well as Elstir are acquaintances made outside
of the family.

At first Marcel is sensitive to the beauty of young women
in general. They are everywhere, in groups, at the Casino,
at the pastry shop, or on the sea wall. He looks upon them
collectively as *la petite bande,* in somewhat the same way
Swann had looked upon the habitués of Mme Verdurin's
salon. Their beauty and their ceaseless activities strike him
forcibly: he compares them to Greek virgins (*vierges hel-
léniques*). Their swift movements, against the background
of the ever-moving sea, accentuates for Marcel the fleeting-
ness of life, the ephemerality of human life. In his imagination he wonders if he will ever be able to penetrate a single
human life, and really to know a human being.

Then out from the fluid, collective, mobile beauty of the
*jeunes filles,* one emerges on whom Marcel begins to fix his
attention. Her eyes are brilliant and sparkling; she wears a
black polo hat and walks beside her bicycle. The sensual
swing of her hips as she walks and the slang of her speech
cause him to imagine she is the mistress of a professional
cyclist, or perhaps a sprite (*une péri*) of fabulous origin.
When he learns her name—she is Albertine and referred to
as "la petite Simonet"—he contrasts her dark hair with the
red hair of Gilberte, who had been for him the embodiment
of the inaccessible ideal of woman. He wonders if he is ever
to become friends with any of these girls, or with Albertine *la brune,* in particular.

The meeting with Albertine will come about in Elstir's studio, and put an end to the purely imaginary life and reverie that she has inspired. But between the pages in which Albertine is distinguished from the other girls of *la petite bande*, and her emergence as a central character in the narrative at the end of *A l'ombre des jeunes filles en fleurs*, an important passage occurs: a brief synopsis of Proust's aesthetics. The meeting with Elstir, first at the restaurant of Rivebelle where Marcel and Robert introduce themselves to him and later in Elstir's studio, occasions the conversations in which Marcel formulates an aesthetic creed centered on actual paintings in Elstir's studio, and on insights into the life of the artist which he gets from Elstir. Fundamentally, the aesthetics of the paintings and the psychological theories concerning the habits of the artist are related to the dominant theme of communication which pervades the entire chapter and which, moreover, is a leading leitmotiv of *A la recherche du temps perdu*.

As Marcel enters the studio, Elstir the "creator" is finishing, with brush in hand, the "form" of the setting sun. *Au moment où j'entrai, le créateur était en train d'achever, avec le pinceau qu'il tenait dans sa main, la forme du soleil à son coucher.* Elstir is referred to as *creator* and the sun he is painting *form* (I, p. 834). With these solemn terms the discussions on art begin. As Marcel examines Elstir's seascapes (*les marines*), he sees them as metamorphoses of objects, a process analogous to the creation of metaphor in poetry. Marcel Proust, the writer, does not hesitate to claim that art is metaphor.

The artist is the man who transforms an object in his mind in order to enter into closer identification with it. Nature is seen by the artist in its core of reality, rather than in minute, physical detail. The artist's poetic vision of nature is the subject matter of his work. In Elstir's painting of the harbor of Carquethuit, the artist used seascapes in painting the town, and landscapes in painting the sea. The painting is a kind of metaphor in which the land is used for the sea, and the sea for the land. This deliberate confusion shocks the spectator's reason, but the painting

imposes its own metaphoric truth and surpasses the mere
reality of the objects represented in it. Art becomes, then,
a recasting of nature by means of the artist's imagination
and his sensitivity. In recreating an object, by making it
into a metaphor, the artist exercises the freedom of his
own spirit. The result of this freedom, the paintings themselves, may in time come to be laws of a style or a movement in art. In Elstir's method, Proust obviously describes
the method of the impressionist painters. Technology, in
its turn, by the process of photography, will vulgarize the
methods and the manners of art. In its simplest form, Elstir's method is reminiscent of the method of impressionism
quite in keeping with Proust's method as novelist: the effort, first, to recapture and rediscover the original impression of a scene or an object, and, second, to reconstruct or
recompose that impression.

In the first chapter of *A l'ombre des jeunes filles en
fleurs*, Marcel received from the writer Bergotte his first
indoctrination in art and the artist, and now in this second
chapter, he has a second indoctrination, more detailed and
more pointedly relevant, from the painter Elstir. The fundamental lesson would seem to be that painting is not an
imitation of nature, but a conscious metamorphosis of nature. (In speaking of the literary art, one would say that
writing is not a transcription but a reordering of life.) In
the philosophical sense, Proust is saying that objective reality is never fully knowable. All that we can hope to have
from it is illusions, and the artist's work is the record of
these illusions.

The laws Proust derives from the painter's art are more
applicable to his own than the literary and musical examples he uses. The painter, he seems to say, reconstructs
the world as a god might reconstruct it. He does not reproduce the world as he sees it with the everyday vision
of men who have been told what to expect when they
look at objective reality. The artist looks at the world
freshly and does not see it in the same way as others,
trained by habit and custom, see it. He sees reality more
as a child sees it when he looks at it for the first time, or

as reality appears in dreams. That is why the artist will find relationships different from those to which his public has become accustomed. The artist as a man and as an individual need not communicate with other men. But his work: his writing, his painting, his compositions, if successful, is communicable to others.

Elstir, whose name is almost an anagram of Whistler but whose work might suggest several painters (Manet, Monet, Renoir, Degas) first appeared in the Verdurin circle, where he was known as M. Biche; in Balbec, he now appears as sage, a genius-figure who will teach the protagonist doctrines that Marcel Proust has already accepted.

The general theory treated in this passage is Baudelaire's dictum that painting is not separate from the literary experience. The Proustian lesson that everything is in an undetermined flux is itself an impressionist theory. And there are echoes of Ruskin here in the discussions on the uniqueness of the vision of each artist, and style defined as the quality of an artist's vision. Elstir himself, as mentioned before, is formed from many models, but his philosophy of art is predominantly that of John Ruskin: for example, the beliefs that beauty resides in humble things, that genius is an act of intuition, that the artist must sacrifice his life to his work, and that the method by which a great artist reveals the universe is to describe it with his own personal vision of it.

Despite these positive expressions of aesthetic belief, Proust does not neglect the harassing problem of communication, never absent for long from his treatment. The essence of things revealed in art, in Elstir's paintings as well as in Proust's novel, is partly subjective and incommunicable because it is recorded in the artist himself. What Proust communicates in his art is what he has understood of reality but it is at best only a fragment of his experience, transposed according to the laws of analogy, metaphor, and symbol. Art translates, records, and perpetuates the most valuable illusions of an artist.

In his discussion of art Swann was concerned with the relationship between art and the familiar objects in the

world, things and beings seen in daily life (Odette reminded him of a Botticelli painting), whereas Elstir emphasizes the relationship between a work of art and the
artist. In Elstir's studio, Marcel experiences the intellectual
excitement and stimulation that Bergotte had spoken of on
one occasion. Yet his mind is constantly turning toward
what he considers the inaccessible Albertine, the girl with
the black polo hat and the black hair. Elstir's contribution
to Marcel's education is not solely aesthetic and philosophical, for a young girl enters the studio to greet the painter:
Albertine Simonet. As Swann had seen Odette in the salon
of Mme Verdurin at the beginning of their courtship, so
Marcel sees Albertine several times in Elstir's studio. Art's
aesthetic discoveries are, in Proust, never disassociated for
long from the concerns of the heart. The communication
of the artist is not treated as a phenomenon totally different from the communication of the lover to the beloved.

Thus the fourth motif of the long chapter on Balbec
(*Noms de Pays: le Pays*) is Marcel's meeting with Albertine, the object of his coveteousness. Fittingly, this motif
emerges from what we have called the third motif, the
revelation of Elstir's art.

The conjunctions of a single scene in Proust are rich
and revelatory. Albertine's appearance in the studio is preceded by Elstir's enthusiastic analysis of the porch of the
church of Balbec, on which the Bible is depicted in stone.
After Albertine's departure, Marcel discovers one of Elstir's
watercolor portraits of a young woman dressed as a man,
which is turned against the wall. The bottom of the picture bears the inscription *Miss Sacripant, octobre 1872.* Elstir quickly hides the picture when he hears his wife coming and modestly refers to it as a document on the theatre
style of the period. In subsequent conversation, Marcel
learns that the figure in the portrait is Odette de Crécy,
whom the reader first encountered as *la dame en rose,* a
friend of oncle Adolphe, and then as Mme Swann. The
mystery surrounding "Miss Sacripant"—her bizarre costume
and Elstir's eagerness to hide it from his wife—faintly re-

calls Albertine, with her contradictions in appearances and
the many obscurities in her life and character.

The mystery that surrounds the origins of a work of art
is somewhat comparable to the mystery that surrounds a
person one meets for the first time. The fortuitous conjunction of "Miss Sacripant" and Albertine in Elstir's studio
is preceded by a series of parallel situations and themes
which have formed the narrative substance of the first two
parts of A la recherche du temps perdu. Combray and
Balbec are two worlds, the first designating the relative
innocence of Marcel, and the second his initiation to a
modest sophistication. The hawthorns of Combray are replaced by the sea at Balbec as a stimulus for Marcel's
meditations. The church of Combray (Saint-Hilaire) is replaced by the more elaborate church of Balbec. The writer
Bergotte, admired in Combray and Paris, is replaced by
Elstir the painter who clarifies many nascent perceptions
on the reality of art. Gilberte Swann, with her red hair and
seeming indifference, is replaced by Albertine Simonet,
with her black hair and tomboyish ways. Charles Swann,
whom Marcel admired as a wiser older friend, is replaced
by a contemporary, Robert de Saint-Loup. Saint-Loup's
friendship raises doubts in Marcel's mind over an artist's
capacity (for an artist-to-be is what he still thinks of himself) of experiencing such simple joys of life as friendship.

The network of themes and relationships is already intricately woven. The frustrating effort of suing for Albertine's love is the final notation on incommunicability. She
becomes for Marcel much less the bacchante riding a bicycle or the orgiastic muse of the golf course than a desira-
ble young lady. But she repulses his advances. This rejection has the mournful background of the end of the season
at Balbec: the departure of the guests from the hotel, the
closing of the Casino, the rainfall, and the first cold spell
of autumn. The manager is seen inspecting the "void" of
his hotel, and Marcel in his now familiar room, remembers
the warmer scenes of the young girls on the sea wall. The
name Balbec now corresponds to a reality for him, and he
reviews in his mind the many ways of human attraction

he has observed during the summer: the habits of tourists and hotel personnel, the dramas of snobbism, and the ill-defined, ever-changing impulses of sexuality. The problem of communication, of speech between one individual and another, is behind all of these observations, and he is, at this point in the narrative, aware for the first time of the insuperable difficulties of mere language in the art of communication, of the prevalence of artifice and insincerity in manners and human behavior, of the defeats both important and unimportant that occur in daily life in a man's desire to express his thoughts to someone else.

## 8. *Le Côté de Guermantes.*
## (*Guermantes' Way*)
### A. The memorialist

The third section of Proust's novel, *Le Côté de Guerman-tes,* is divided into two parts, both dominated by a vast social fresco, the setting of French society: the first at the Paris home of Mme de Villeparisis, and the second a dinner party at the Paris residence of Mme de Guermantes. In each part there are several shorter scenes that recapitulate and develop earlier experiences: in part one, the scene at the Opéra where he observes the princesse de Guermantes in her box, the visit to Robert de Saint-Loup at Doncières, his meeting in Paris with Saint-Loup's mistress Rachel, the carriage drive in the Champs-Elysées with his grandmother; in part two, the scene of his grandmother's death, a strange scene in the salon of M. de Charlus, and the final scene involving Swann and the duchesse de Guermantes, referred to as the "red slippers of the duchesse."

In the opening pages, by an extensive use of Françoise's jumbled, strange misconception of social classes and individuals within them, we are introduced almost without our realizing it, to the idea that our perceptions are unreliable in our attempt to understand social relationships. Marcel's family has moved into a wing of the large house of the duc de Guermantes in the Faubourg Saint-Germain. This is a new neighborhood in Paris for Marcel, synonymous for him with the Guermantes' world, where he falls in love with the duchesse, his neighbor and the proprietress of the house in which he lives.

The prevailing emphasis in *Le Côté de Guermantes* is on society's forms and the false perceptions we constantly cultivate because of our limited knowledge and our misconceptions of human relationships. We are led to these scenes by individuals whom Marcel knows. There is, in reality, only one character—Marcel—in *A la recherche du temps perdu* in the triple role of protagonist, narrator, and novelist, but he succeeds, despite the staggering subjectivity of the work, in bringing countless characters to life outside himself, yet formed by his perceptions and seen through his rich and tolerant sensitivity.

One of the most fully developed of these Proustian characters is the duchesse de Guermantes, Oriane, who presides over the beginning and the ending of *Le Côté de Guermantes* and who introduces us, more dramatically than any other character, to the complexities and the cruelties of society. In the early part of the first chapter, Marcel loves the duchesse at a distance, in the classical way an ardent young man loves an inaccessible older woman whose beauty and social distinctions elevate her to the status of goddess. Marcel's infatuation for the duchesse does not last very long, but it has its place in the sequence of love stories in the novel. Swann's love for Odette was the prelude. It precedes the novel in which Marcel is protagonist, in somewhat the same way that the Pagan temple preceded the Gothic cathedral. *Un Amour de Swann* is the foundation and pattern of all subsequent loves in Proust. The boy's love for the girl Gilberte is quite easily and naturally metamorphosed into the boy's amorous admiration for Mme Swann. (This episode in itself is a prelude to Marcel's love for the duchesse.) At Balbec, one remembers, Marcel fell quickly in love with all of the young girls on the beach, until Albertine Simonet emerged from the group, captivating his imagination. But the hiatus between the closing of the hotel at Balbec (*A l'ombre des jeunes filles en fleurs*) and the new apartment in Paris (*Le Côté de Guermantes*) has interrupted Marcel's obsession with Albertine, and he

can now observe the duchesse coming and going, and make
her once again into the heroine of his imagination.

At Combray, when he was a boy, the duchesse had been
a distant worshiped figure, a kind of queen in a fairy story,
whose eyes were blue like the blue stained glass windows
of Saint-Hilaire, whose role was the role of a mediaeval
suzeraine. That was the age of names, with no reality to
substantiate the dreams. In one sentence (II, p. 11) Marcel
indicates the significant change that has taken place. It
refers to the famous fairy Mélusine, of the Poitou legend,
founder of the mediaeval family of Lusignan who figures
in Rabelais and in the writings of André Breton. Mélusine
has already been used by Proust to describe the dual heritage of Gilberte, but here, in the analogy with Mme de
Guermantes, he indicates much more. In the fairy story,
when Mélusine (half dragon and half woman) disappears,
the family of Lusignan is extinct. Now Marcel's neighbor
the duchesse ceases to be merely the *name*, the fairy Mélusine, and becomes something closer to a real woman. In
the most delicate way possible the analogy is expressed in
the announcement of the end of the Guermantes line, and
of the gigantic change in French society which marks the
dissolution of the aristocracy. In his novel, Proust uses as
one of his leading illustrations of the action of time the disappearance of the French nobility as a class. Epitomizing
this class, the duchesse de Guermantes is seen variously, in
the changing roles of her relationships with Marcel, Swann,
Robert, her husband, and with the lesser and greater members of the Guermantes family.

As with every major character in Proust, scholars have
tried to discover the model for Oriane de Guermantes. But,
as always, the novelist drew traits from many ladies he
knew: Mme de Chevigné, la comtesse Greffulhe, Mme
Straus and others. Proust affirms the principle of this kind
of fictional composition in a letter to Lucien Daudet where
he claims that there are so many keys to each door in his
novel that in reality there is no one key . . . *il y en a tant
[de clefs] pour chaque porte qu'à la vérité il n'y en a
aucune.* The duchesse is a composite figure, and she bril-

liantly represents her class as observed by one outside of
it. Marcel will be drawn in various ways to many members
of the Guermantes, but to none more ardently than to
Oriane.

As a boy in Combray, she represented for him the past
of France, the beauty of woman, the inaccessibility of the
beloved. Then a few years later, in the early pages of *Le
Côté de Guermantes,* when he had temporarily forgotten
Gilberte and Albertine, he remembers his previous love for
the duchesse in a memorable scene at the Opéra. A ticket
to a gala performance, at which La Berma will again appear in scenes from *Phèdre,* is received from A. J. Moreau,
a friend of his father. The slight detail of this proper name,
with its final syllable *-eau,* initiates the development of a
leading theme of the episode. The Opéra becomes a sub-
merged water scene with greenish light from the stage,
and the dazzlingly dressed ladies in the loges (called
*baignoires*) who resemble water nymphs or mermaids,
white deities, half-naked bodies, before which foamlike
fans move back and forth slowly. The Opéra in a long-
sustained metaphor becomes an aquarium in which the
princesse de Guermantes, cousin of the duchesse, is seen
in her *baignoire,* fastidiously described as reclining on a
red divan (a coral rock), as on a halcyon (kingfisher) nest.
The pearls and feathers of her gown lend to her the air of
being a huge bird of paradise.

After La Berma's scene, during which Marcel is able to
judge her more critically and more appreciatively than on
the earlier occasion, when, expecting so much from her art,
he was bitterly disappointed, he notices a commotion in
the box of the princesse. The cause is the entrance of the
duchesse de Guermantes, enveloped in white muslin, who
greets the members of her family and friends with the ceremonial gestures of a goddess. She takes her place at the
front of the loge with as much art as La Berma has just
demonstrated in playing *Phèdre,* and Marcel can see the
simple aigrette in her hair, her fan of swan feathers, the
sparkling corsage on her dress, and her arched nose. Marcel
is not alone in seeing the contrast between the two cousins,

the princesse and the duchesse, for Mme de Cambremer, whose greatest social ambition is to know them, watches them avidly from her seat. The princesse, a Bavarian, is compared to a softer bird, more flowerlike, and the duchesse, with her sharper beaked nose and more closely fitting dress, is compared to another kind of bird, more dangerous, more swift.

Marcel, who had met the duchesse only once, has no hope that she will recognize him. But she does. She raises her white-gloved hand and waves at him, and her eyes shower over him the dazzling celestial ray of her smile . . . *et celle-ci . . . fit pleuvoir sur moi l'averse étincelante et céleste de son sourire* (II, p. 58). The sentence, with its allusion to the color blue in the word *céleste,* is very similar to the smile of the duchesse in the church of Saint-Hilaire. This new recognition excites Marcel to new fervor for his goddess become woman, and he posts himself day after day at some point along her walk, in order to confront her face to face, and ludicrously manifests surprise at their encounter. In these street scenes the color blue returns, in her toque hat and in her eyes. In this calculated closeness to her, Marcel is more aware than ever of her birdlike features, her small head, and the arched nose resembling a beak.

Marcel's amorous inclinations quickly grow into an obsession, and with the art of a strategist he plots ways of carrying out his conquest, never precisely defined. Marcel's principal reason (which he conceals) for visiting Robert de Saint-Loup at the garrison town of Doncières is to solicit his friend's aid. The Doncières episode provides a full example of what Proust means by the mysteriousness of human relationships because Marcel's real motive is never expressed to Robert and is covered up by several subsidiary motives and themes. Marcel does not wish to deceive his friend, but he is ashamed to acknowledge to Robert that he is in love with Robert's aunt, the duchesse. The comedy is one of misunderstandings and half-expressed truths. The friendship of the two young men grows closer. They begin to use *tu* in speaking to one another. Robert is proud of Marcel's intellectual attainments and conversation, and shows him off to his military friends. He is solicitous of Marcel's physical comforts and surrounds him with every possible attention.

Much of the conversation is about military art, and, at the same time, in an indirect way, Marcel is practicing a kind of military strategy, by drawing out from Robert a promise to speak of him favorably to Mme de Guermantes, by securing an invitation to call on the duchesse on the pretext of seeing some of Elstir's paintings which she owns. Marcel even goes to the point of asking for the duchesse's photograph which her nephew keeps in his room, but here the strategy fails—and there ensues a somewhat humiliating retreat. What we are describing here as Marcel's "strategy" is not unrelated to his enjoyment of his conversations with Robert and the military men, of the town of Doncières and the Hôtel de Flandre. The narrative, as always in Proust, promulgates several themes at once, but we as omniscient readers understand more of Marcel's fundamental motivation than his friend Saint-Loup.

The originality of Proust's art as novelist lies in the extraordinary skill with which he is able to present so many themes simultaneously: the personal dramas of individual characters (the adaptation of Françoise to a new house, Marcel's infatuation with Mme de Guermantes, Saint-Loup's stormy liaison with his actress-mistress); the large social settings, the tableaux of characters involved in a comedy of manners and class distinctions (the Opéra where the *baignoire* of the princesse de Guermantes is the center of attention, the descriptions of the life in a garrison town, the matinée at Mme de Villeparisis', the first very detailed social fresco in *A la recherche du temps perdu*). Other novelists, Stendhal, for example, emphasize either society or the individual. At no point in the closely woven texture of Proust's writing is any demarcation visible between society and the individuals interacting within the society.

In accordance with the usual preoccupation of the novelist, Proust shows us what is actually seen in such a town as Doncières: streets, shops, hotel rooms, military men. But he is constantly adding to what can be seen by everyone, an artist's personal subjective vision. In other words, he is interested in telling us in what way he was led to see what he does see. For example, in describing a tawdry second-hand novelty shop in Doncières (*un petit magasin de bric-à-brac.* II, p. 97), the light of a candle and the light of a lamp fall in such a way on various odd objects that, for Marcel, the drabness of the scene is momentarily transformed into a Rembrandt painting.

In addition to these two kinds of writing—the description of what can be seen and the peculiarly subjective way in which Marcel Proust sees it—there is a theoretical kind of writing far more occasional than the other two, in which the writer tells his reader why he has chosen to describe his society and the customs of his time. This is the function of the memorialist who, more than the historian, seeks to understand the meaning of individual and social behavior, to derive general theories concerning the relationship between man and man, and man and society. The writing of a novel would never be sufficient for Marcel Proust. Consciously, and at times unconsciously, he makes the novel a justification for writing, and, more than that, a justification for his own life. The protagonist in *A la recherche du temps perdu* is never seen alone: he is portrayed in conjunction with some object (such as the porch of a church), or with some human being, or with some social group. In the same way, Marcel Proust is never solely the novelist. He is the novelist who is at the same time aesthetician and memorialist.

The two social worlds Marcel had thought about as a boy, because he knew them to be very different from the social world of his own family, were that of Mme Swann and that of Mme de Guermantes. In fact, he uses *Swann's Way* and *Guermantes' Way* as titles of the first and third parts of the novel to designate two dreams to be realized, two aspects of reality he wants most to know. Though it was comparatively easy for Marcel to meet Mme Swann and enter her world, he still had to pass through various preliminary phases: games with Gilberte in the Champs-

Elysées, close observance of Mme Swann in her walks or
when she was out driving. The phases that precede Marcel's reception into the home of the duchesse are more elaborate and difficult: her seignorial smile in the church of
Saint-Hilaire, the recognition she gives to him from her
cousin's box at the Opéra, the calculated encounters on her
Paris walks, Marcel's plea to Robert to speak on his behalf
and secure an actual invitation, and, finally, his social encounter with the duchesse at Mme de Villeparisis' matinée
where their conversation is brief and painfully perfunctory.
This much is accomplished in part one of *Le Côté de Guermantes*. In part two, Marcel dines at Mme de Guermantes'
and participates in the important scene between Swann
and his great friend the duchesse—the scene of the "red
slippers."

Before he gets to know them, Marcel entertains illusions
about the milieu of the Swanns and the Guermantes. The
action of the novel, in part, is the dissipation of these illusions and the protagonist's objective attempts to describe
the two ways of his childhood when he knew them as a
young man. The revelations made about social reality un-
fold slowly. Proust's reader is always just a bit ahead of
Marcel in his recognition of this or that fact about human
relationships and social traits, but on the whole the reader's understanding is delayed almost as much as Marcel's.
When the understanding is finally reached, the general
conclusions, Marcel's conclusions, are probably more pessimistic about the human condition than the reader's. The
great salon scenes in Proust, such as the one we are coming
to at Mme de Villeparisis' matinée, are elaborate testimonials to the vanity of social activity. And they provide in
the deepest sense the background to one of the novel's major themes, the most pessimistic and the most disenchanted
of all of Proust's themes, the vanity of love. The relationship
by analogy between the emptiness of social activity and
the foreordained defeat of love is one of the most subtly
drawn lessons in *A la recherche du temps perdu*.

Though no concept specifically sociological or psychological is announced, we are forced to explore and reach

socio-psychological conclusions in somewhat the way Marcel does, by penetrating their mystery in a very gradual way. We watch the characters in a social scene and listen to their conversation before we become conscious of their ignorance about one another. The basis of Proust's understanding of society and individual psychology is the impossibility of man's knowing anyone outside of himself. Man's incongruous behavior, of which there are so many examples in Proust, is explained in large part by his ignorance, by the impossibility of correcting this ignorance, and by an unwillingness on the part of most people to know what can be known about anyone else. No writer has gone as far as Proust in analyzing the terrifying limitations which isolate man as a human being. Because the limitations are for Proust a composite of the conscious and subconscious, both willed and unwilled, the harsh manifestations of stupidity, vice, snobbism, and ignorance are treated with considerable tolerance.

By instinct and by habit, Proust is an observer never satisfied until he has divided any phenomenon he is studying into as many elements as possible. The worlds he knows and observes are the worlds in his novel. A futile criticism often levelled against Marcel Proust is the narrowness of the world he chose to depict. This criticism is not accurate because, in the first place, Proust did not limit himself to one world in Paris. Several different, interacting classes are present in his novel. But wisely, in keeping with the most permanent tradition of art, he focused his attention on those worlds he knew the most intimately: the aristocracy, the upper bourgeoisie, and the servant class. The universality of genius lies in the profundity of its understanding, and not in the mere multiplicity of its themes. The major novelists have quite consistently sought that historical moment and that social world most favorable to their talent. Dickens, Balzac, Henry James carefully chose a world they knew or could easily document: they recreated these worlds into what is recognizable today as a Dickensian, a Balzacian, a Jamesian world. Proust belongs to this category of novelists whose power of observation is coupled with an imaginative visionary power which exaggerates and deepens and clarifies the observable and the documented elements of their writing.

The restaurant scene outside Paris when Marcel meets Saint-Loup's mistress is a prelude to the larger social scene of Mme de Villeparisis' matinée. It contains, in a more modest dimension, some of the basic themes on which Proust elaborates in his major scenes—especially the theme of surprise recognition and the change in character that results from change in time or place. Marcel is surprised to discover that Robert's actress friend is Rachel, the girl he had once seen in a house of prostitution and whom he used to call "Rachel, quand du Seigneur." At this unhappy dinner Rachel reveals traits of maliciousness toward other actresses and traits of sadism in her behavior toward Robert. She tortures him by responding to advances from other men. But abruptly those moments of cruelty are forgotten in an intimate scene—which Marcel witnesses—of reconciliation between the lovers.

On a far grander scale, and with an elaborateness impossible to summarize, these contradictory traits in a human being, these abrupt changes in manner, these ambitions of conquest and love and snobbism form much of the one-hundred-page salon scene of Mme de Villeparisis.

At Balbec, Mme de Villeparisis' social position seemed unchallenged, but in Paris, despite her Guermantes forebears, she no longer occupies one of the highest ranks in society. Her long liaison with M. de Norpois does not explain this fall from favor as much as her intellectual interests. She is a "blue stocking," a painter of flowers (she continues to paint as she receives her guests), and a writer of memoirs. Several of her guests do not appear at any other Guermantes party (save for the final gathering which is no longer purely Guermantes): Bloch, who is now a rising young dramatist so awkward that he knocks over a vase of flowers; Norpois, who goes through a mock entrance scene in order to convince the others he is a formal visitor; Legrandin, always portrayed as the social climber, who is surprised to find Marcel in the group; M. Pierre, who is writing the history of La Fronde, an academic figure in a worldly setting.

Through fidelity to one of their own, a few of the Guermantes briefly attend the reception: the duc and the duchesse, Robert and his mother, Mme de Marsantes, and the baron de Charlus. Their coldness, their wit, their dissembling ceremonial gestures form a large part of the cruelly comic aspects of the scene where they are forced to mingle with people they look down upon. The duchesse, the woman whom Marcel longs to know as a friend, is probably the most representative member of the aristocracy. Wealthy and beautiful, she is favored with the highest prestige, is famous for her wit, and for the amusing qualities of her speech and observations. Heretofore in the novel we have seen her largely through Marcel's eyes, but in the matinée scene she appears in fuller relief, more naturally, and with conflicting traits of goodness and malice. Her vanity is obvious in her attraction toward those people who will throw her beauty and wit into greater prominence. Her wit appears fairly banal when it is not pointedly cruel, as in the remarks about Mme de Cambremer's corpulence. (*Je reconnais qu'elle n'a pas l'air d'une vache, car elle a l'air de plusieurs.* II, p. 232.) But she establishes, by means of her name, her beauty, and her cast of mind, a standard of fashion and behavior. She is not without courage. She accepts the innumerable infidelities (*mil e tre*) of her husband without complaint. She has resigned herself to what cannot be in the way of personal happiness, in order to enjoy and to represent, as an actress might, the social amenities: the vanity of attire, impeccable public behavior, a brilliant wit. As a representative of her class, she exemplifies her type with the never fully articulated knowledge that she is the last of her line, the fairy Mélusine, who will, with her death, bring to an end a lineage in history. Proust's novel, as it moves ahead, is always moving toward death and dissolution and toward what lies beyond death and dissolution, which is redemption by art.

Despite the large number of guests at Mme de Villeparisis' reception, each one described is a distinct personality and set off from all the others. In such a scene as this, Proust's art is endowed by an aesthetic pleasure in noting the minute dramas and characteristics of the players and a very serious scientific curiosity. Each new arrival has some kind of effect on the entire scene. All the guests present are constantly being rediscovered and seen in a different light and in different conjunctions. In the matinée scene, and in other comparable scenes, the power of Proust's imagination is clearly subordinated to his direct experience with, and his observations of, society.

The members of the Guermantes family, except for Mme de Villeparisis herself, will be described in greater detail in subsequent scenes. But even here, where the notations are brief, the Guermantes are recognizable in many ways. In their physical characteristics, for example: their skin with its rosy-violet complexion, their blond hair, their distinctive clothes, their flexible gait, their stiff peremptory bow—all such traits define them as a related blood group. Proust often uses the analogy with a bed of flowers, in order to accentuate their distinctiveness. Because of such striking, apt analogies, Proust has often been compared to an entomologist or a botanist. (One thinks of Balzac's theory of human species and his dependence on the zoological species in Buffon's *Histoire Naturelle*.)

The rich comic traits of the matinée scene become more and more apparent in successive readings. The length of Proust's novel requires such moments of comic relief. The humor is not only in the *mots* of Oriane, which at times verge on the cruel; it is everywhere, in Legrandin's and Bloch's snobbishness, in the duc de Guermantes' forced amiability, in the confusions and difficulties arising from the presence of the multiple hierarchies in the salon. Only the Guermantes have no reason to move in any direction. The others are seeking change and advance: an entrance into a coterie or admission to an academy. Gestures and speech imply one thing and reveal another—as with the princesse de Luxembourg at Balbec who, when she extended her hand to Marcel or to his grandmother, seemed to be giving a piece of bread to an animal in a cage. In

order to avoid shaking hands with Bloch on his departure
from her salon, Mme de Villeparisis pretends to fall asleep.
It is part of the role of a grand lady to dismiss a visitor in
such a way as to leave him little hope for a return visit.

The timbres of voices, posturings, attitudes are all minutely described through the scene. M. de Norpois, for example, never says anything that could possibly compromise
him. The exaggeration of traits can easily become caricature in a novel. It seldom does in Proust who treats comedy
more deftly, integrates it more closely with the main stream
of the narrative than Dickens or Balzac. The purely comic
effect in Proust is always being offset by traits of scorn or
satire or irony. However, Bergson's theory of comedy is applicable to Proust: he often stresses the mechanical aspects
of the human body and the human voice, and human resemblances with animals. Minute social dramas are relentlessly acted out in the course of the matinée: the effort on
the part of the prince de Faffenheim to solicit the help of
M. de Norpois, Oriane's refusal to meet Mme Swann, Mme
de Marsantes' worshipful love for her son Robert and his
seeming callousness toward her. What unifies such a complex scene is Marcel Proust's consciousness of the ancient
problem of appearance and reality, and his sensitivity to
the tragic and despairing dichotomy between our social
personality (what others think of us) and our real personality (what we know to be true concerning ourselves). One
sentence in the scene itself states the problem quite succinctly when the narrator speaks of the impression others
have of our acts and gestures, an impression contradictory
to what we have of ourselves . . . *l'image que les autres se
font de nos faits et gestes ne ressemble pas à celle que nous
nous en faisons nous-même* (II, p. 272).

M. de Charlus is not a prominent figure in the matinée
scene until the very end when he plays once more the role
he has played thus far in the novel: that of a gentleman
with eccentric manners, whose speech and actions Marcel does not understand. Just when Marcel discovers that
Charlus is the duc de Guermantes' brother, the baron suggests they leave together. When Mme de Villeparisis learns

of this from Marcel, she urges him to leave alone and pretends that the baron has already forgotten his invitation.

The mystery continues through the following pages when Charlus catches up with Marcel on the stairs, briefly upbraids him, and then, as the walk continues, tells him that he wants to help the young man. In the ensuing conversation he shows an extensive knowledge of the world and of politics. He talks about his wife and her death, about whether Marcel is worthy of his attention, about friendship and mistresses. The scene ends abruptly as the baron hails a cab with a young half-intoxicated driver, and sitting beside the driver, takes the reins and drives off.

Marcel's amazement at Charlus' speech and behavior is probably not matched by the wary reader. Charlus' piercing, roving eyes, which Marcel had first noticed in Combray behind the hedge of Tansonville and then later at Balbec, he sees again during this Paris episode. He notices again, as at Balbec, the vacillation of Charlus' temperament between excessive kindness and a furious peremptory curtness. His speech is at times eloquent and high-pitched, and at other times resembles Swann's less elegant speech. *J'étais frappé par combien de côtés sa diction, plus encore qu'à Balbec, ressemblait à celle de Swann* (II, p. 286). His language is for the most part courtly and noble, but he can also use current slang words (such as *truqueur*) unknown to Marcel.

Every scene in Proust bears some relationship, slight or significant, to every other scene. The narrative progresses by an elaborate series of recapitulations which widen and deepen. The action of the novel is Marcel's gradual awakening to the world and the characters in it. Mme de Villeparisis' matinée recapitulates Mme Swann's luncheon; and the walking scene, which follows, of Charlus and Marcel, resumes themes faintly announced at Combray and at Balbec. This last scene culminating with Charlus' driving off absurdly with the half-intoxicated cab driver, is actually a very precise, complete introduction to several important later scenes where Charlus' tragically disguised life becomes the focus of interest. All the elements of dissimulation and

tragedy and love are touched upon in the walking scene,
but Marcel is not as yet aware of this in the narrative.
However, the novelist has laid the foundation in this episode for some of the major revelations in *A la recherche du
temps perdu.*

Marcel's bewilderment at his talk with Charlus is in itself a recapitulation of the entire matinée scene at which
no one knows exactly what anyone else is thinking or plot-
ting. Every one knows only partially, or suspects, or believes he knows. Such approximations of knowledge and
ignorance account for the human comedy and the human
tragedy. These two terms have to be used simultaneously,
because in Proust comedy is always tragic.

This duality is explicitly illustrated in the final development of the chapter when Marcel, on his return home, finds
his grandmother ill. Dr. Cottard (first introduced in the
Verdurin clan) is called in, but the milk diet he orders is
not successful. This is an occasion for Proust to attack the
medical profession and to develop a beautiful passage on
the mercury in a thermometer. An even more eminent doctor—Dr. du Boulbon—is then called. He holds not so much
a consultation as a literary discussion with the patient. He
advises her to forget her temperature and walk in the
Champs-Elysées. He explains her illness by the magic word
"nerves," and places her among the great of the earth who
live on their nerves. *Supportez d'être appelée une nerveuse*
(II, p. 305). It is select company, for those in it are the
ones who found religions and compose masterpieces. The
diagnosis, it seems, is brilliantly subtle or outrageously
pompous—it is difficult to know which.

As a result, the grandmother accedes to a carriage drive
and a short walk with her grandson in the Champs-Elysées.
Abruptly she leaves Marcel to go into one of the public
toilets supervised by "la marquise," an old woman whom
Françoise knew. While the grandmother is inside (Marcel
has the faint apprehension that the reason is more than
mere nausea), the "marquise" describes her profession to
the young man, refers to her toilets as her salons and indicates her preference for her regular clients. It is the carica-

ture of the great salon scene we have just witnessed, and the reader feels it is more than mere caricature. When the grandmother comes out, Marcel knows a change has taken place in her. After a feeble attempt to make conversation, he suggests they go home immediately. He realizes his grandmother has just suffered a slight stroke.

This news is delivered in the final sentence of the chapter, sobering after the comic speech of the "marquise," poignant and personal after the erratic unpredictability of Charlus on the street and the social behavior of the guests in the salon of Mme de Villeparisis. Marcel is back again with his family, with the grandmother who had shown such kindness and intelligence at Balbec, and who transports us in this scene of illness back to the beginning of the novel, to Combray, where tante Léonie, the hypochondriac, had feigned illness and tyrannized those around her. A complete circle has been made, beginning in Léonie's bedroom with medicines and missals when Marcel was a boy and ending with Marcel's ominous realization on the Avenue Gabriel that his grandmother is seriously ill: at this moment in his life, Marcel passes through the two initiations to Swann's Way and Guermantes' Way.

## 9. *Le Côté de Guermantes.*
### B. Death under the shadow of society

A short chapter of only thirty pages opens part two of *Le Côté de Guermantes*. The saddest section of the novel, the death of Marcel's grandmother, announced at the end of the preceding section, is narrated with fewer interruptions than other scenes. Before he knows with certainty the seriousness of his grandmother's attack, Marcel's emotions are described. On the Avenue Gabriel, while his grandmother is seated on a bench, he dares to approach a famous doctor, le professeur E, who knows his family, and asks permission to bring his grandmother to the doctor's office. Professeur E consents but is more concerned with the evening's social engagement, and with having his dinner jacket repaired so that he might wear his decoration. During the examination he resumes his cultivated manner and treats the grandmother with courtesy and good humor. Marcel's fears abate a little, but he has already meditated on the possibility of unexpected death, on our regularized life of appointments and activities, a routine flagrantly flouted by death, our constant silent companion. He has seen the change in his grandmother's face and knows she has already entered another phase of existence. In one sense, she has already left him, and he knows this. Professeur E's final word does not totally surprise him: "Your grandmother is beyond help." *Votre grand'mère est perdue* (II, p. 318). Marcel's feelings on death are so detached and remote that he is almost philosophical, and, when he hears from behind the doctor's door an outburst of anger over a trivial buttonhole in a coat, he only speculates on man's isolation.

Swiftly and philosophically he lives through the experience of loss which he will know with his grandmother's
death. From this point on, throughout the chapter, he feels
very little of the anguish his mother and Françoise feel.
The observer of the drama of death, he is the narrator of
all the final phases of the illness and the final episodes leading up to death. His suffering will come later, in accord
with that unusual and unpredictable Proustian chronology
of grief.

The procession of doctors throughout the scene is decidedly and pointedly Molièresque. Though they provide a
high point of comedy, they depict the anxious hope of the
family that medical art will prolong the grandmother's life.
The introductory scene with Professeur E initiates consul-
tations where pomposity vies with helplessness, where attentiveness and ignorance form an impossible alliance. Dr.
Cottard, the "family" doctor, is in charge of the case and
is constantly puzzled over the amount of morphine he
should administer. The illness is uremia, and the physical
suffering of the aged lady is fairly constant. A doctor called
Spécialiste X comes with elaborate paraphernalia, and the
next day everyone in the family has colds. At the very end,
the celebrated Dieulafoy [a real person, Professeur Georges
Dieulafoy, 1839–1911] is called in for consultation. With
his *grand seigneur* manners, Proust does not hesitate to
evoke the name of Molière.

There is also a procession of friends, both helpful and
importunate. Bergotte, ill himself, comes; so does Mme
Cottard, wife of the doctor, and the duc de Guermantes.
They all come at the moment when the grandmother is
dying and therefore at the worst time for a visit. A monk,
brother-in-law of the grandmother, who received permission from his order in Austria to come to the deathbed,
also visits. To complicate matters, the arrival of an elec-
trician, hired before the illness, captivates, while he is in
the house, Françoise's full attention.

The theme of death, despite the prodigious amount of
activity, professional and otherwise, that fills the last days

of the grandmother, is never obscured. Without any melodramatic emphasis, the narrator comments on death, on its
mysterious presence in the dying, and on the premonition
of this solemn event in all those who approach the bed-
side. This theme of death, as far back as one can go in
history, is a constant universal source of terror. And because of this fatal deep-seated terror, mankind has always
felt the need to offset it by comic relief. *La danse macabre*
is precisely that strange combination of death and humor,
of humor solicited so that man can bear the solemn event
of death. Proust makes a brilliant use of the *danse macabre*
in this chapter, as in the appearance, for example, of Dieulafoy when one forgets momentarily the grandmother's
death-agony. The black figure, standing at the foot of the
bed, dominates the funereal protocol. For such an event,
he—and not the duc de Guermantes—is the leading actor,
the *grand seigneur. Aux pieds d'un lit de mort, c'était lui
(M. Dieulafoy) et non le duc de Guermantes qui était le
grand seigneur* (II, p. 342).

The pathos of the scene is stated economically and spar-
ingly, and is therefore all the more moving, particularly in
the quiet inarticulate suffering of Marcel's mother, and in
the instances when the grandmother is described. At the
beginning of the death agony Marcel's mother tells him in
the simplest possible way that his grandmother is dying.
They go into the bedroom and witness the terrifying death
struggle. The grandmother is like an animal, twisted in a
half-circle, moaning in her convulsions. *Courbée en demi-
cercle sur le lit, un autre être que ma grand'mère, une
espèce de bête* . . . (II, p. 336). This physical transformation brought on by death is very briefly noted by Proust,
but it is part of the extensive network of analogies between
human beings and animals, birds, plants and even minerals.
A few pages later when the grandmother is dead, and Françoise has prepared her body, she appears again transformed
by death, but this time serenely, with life, as it left her,
withdrawing all its disillusionments. The novelist compares
death to a mediaeval sculptor changing the features of
the grandmother into those of a young girl . . . *la mort,*

*comme le sculpteur du moyen âge, l'avait couchée sous
l'apparence d'une jeune fille* (II, p. 345). Within just a
few hours this elderly woman whom we have known for
her sane outlook on life, her cultivated mind, and her affectionate ways, has been metamorphosed into a beast, by
the physical onslaught of death, and then changed back
into a figure with the clear innocent traits of a young girl.
The bewildering physical transformation of a human being
in Proust parallels spiritual and moral transformations.
Time destroys and restores and reveals, but outside of the
laws of time fixed by human beings for the ordering and
the unfolding of their lives.

The opening pages of chapter two, which follow this
brief poignant episode on the inexorability of death, seem
on first reading rambling and even formless. But actually
they serve a very specific purpose. They reflect a resumption of life, in its fluidity and changeableness, and the resumption of Marcel's rich mental development. He is in
bed, in the Paris apartment. It is noon of a day in autumn.
He notices the transformations in nature outside, and inside
himself he follows the development of desire, the oldest
desire in the world—the desire for a companion. He thinks
of an open fire at night and a bed shared. And he calls
himself Adam, sensitive to the cold, and searching for a
sedentary Eve, who would keep him company. *Adam fri-
leux en quête d'une Eve sédentaire* (II, p. 346).

The recollection of memories, as Marcel lies in his bed,
reminds us of the first theme of the novel, and the same
leisurely tempo prevails again here in the writing. But the
memories now are far more sensual than Marcel's memories
as a boy. Only Françoise is in the house. At his feet lies
*Le Figaro,* to which he has sent an article, as yet unpublished. Earlier in the morning he had sent a letter to Mlle
de Stermaria. Thanks to Robert de Saint-Loup (now in
Morocco where his family hopes he will forget Rachel)
who had met the young lady, Marcel learns of her address
in Paris, of her marriage and divorce, and of her availabil-
ity. Robert is vaguely playing the role of a panderer, and
the thoughts of a possible conquest float through Marcel's

mind. But still the afternoon seems unbearably empty to him.

Suddenly, unexpectedly, Albertine enters the room, ushered in by Françoise. She has somehow changed. In his mind, Marcel contrasts two girls—the one he knew and desired at Balbec, and the new Albertine in Paris with whom he has fallen out of love. It is now Albertine who approaches him, who comes into his bedroom, sits first close to his bed and finally on his bed. It is true he is not in love, but Albertine is the past and she brings back Balbec and the sea to him. She is the poetic evocation of a girl once loved in a beloved setting. He notices changes in her vocabulary and way of speaking, and wonders vaguely about what changes have taken place in her life. An erotic play begins between the two: Albertine initiates it and Marcel is—or pretends to be—reluctant and indifferent. The play reaches an important pitch when it is interrupted by Françoise. A loveless physical passion grows as an idea in Marcel's mind, and with it, the scenes of Balbec: the beach, the sea, the waves. It is the reverse of the scene in the Grand Hôtel de Balbec when Marcel had tried to embrace Albertine. Her caresses finally give him an erotic satisfaction. He marvels at her new docility and sees her as an incarnation of a French peasant girl, such as he had seen sculptured on the church of Saint-André-des-Champs. In some ways, she is a feminine Théodore, the grocer boy at Combray, whose features Marcel found in stone in the church. Though she is reluctant to leave, he sends her off with Mlle de Stermaria very much on his mind. One dream of sensuality leads to another. And the sexual consummation Marcel has just experienced does not diminish the sensual dream of conquest.

At Albertine's departure, he receives a letter from Mlle de Stermaria accepting his dinner invitation. That evening —it is on a Sunday—he briefly attends a function at the home of Mme de Villeparisis. The tide has decidedly turned for Marcel, because this brief episode and, in fact, all of this passage which leads up to his first dinner at the duchesse de Guermantes', indicate that the members of the

Guermantes family are interested in him and are cultivating his friendship. At one time in his life, even to approach a Guermantes seemed an impossibility, but now he is showered with obvious signs of affection and interest.

The duchesse, whom he sees at Mme de Villeparisis', invites him to dinner. By this time, he has recovered from his infatuation for her. A few words from his mother, who had pointed out that he was being made fun of by the servants, had been sufficient to dampen his ardor and discontinue his mute courtship along the streets where the duchesse walked. He admires her still, of course, and wonders about her personal life because he knows of the duc's constant infidelities. In her invitation for the Friday dinner, she tempts him with the promise that he will meet the princesse de Parme. Marcel is amazed that the once forbidden, the once inaccessible salon is now open to him. Oriane reminds him, as if he had not realized it, that she is the aunt of Robert de Saint-Loup. He replies that he now also knows M. de Charlus. The mystery of Charlus' character is heightened when Oriane says that her brother-in-law (Charlus) claimed not to know Marcel. She calls him *cachottier* (a mystifier) after suggesting the nickname for Palamède used by the family: Mémé. (In the novel, the chameleonic Charlus is invested with the greatest number of names and the largest number of personalities!)

These pages are suffused with Marcel's thoughts of women: of Albertine, Oriane and Gilberte, the three women he had once loved, and of Mlle de Stermaria whom he has hopes of seducing. The dinner rendezvous with Mlle de Stermaria is to take place in a restaurant on the Ile du Bois. But a letter reaches him just before the appointed time for the rendezvous. Mlle de Stermaria is unable to come, and the disappointment is so acute (for days Marcel had thought of little else) that he actually breaks down and sobs. *Je me mis à sangloter* (II, p. 393).

At this moment of collapse, Robert de Saint-Loup unexpectedly enters to ask Marcel to dinner. The consoling role of friendship is here very dramatically used. Friendship, then, becomes the principal theme of the intervening

pages between Mlle de Stermaria's letter and the dinner at
Oriane's. It is one of the subtlest and most philosophically
reasoned of all the themes in *A la recherche du temps
perdu*, and unquestionably one of the major preoccupations
in Proust's personal life. Much of what is known concerning
the ardent friendship shown to Proust by several young
aristocrats, who served to some degree as models for Saint-
Loup, is recast in these pages of *Le Côté de Guermantes*.
Proust's philosophy of love is far more specifically developed and stated in the novel than his philosophy of friendship about which he hesitates to draw conclusions.

In this particular scene with Robert—a prototype of all
such scenes—Marcel gratefully feels the warmth of friendship and its disinterested kindness. At the beginning, he is
rescued by Robert from a serious moment of depression.
Later, at the restaurant, Robert administers to him constantly: he remembers to close the door to avoid a draft,
he wraps Marcel in a coat to fend off the cold. The role
of friendship is here played against a spectacular background of young aristocrats who surround the prince de
Foix. Robert belongs to the coterie, but gives all his attention to Marcel, while Marcel tries to understand the coterie,
their behavior, and the legends he has heard about them.

The theme of friendship in Proust inevitably brings with
it the theme of work, of the writer's vocation. One theme
calls up the other, in much the same way as, in the theme
of physical love, the image of one girl calls up the image
of another girl, and the orgy of the senses is re-enacted
mentally. The theme of friendship does not cause the acute
kind of suffering that love does: neither the prolonged frus-
trations or the bitterly dramatic disappointments. Already
Marcel is somewhat spoiled by Saint-Loup's friendship. He
accepts the indulgences, the favors, the sometimes elaborate attentions. (These attentions Marcel Proust the man
bestowed on, and received from, others, but in the novel
he is the passive friend who receives more than he gives.)
The key phrase in the passage, the words which explain
succinctly Marcel's feeling of guilt about friendship, appears when he remembers the attentions Robert paid him

at Doncières, the lonely evenings at Combray when he had no real friend, and the dinners at Rivebelle by Balbec when Robert first befriended Marcel. Suddenly the narrator speaks in this passage and one forgets momentarily Marcel the protagonist. One is now aware only of the omniscient narrator who knows that empty useless years lie ahead for Marcel. With candor and clarity, he discloses that the work being read is the history of the imperceptible progress of his vocation . . . *la vocation invisible dont cet ouvrage est l'histoire* (II, p. 397).

One of the few significant clues to the meaning and the genesis of *A la recherche du temps perdu* that appears before *Le Temps retrouvé* is to be found here in this passage of *Le Côté de Guermantes.* Long before Marcel's full assurance that he has a writer's vocation, he wonders whether he has the right to spend hours in conversation with a friend, and to expend the energy required in such warm relationships. The achievement of a work of art inevitably requires a sacrifice of human pleasures. The artist is compelled, to some degree, to abandon life in order to recreate it.

For Marcel, the evening at the restaurant, when Robert talks to him about many things—the dinner at Oriane's to come, a message from M. de Charlus asking to see Marcel at his apartment after dinner, Robert's admiration for the men of Morocco—is an "evening of friendship." (*Ce fut le soir de l'amitié.* II, p. 413.) He states this with a tone of nostalgia, as if it might be one of the last of such evenings. In truth, Robert is the active friend during the scene, the one who serves, the one who gives of himself unceasingly; by contrast, Marcel appears the passive recipient of his friend's attentions: he is more the recording observer, the one who analyzes the motives of human actions rather than the one who participates in them.

Marcel's role as observer has, of course, always existed to some degree. With the dinner scene at the duchesse de Guermantes', it becomes more marked. His first dinner at the Guermantes', the description of which occupies approximately one hundred and forty pages, is a narration of many

themes and characters, where Proust is primarily the observer of society, its memorialist and commentator. Marcel
is treated as a privileged guest. On arrival, he asks to see
the Elstir paintings which the Guermantes own, and spends
so much time looking at them that he delays the dinner by
three quarters of an hour. But no reproach is made. He is
introduced to the princesse de Parme who pretends she
knows his family. In particular, throughout the evening, he
watches the Guermantes, their manners, their speech, their
action, the color of their skin, their hair. With the care of
a biologist, he studies their characteristics in order to understand what makes them different. The duchesse herself,
Oriane, is, of course, the dominant figure. He focuses on
her in an effort to analyze the spirit of the Guermantes
(*l'esprit des Guermantes*). And this is the principal theme
of the dinner party: in a long passage, Marcel, forgetting
himself and his personal problems, describes a rare species
of human being in its relationship to French society.

From the very beginning of the novel, the Guermantes
represented for Marcel a distant and seemingly impossible
goal. With the dream now realized, he is free to explore
more deeply than in the past all the subjects he associated
with them: the meaning of aristocracy, the poetry of lineage and history, the hallmarks of tradition in their faces.
Marcel's rarefied, only mildly sensual love of Oriane de
Guermantes now ended, he is able to look at her more objectively. He sees her now not through any romantic attachment, but in the lesser role of a young friend who,
though sympathetic, can still be objective.

Nothing is ever static in Proust's novel. What had
seemed stable—Guermantes' way—shows for the first time
signs of change and dissolution. The real process of disintegration has not yet begun, but one feels that behind the
brilliant façade, the social tensions, and the sentimental
tensions, the change has been prepared. In the next volume, the subject of inversion, as manifested in other Guermantes scenes, will clearly represent the actual beginnings
of decadence and dissolution in the reign of Charlus in
*Sodome et Gomorrhe*. But as long as Oriane dominates the

scene, which she does up to the very last page of *Le Côté de Guermantes*, the real process of disintegration is held in abeyance. In veiled ways, both Mme de Villeparisis and Oriane de Guermantes have expressed a desire to discourage friendship between Marcel and Charlus. The reasons for this they keep to themselves. Oriane is, more than Mme de Villeparisis, the last of the Guermantes, for she is intact in a social sense and cannot be seriously reproached morally.

As Marcel leaves the Elstir paintings to join the dinner guests, he is momentarily dazzled by the low-necked gowns of the ladies and thinks of himself as Parsifal among the flower girls. *Parsifal au milieu des filles fleurs* (II, p. 423). Each of the great social scenes in Proust is an initiation for Marcel, a testing of his powers of intellect and spirit, a revelation of some aspect or several aspects of society and the psychology of individuals. The development of the dinner scene in *Le Côté de Guermantes* is a long labyrinthine unravelling of the intricacies of social caste. In Oriane herself one finds the contradictions, specifically, of the aristocracy as well as the contradictions, generally, of humanity. She claims socialist beliefs though she continues to refer to her husband as "Monsieur le Duc." She demonstrates, as all the Guermantes do, a marked politeness to others, but it is politeness which can be quickly retracted with separation. The bow, the handshake, the kissing of the hand have a mechanical precision that easily establishes a desired distance. Marcel observes the Guermantes' mechanical reflexes and sees them as if participating in an elaborate choreography.

During the evening Marcel analyzes every possible clue to the Guermantes, to the sources from which they derive and have derived through the centuries their *esprit*, which is spirit and mind and motivating force and characteristic. If Marcel can understand the *esprit des Guermantes*, he will understand Robert de Saint-Loup and his handsome horses and carriages, Oriane and her magnificent gowns. He moves cautiously around this word *esprit* in an almost futile attempt to understand its complexities. At times he abandons it for the even more mysterious phrase of *génie de la famille,* the particular genie which explains the perpetuated unifying forces characterizing all the members of the dynasty. If contradictions are permitted within the code of behavior, with its often flagrant contradictions, this vigilant genie prevents any infringement against the code, any lessening of the inherited social values. M. de Guermantes, Basin, is presented as a wily duke, *un rusé seigneur,* and as a bad husband with a long line of mistresses; but he is in part redeemed by his admiration for his wife, for her intelligence and wit, her kindness in seeing people, and the remarkable way in which she enhances his own name and position. He does not love her as a husband loves his wife, but he uses her. She is indispensable in maintaining the primacy of their salon in the Faubourg Saint-Germain. Her power, in representing the *esprit des Guermantes,* is such that she is able to break social customs and establish new fashions, new modes of conduct.

Most of the observations Marcel makes on the Guermantes and their *esprit* are fairly objective analyses, but in a few very important instances in the narrative of the dinner, he relates this study to himself and thus attaches it firmly to the leading theme of the novel—Marcel's initiation to the great concepts of time and eternity. In his description of the attractive suppleness in the ceremonial physical movements of the Guermantes, we are led to feel that this is a special attribute which separates them from Marcel whose own physical movements are somewhat bourgeois. He realizes that Oriane's mind was formed long before his own and he realizes in particular that Oriane, being a Guermantes, possibly the highest representative of her family, cannot understand what he had first looked for in her, in Combray, when he was a boy, and what he is now looking for in Paris: the magical spell (*le charme*) of the Guermantes name. In a sense, their relationship is between a highly imaginative young man and a highly sophisticated lady of the world. Oriane de Guermantes creates for Marcel a magic spell that exerts a strong attraction over him. She incarnates it every day so naturally, so unthinkingly, that she could not possibly understand what it is to be someone else.

Marcel sees in the Guermantes the persistence of the past. Geography, history, trees, and Gothic spires are in their name. All of these elements, and many others, have shaped their faces, the characteristics of their minds and attitudes, their prejudices. Their history is of far more interest to Marcel than to the Guermantes (despite their endless discussion of genealogies). Marcel, in this regard, compares himself to an anticlerical archaeologist who knows far more about the history of a church than the curé who celebrates his daily mass in the church . . . *un archéologue anticlérical pourra souvent en remontrer à son curé sur tout ce qui concerne même l'église de celui-ci* (II, p. 533).

One short sentence, not very far from the end of the dinner episode, succinctly recapitulates the meditation on Oriane and the drastic difference between Marcel's image of Oriane and that of the nobles surrounding her. Oriane was first, for Marcel, the fairy, reminiscent particularly of Mélusine (although she is not named in the passage)—the doomed fairy. This additional remark confirms the reference to the story of Mélusine. But Oriane is a woman for the nobles of her castle. She will become more human for Marcel as time continues and as human defects become apparent. This is an important part of the action of the novel, an almost imperceptible part, whereby the ideals and the illusions of Marcel are dissipated by time. *J'avais commencé par la fée, dût-elle bientôt périr; eux, par la femme* (II, p. 533).

In contrast with the elaborate dinner scene, Marcel's encounter with M. de Charlus in his house is brief and dramatic. Occupying twenty pages, it is the first time in the novel that Charlus appears in full relief. Many of his traits, only briefly sketched before, are here more fully developed. We witness in this latently comical, highly charged scene with Marcel, the full traits of haughtiness, irascibility, megalomania, affectionateness, and neurotic capriciousness. Marcel himself goes through a whole gamut of feelings:

surprise, indignation, fury, and finally resignation. He accepts the inconsistencies of this older man who attracts him on many counts: his name, his knowledge, his offers of help and friendship, and his mysteriously mercurial behavior.

The scene serves two purposes. It is an interlude between the long dinner scene where there has been so much discussion of the *esprit des Guermantes* and where we have watched Oriane in her complex role of hostess, and the final scene of *Le Côté de Guermantes* where Oriane will appear again, not as hostess but as a woman exercising a very special kind of cruelty over the man she calls her best friend. In itself, this interlude, by the greater revelations made concerning M. de Charlus' temperament, is the preparation for the opening of *Sodome et Gomorrhe*, an almost silent pantomime to which Marcel is witness and one of the key scenes in the plan and architecture of the entire work.

Brief as it is, the Marcel-Charlus episode has its own introduction, the carriage drive from the house of Mme de Guermantes, late in the evening, to the baron's house. Marcel is reminded of the other carriage drives in his life, one at Combray with Dr. Percepied when he saw the steeples of Martinville, and the other, at Balbec, with Mme de Villeparisis, when he saw the group of three trees. Nothing quite as important happens to him during the Paris drive, but he continues in his mind the conversations he has just heard and enjoys in perspective the pleasure of relating them to M. de Charlus. The social visit he is about to make interests him in many ways but especially for the reason, articulated quite clearly to himself, that a young bourgeois like himself learns more from members of the aristocracy and the peasantry than from his own class. *Les grands seigneurs sont presque les seules gens de qui on apprenne autant que des paysans* (II, p. 550). In truth, Marcel is destined to learn more in his quest for lost time from Oriane and from Charlus than from any other characters.

He is kept waiting in a small salon for twenty-five minutes before he is ushered into the presence of M. de Charlus. The term *mise en scène* is used in the text, and the scene does resemble a play where a costume is described (Charlus is in a dressing gown) and where a prop is pointed out (a tall silk hat on a chair). Without preamble, Charlus denounces Marcel for having spoken against him. Guiltless, Marcel protests his innocence without realizing that that is precisely what Charlus expected him to do. Falsely accused, Marcel flies into a rage himself and tramples on the tall hat and tears it apart. This violence calms Charlus, who, in turn, comforts Marcel and reiterates all his promises to help him. Once again, Marcel hears in Charlus' softer intonations, the voice of Swann. As the supreme example of his power in society, Charlus proclaims that the princesse de Guermantes invites no one unless recommended by Charlus, even though she occupies, according to the baron, the most exalted position in French society. He acknowledges Oriane's charm and finesse, but accords the higher rank to her cousin the princesse.

The phases of the episode are clearly indicated, like a series of dramatic scenes: the long wait, the unexpected kind of reception, the tirade of denunciation, Marcel's loss of temper, the reconciliation, which is also a leavetaking. So dazzled by Charlus' glamor and prestige, Marcel understands less of what is happening than the reader. His relative innocence keeps him from realizing that the unjust accusation is a trap, a sign of Charlus' suspicious mind, a mind not accustomed to Marcel's ingenuous respect. Then, as the compromises begin and the renewed offers of help are made, Marcel does not understand that Charlus is using a mild kind of blackmail and that, in reality, the entire scene is a travesty, a caricature of an amorous proposition.

The link between the Marcel-Charlus scene and the final "red slippers" scene, is Marcel's invitation to a soirée at the princesse de Guermantes'. Charlus had made it clear that he chose the new guests for such occasions, and Marcel, half believing the invitation to be a joke, decides to check on its authenticity with Oriane. The duc and the duchesse are at Cannes when he tries to speak with them, but they will return on the day of the princesse de Guermantes' party. Spying on the duchesse from a stairway, he comes upon the revelation that will form the opening of *Sodome et Gomorrhe*.

This culminating scene of *Le Côté de Guermantes* is complex and revelatory. In a documentary sense, it is Oriane's most important scene, and emphasizes, more than any other, though in an extremely subtle way, the meaning of Oriane's dominant role in *A la recherche du temps perdu*. At the beginning, when the duc greets Marcel and announces the arrival of his wife and Swann, he claims that Oriane is more interested in the Order of Rhodes and the Templars than in the history of the Lusignan family, from which the Guermantes are descended. This rejection of her own family, and hence of the fairy Mélusine, is clearly a presentiment. Oriane's action, the heartless way in which she treats the sad news Swann gives her, is the beginning of an end.

In this scene, Marcel is again, merely an interested observer. When he asks about the invitation, the duc is displeased: he is given no satisfactory answer and is forbidden to ask Oriane. He asks Swann about the Guermantes' anti-Dreyfusism, and here also the answers are complex and contradictory. The appearance of Swann, who has been absent for some time from the narrative, is carefully described: the elegance of the impeccably dressed clubman; the ravages that illness (the same which killed his mother) has brought about on his face. His clothing, his affable witty speech, are only disguises for the mortal illness which he acknowledges with reluctance.

The moments in a Proustian scene, however poignant and dramatic, and though they modify and affect the action of the narrative, are actually very brief. But they are prepared for meticulously and elaborately. Oriane's breathtaking entrance is dramatic in an unforgettable way: dressed in red, red satin with glittering sequins on the hem of her skirt, a dark red ostrich feather in her hair, a red tulle scarf on her shoulders, and a necklace of very large rubies. Affably sweet with Swann, she reminds him of her cousin's beautiful gardens. After cruel and kind references to the princesse, reminders to Basin that they are due for dinner at Mme de Saint-Euverte's, complaints in general of the number of social engagements in her life, she suddenly suggests to Swann (*"mon petit Charles"*) that he accompany her and her husband to Italy in the spring. A little later she returns to this suggestion and, thereby, forces Swann to say that he will not see the spring: that the doctors have given him only a short time to live.

The climax of the scene is brief. Because of their dinner engagement, neither the duc nor the duchesse wants to be affected by this tragic news, so they refuse to believe it. Mme de Saint-Euverte's dinner and Swann's death are put in the balance, and the dinner is judged as of greater importance. As the duchesse is about to mount the running board of the carriage, the duc is horrified to see she is wearing her black slippers. *Vous avez gardé vos souliers noirs! Avec une toilette rouge!* (II, p. 596.) He insists that she put on the red slippers, and she goes upstairs forthwith. Then, in order to spare his wife any further embarrassment, he sends Marcel and Swann off. His last words, said to ease his conscience, refer to the ignorance of doctors: Swann, he says, is as strong as the Pont Neuf and he will bury them all. *Vous vous portez comme le Pont-Neuf. Vous nous enterrerez tous!* (II, p. 597.)

The color red, already emphasized in Oriane's dress, and made even more dominant by the episode of the "red slippers," symbolizes Swann's impending death, a death which has been hastened by his best friend. One sees in Oriane once again the figure of Mélusine, the wicked fairy, half dragon, half enchantress, who consummates, in this scene of social banter and superficiality, the death of the friend, mysterious by his name, disguised by the signs of approaching death, haunted by the numbered days which remain in his life. The death of Swann and the end of the Guermantes are joined before Marcel's very eyes: he witnesses, without fully understanding it, one of his most important initiations to life and to time.

## 10. *Sodome et Gomorrhe.*
### (*Cities of the Plain*)
### A. Morality and art

The title of the fourth section of *A la recherche du temps perdu* calls attention to a new theme which the section is to be concerned with—a theme only briefly and intermittently referred to previously in the novel. By using the biblical title, with its implicit disapproval of sexual inversion, Proust announces an attitude that would seem moralistic. And yet he is hostile to the moralizing novelist. The drama of inversion is an important part of his novel. By "drama" is meant the suffering and the social ostracism inversion entails. All the vices exist to some degree in Proust's work, but they are not condemned as vices. Proust affirms them, and he studies in particular the subconscious role they play in the moral and spiritual and social make-up of his characters. Proust is far more fully conscious of the vice of inversion in Charlus than Charlus himself. According to Proust's canon, only the artist, when functioning as artist, is fully conscious.

Inversion is only one reflection, however strong and dramatic, of the entire moral problem of the protagonist, and hence of the entire novel. Almost as if he were the protagonist of a mediaeval morality play, Marcel faces two sets of alternatives throughout the history of his life: the virtues of Combray, on the one hand, and the vices of society, on the other. The novel asks the question: Which will win Marcel's heart? The answer to this leading question is saved for the very end of the work.

In the opening episode of *Sodome et Gomorrhe,* which
is the prelude to the second half of the novel—as the episode on sleep at the beginning of *Du Côté de chez Swann*
is the prelude to the entire novel—Marcel is the hidden
observer, the mute witness to an extraordinarily bold scene
of sexuality. No mention of temptation is made, but in a
way Marcel stands in the position of one who might have
been tempted or tested by what he has seen accidentally.
In terms of his comments and recordings and analogies,
he is always the observer, astonished yet astonishingly
tolerant. And it is a tolerance to which the reader is—at
this point in the narrative—accustomed.

The grotesquerie and the jolting quality of the encounter
between M. de Charlus and Jupien, the waistcoat maker
(*giletier*), in the courtyard of Mme de Guermantes (and
hence in Marcel's own courtyard) is offset, first, by the
other scene Marcel watches: the fertilization of a flower
by a bee; and, second, by the long passage that follows
the scene, on the history of the descendants of Sodom.
Four subjects are developed during the thirty pages of
this prelude: (1) the chance meeting of two men, Charlus
and Jupien, and their utterly banal phrases and signals
(*je vous demande du feu*) and gossipy exchanges of information; (2) the botanical scene, so strikingly related
to the human scene in its grotesqueness and chance (the
large bee's—Charlus'—visit to the solitary waiting flower—
Jupien); (3) the lengthy exegesis on inversion in which
the narrator becomes historian, contemporary observer, and
sociologist; (4) a discussion of the reason for Marcel being
posted as observer of the court—to watch for the duchesse
whom he wishes to question about the soirée at the princesse de Guermantes' which will take place that night. The
entire scene therefore precedes in time the ultimate sequence of the "red slippers of the duchesse" of *Le Côté
de Guermantes.* For Marcel the two are major scenes of
revelation: the first, on the character of Oriane, the second, on the character of Charlus. They are two aspects of
the sin of pride: one, Oriane's, which the world would call
the sin of selfishness; the other, Charlus', which the world

calls the sin of concupiscence. In each case, Marcel first knew the character involved as noble, brilliant, illustrious. The way in which he adjusts to such violent revelations and reversals of value, is the Proustian way of his novel: not by moral condemnation, but by the artist's conviction that life never teaches one lesson singly, but rather that many lessons have to be assimilated together. Oriane's selfishness is the result of so many conditionings, so many inherited traits of family and history, so many subconsciously acquired habits and reflexes, that finally the word *selfish* has little meaning, and Proust will in fact refuse to employ it or any other such simplification. Charlus' inversion likewise is, for Proust, the result of traits that long preceded Charlus, that formed leading traits of his temperament and character which would remain no matter what his moral conduct was, and Proust, in his effort to place Charlus within a human context, uses such phrases as "the numerous posterity of Sodom," "a freemasonry of every country," "a race that is cursed."

It is not difficult to realize the major importance of this scene for Proust in terms of the general conception and architecture of his novel. Nor is it difficult to sense the aesthetic and moral danger Proust the novelist must have felt in attempting such a scene. The boldness of the pantomime episode and the breadth of treatment in the historical passage had not been attempted before in any serious novel. There are allusions and implications in the *Comédie Humaine* of Balzac, especially in episodes concerning the character Vautrin, who bears some resemblance to Charlus, though Balzac avoided on the whole any direct depiction of inversion. Proust was well aware of the risk he was taking of possibly alienating his public, and within the scene itself he explicitly alludes to the horror many readers feel for such a theme and tries to justify its inclusion on aesthetic grounds. The orchid, the flower in the fertilization scene, appears grotesque and abnormal when associated with Jupien. Marcel thinks of a jellyfish (*méduse*) he had seen at Balbec which had revolted him. But the historian Michelet, in a passage he had read on

the jellyfish within the realm of natural science, caused
Marcel to see the medusa as a "beautiful wheel of azure
flame." *Méduse! Orchidée! Quand je ne suivais que mon
instinct, la méduse me répugnait à Balbec; mais si je
savais la regarder, comme Michelet, du point de vue de
l'histoire naturelle et de l'esthétique, je voyais une dé-
licieuse girandole d'azur* (II, p. 626).

By comic effects and sociological notations, Proust softens the effect of unnaturalness in the Charlus-Jupien encounter. He never allows the attention of the reader to
focus for long on the sinister, the humorous, or the scientific. In a few pages, without ever moving away from
the narration of the encounter between Charlus and Jupien,
and the action which Marcel observes, he describes so
many minute details on the historical, sociological, and
psychological aspects of the problem of inversion that the
reader may easily believe the consideration to be exhaustive. Even the theological point of view is touched on in
the rehearsal of the chapter in Genesis that describes the
cities of the plain.

The necessity of this prelude, in spite of its seeming
"miscellaneousness," becomes increasingly apparent as the
novel continues. It was no indulgence on the part of
Proust, no melodramatic tendency to scandalize. Charlus
will be the major representative of Sodom in the novel,
but he is also one of the major representatives of the
Guermantes, and his personal anomaly will designate meta-
phorically the decadence of the French aristocracy and,
beyond that, a point in the cyclical movement of history
when the weaknesses and defects of man suddenly show
themselves under the hard carapace of continuous tradition. In fact, it would be difficult to find a major theme in
Proust's novel that Charlus does not incarnate.

Everything Proust says about personality is exemplified
in Charlus. He is both changeable and unchanging. He is
one man, and he is all men. This dual aspect of human
character, in one man, Charlus, means that everything that
can be said about personality is true. Truth is, for Proust,
the container of contradictions. And this is one aspect of

Proust's concept of the absolute. Charlus' impeccable good taste, his knowledge and love of the arts, his magnanimity and kindness, revealed on many occasions, his understanding of history and politics and the ways of man, have been acquired during his conscious life as a highly privileged French aristocrat. When sexual desire transforms him into a reprobate, he is the same man, responding to a bestial trait inherited from some distant ancestor. No part of past human conduct is ever completely lost. Our instincts and our feelings are predetermined, even if our will is free to carry out or repress these instincts, to submerge or express these feelings. The love Charlus has doubtless already felt for Marcel in the first part of the novel—not exactly the same attraction he demonstrates for Jupien in the courtyard scene—is the adventure of a stranger alienated from himself. This is the persistent Proustian formula for the experience of love. Its full analysis comes in time, with Marcel himself, in his love for Albertine. But in Charlus, more than in Marcel, we are able to follow a conscience, actually a consciousness in perpetual motion, traversing all the levels of an awareness of the past, an awareness implicit in the living conscience, and able, under certain conditions, to take hold and direct the present.

M. de Charlus is elaborately described in his exterior mannerisms, appearance, and behavior. Marcel is never described in this way. The reader has seen a different Charlus at each of his appearances: behind the hedge at Tansonville (in *Du Côté de chez Swann*), at Balbec near the hotel (in *A l'ombre des jeunes filles en fleurs*), at the soirée of Mme de Villeparisis (in *Le Côté de Guermantes*), in his own house (in *Le Côté de Guermantes*), and now in the courtyard of the duchesse (*Sodome et Gomorrhe*) where he believes he is not seen and where he reveals before Marcel a very important aspect of his character. Each of these scenes uncovers more and more about Charlus, up to the final strong illumination in the courtyard. And he appears on several more occasions later, always in a slightly different light. Charlus is the most dazzling representative of Proust's belief that each personality is in reality many personalities, because he needs to conceal the fact of his inversion. From this point on, Marcel understands Charlus much better, and in the next scene, at the reception of the princesse de Guermantes, Marcel recognizes more readily, probably because of his newly acquired knowledge, the traits of the invert in the baron's social appearance and conversation. But inversion alone, as important as it is, still does not fully explain Charlus. No one quality is the absolute key to personality.

The habits and the souls of the past, which survive in us as mysterious and often invisible components of our personality, may be suddenly revealed under certain conditions or certain states of feeling. The appearance of Jupien at the door of his shop in Mme de Guermantes' courtyard at the moment when M. de Charlus came out from paying a visit to his aunt, Mme de Villeparisis, was the unexpected, unpredictable condition for the revelation that Marcel relates. The chance encounter caused one part of Charlus' character to come to the surface and declare itself, just as other conditions or experiences would reveal other aspects of his character: ecstasy, for example, or sleep, with its revealing dreams, or death.

The theory of multiple personality is discussed at length by Marcel when he is in love with Albertine (in the next two sections of the novel), and more briefly alluded to in every character: Françoise, Oriane, Odette, Saint-Loup. But it is staged, as it were, in the character of Charlus, and dramatized by his actions and by his speech. Each moment, for Proust, combines two seemingly contradictory characterizations. First, it is autonomous. It is unique and separated from every other moment in time, in the sense that the first strange meeting between Charlus and Jupien can never again occur in exactly the same way. But, second, a moment is also eternal. Its effect on the world can never be completely effaced. A record of every moment exists somewhere in the physical or the mental world. This is one of the philosophical bases of the novel and allows Proust to claim that a certain quality of laughter in Charlus is the echo of the laughter of some forgotten Bavarian

ancestor. The greater historical emphasis in Balzac's treatment of Vautrin, and the greater psychological emphasis
in Proust's treatment of Charlus, explains the ambiguity
and vagueness in Vautrin and the extraordinary precise
and rounded depiction of Charlus.

For Proust, inversion is, if we summarize what seems to
be the main point in the prelude to *Sodome et Gomorrhe,*
a biological condition. He makes no defense for it, but
points out that when it is, it is natural and separated from
the norms of human behavior. Up to this point in the narrative, Charlus has successfully concealed his inversion
from most of his friends and family, from Swann, for example, and from the princesse de Guermantes, from Marcel,
and from Robert de Saint-Loup. But this stage of con-
cealment changes during the course of the ensuing narrative. At the beginning of the pantomime scene in the courtyard, Marcel remembers a similar scene he witnessed as a
boy, at Montjouvain in Combray, when he had looked
through Mlle Vinteuil's window. Again he is the hidden
observer.

Proust analyzes in considerable detail the phenomenon
of male inversion in *A la recherche du temps perdu,* but
he does not discuss female inversion. It is important in the
case of Albertine, but it is never studied. In his treatment
of inversion, Proust avoids any tone of sarcasm or castiga-
tion, and emphasizes, even when there are semicomic
idiosyncrasies, the suffering of the invert in being different, and the tragedy of his destiny.

Both in the discourse on inversion and in the illustrations of the discourse in subsequent episodes throughout
the novel, Proust stresses the varieties of inversion, which
are as numerous as the varieties of normal love. In Proust
the longing for an impossible happiness is the same for the
invert and the normal lover. The descendants of Sodom
form a society within society. And for them the suffering,
the jealousy, the fantasies that torment the normal lover
are drastically increased. In the case of Charlus, the tensions and the ravages created by his sexual proclivities
culminate in madness. The symptoms of his madness and

his moral collapse are visible long before the end of the novel. In the case of Proust himself, whatever his suffering was, whatever need he may have felt to conceal his anomaly, whatever personal disillusions he may have known in love (our verifiable knowledge on all these points is extremely limited), he used the sensibility that came to him from his character, his understanding of man and society, and his record of this understanding: his novel. In the classical sense of the tragic hero, Charlus qualifies far more easily than Marcel Proust.

At this stage in the novel, the opening of *Sodome et Gomorrhe,* the Guermantes, including not only Charlus but the others as well, have triumphed over time. They have resisted its power of change more successfully than others. They form a bastion of prestige and strength and invincibility. But the revelation of Charlus' character, made to Marcel as he watches the courtyard and the fertilization of the flower, marks the beginning of change, the first crack in the bastion wall. The depiction of Charlus' moral defect is the sinister sign of change and evil which will spread, in similar and other manifestations, to an entire family, a caste, and even, it can be argued, a civilization. With the Charlus-Jupien pantomime scene, a new epoch begins: one characterized by disenchantment, decadence, and vanity.

After the incisiveness, the glaring crudity of the action, the sinister quasi-comic, quasi-tragic quality of the prelude comes the opening chapter of *Sodome et Gomorrhe,* one of the most elaborate in the novel: the reception at the princesse de Guermantes' which Proust sees as dominated by the position of M. Charlus in society. There are so many characters, so many dramas—trivial and significant— that begin or continue during the soirée, so much falseness and wit are exhibited and so much humor at the expense of human feelings, that no theme, no character is given the stage for long. The subject of inversion does, however, occupy the attention of the observer Marcel more persistently than any other. His new awareness permits him to see signs, to understand allusions and conversations that he

would not have seen or understood before the courtyard
scene.

But Proust's art never allows one theme, in such an elaborate social function as this, to appear alone. The texture
of the scene is woven tightly. Most of the characters we
have already met, most of the incipient dramas we are
aware of, but everything moves ahead for the reader with
greater clarity, as Marcel acquires his knowledge and
deepens his understanding. The reader, in this regard, is
easily assimilated to the protagonist-observer in the soirée.

Deliberately, with marked overtones of comedy, the
theme of inversion starts with the duc de Châtellerault.
The duc had hidden his identity from a young man he
had known, who turns out to be the doorman, the *huissier*
of the princesse, whose function is to announce the duc's
name to the assembly. This confrontation is followed by a
conversation between the duc de Sidonia and M. de Charlus, each of whom guesses the vice of the other. Then
there is a return to the subject of medicine considered early
in the evening, to accommodate Professeur E who is very
much out of place. He was invited because he had cured
the prince. With Marcel, the only guest he knows, he talks
affably, checking on the fact of the grandmother's death,
so that he could verify his prognosis. Marcel's approaches
to the prince are comically hindered in several ways, but
when the introduction does occur, he realizes the superiority—the greater simplicity and dignity—of the prince
over the duc de Guermantes.

Guests move in and out of the gardens, with its famous
fountain created by Hubert Robert. Marcel overhears comments on widespread inversion in diplomatic circles, and
he listens to biting insolent remarks from Oriane whose wit
verges on calumny. Marcel's inexhaustible curiosity and
aptitude for detail, without ever obscuring the action or
the characters or the points of reference, fuse the important with less important themes. The reader is forced to
submit to Marcel's omnivorous appetite which is able to
absorb the multivarious dramas of a complicated social
function. Like Marcel, the reader recognizes the return of

themes and personages and plots and is unaware of which among the new themes and characters will become important in the future action of the novel. Marcel, in such a scene as this, is the protagonist-hero being initiated to life, who forces the reader to follow the novel in the ever-continuing present.

There is, first, like a dark thread weaving through the entire text of the scene, the references to inversion and Marcel's new awareness of signs exchanged between characters. There is M. de Vaugoubert's inversion, long concealed because of his diplomatic career, and a brief sketch of his masculine-looking wife. There is Charlus' complicated game of engaging and disengaging the two handsome sons of Mme de Surgis, and his affable attentions to their mother. At two moments in the evening Charlus' inversion is denied, once by Robert de Saint-Loup and once by Swann, both of whom believe they know him well. Marcel, as he listens to these two denials, realizes he is better informed than they are. Family and social relationships are often based on misconceptions and errors—a truth Proust never tires of illustrating.

The harshness and terrifying precision of the social hierarchy are illustrated in many ways, but especially in the presence, at the soirée, of Mme de Saint-Euverte. Some people in Paris believe her salon to be among the highest ranking, whereas it is, in reality, among the lowest. She has lost favor with the Guermantes, and has come to the soirée of the princesse in the hope of recruiting people for her own garden party the next day. Charlus' diatribe against her, spoken within her hearing is one of the vilest passages in the novel, and the only passage where scatology dominates. But Mme de Saint-Euverte's greed for social success is so great that she demeans herself before Charlus and accepts his scorn.

We learn that the duc de Guermantes' newest mistress is Mme de Surgis. At points throughout the scene we are reminded of his forced and rehearsed joviality. Before Swann's arrival, the duc attacks Dreyfus and also Swann's loyalty to Dreyfus, and points out that this has hurt Oriane.

There is a rather touching, strained scene between the
two brothers, Basin and Charlus (Mémé). The contrast
between the two brothers is not analyzed in detail, but the
reader can sense it.

The role of Swann at the reception, his last appearance
in the novel, is most subtly developed by Proust, most
pointedly analyzed by Marcel. Marcel has seen Swann
early in the evening, but the prince de Guermantes had
led him off to a distant point in the garden. Oriane is one
of those present whose curiosity is aroused by the subject
of the conversation between the prince and Swann. When
Swann returns to the large room where the reception is
being held, Marcel sees Swann's death on his face, and we
remember the announcement of his death he has already
made to the duchesse. His face is swollen now and redder
than usual, less the face of the Paris clubman than of an
old Hebrew. At this moment, at the end of his life, the
physical traits of his race are apparent in Swann, not only
because of his illness but also, possibly, because of his
strong defense of Dreyfus and the sadness and torment he
has felt over the anti-semitic propaganda in France. The
harsh word used in *Du Côté de chez Swann* to describe
him, that of *mufle* (cad), is repeated here, but joined with
the new word of *prophète. Swann était arrivé à l'âge du
prophète* (II, p. 690). This man who was once a god for
young Marcel, and who inspired Marcel with excitement
when he saw him on the Champs-Elysées, now at this
solemn meeting chez la princesse, no longer represents the
same divinity for Marcel. What remains is friendship and
respect, and Marcel marvels at the change of feeling that
has come about with time.

A bit later in the evening, Swann asks Marcel if he knows
the experience of jealousy, and Marcel explains that he has
never known it. The conversation between the younger and
the older man becomes quite intimate when Swann analyzes
his own character and describes his life. He claims he was
never capable of prolonged reflection, and that, despite
his intermittent suffering from jealousy over women, he
has loved life and art deeply . . . *c'est que j'ai beaucoup*

*aimé la vie et que j'ai beaucoup aimé les arts* (II, p. 703).
One thinks almost of the aria *Vissi d'arte e d'amore* of
*Tosca* as Swann speaks to Marcel, and the two move into
the garden. Marcel is conscious of Swann's moment of lust
for Mme Surgis, when he looks into her corsage and even
puts on his monocle in order to see more clearly. But the
conversation turns to the serious topic of Dreyfus, and
Swann reveals that both the prince and princesse, inde-
pendently of each other, have become convinced of Dreyfus' innocence and are working on his behalf.

Swann's farewell to Marcel is described in one short
paragraph of twelve lines. He does not shake hands with
Marcel in order not to have to do so with the large number
of friends he has in the company. His last words are about
Gilberte. "You should come to see her," her father says.
"She has changed. She would be so pleased." Swann's
departure is sober and undramatic. He thinks of Marcel as
the friend of his daughter, and he attempts, deftly, to
bring about a reconciliation between the two young people. In the previous scene he was "mortally wounded" by
Oriane, and in this scene he appears with the marks of
death and suffering on his face. Though hurt by his dear-
est friend, he is more than ever the loving father. Swann's
name, which Proust gave to the first part of his novel, will
never be lost sight of, and its meaning will become all the
more profound after his death, when, as Mallarmé said of
Poe, eternity changes him into himself. *Tel qu'en lui-
même enfin l'éternité le change.*

Marcel is no longer moved by the name Gilberte. He
has ceased loving her, and records, at the moment when
Swann names her, that "oblivion" has set in. This word,
*oubli,* is one of the solemn terms in Proust's vocabulary,
and designates the death of an affection. Throughout the
entire soirée, Marcel's attention wavers often as he thinks
of Albertine, who has promised to come to him at the end
of the evening (she is attending a performance of *Phèdre*).
In a vague erotic reverie he also contemplates girls in general, and one in particular, baron Putbus' chambermaid
whom Robert de Saint-Loup has praised and promised

him. The princesse de Guermantes' soirée is a transitional
moment in Marcel's love life. Behind him are two great
loves, very different from each other: Gilberte, his play-
mate of the Champs-Elysées, and Oriane, the inaccessible
Guermantes fairy queen. Ahead of him is Albertine who
thus far is merely a convenient object of erotic desire.

Oriane herself, far more than her cousin the princesse,
is the principal female figure of the soirée. Her role is the
continuation of that announced in the incident of the red
slippers. She is still wearing the red slippers, a striking
symbol of her magical beauty, her selfishness, and her ruthless power. Her conversation during the soirée is almost
exclusively comprised of malice and aristocratic insolence.
At the end, as she stands on the stairway, she makes one
gesture of mitigated courtesy to Mme de Gallardon, a
cousin whom she scorns and has avoided throughout the
evening. The duc, who has insisted that his wife wear the
red slippers, urges her, as they leave the home of the
princesse to attend a late costume party (une redoute),
not to wet the slippers in the rain which had fallen during
the evening.

The Dreyfus Case, which affected Proust very deeply,
is wedded to the narrative of the soirée, and continues
throughout the novel until the war takes over the primary
political focus. It is treated as a phenomenon that helps
to explain the social hierarchy, the class distinctions, in
France. It is, at times, a fixation; at others, merely a passing
topic of conversation. As the Dreyfus Case affects the
Guermantes, so it affects the novel. Many of the good
qualities Proust sees in the aristocracy are illustrated by
the often unexpected approval of Dreyfus, first by Saint-
Loup, then by the prince and princesse, and, later, by the
duc himself.

The entire social scene of the soirée, if one considers it
without isolating the separate themes, is a kind of purga-
tory, where there is no happiness, but the visible beginnings of atonement. The society Proust describes has just
passed beyond its moment of power and vitality. It is still
living on its strength and prestige, but the vital force has

been extinguished, and we are witnessing the very slow, very gradual diminution of greatness. The movements of supple bodies are beginning to show the first signs of stiffness. The thoughts and gestures of the nobility are being repeated too automatically. The habits of this part of society are now being performed without feeling, like the habits of a dream.

In the elaborate hierarchy of French society, the two strata of the bourgeoisie—the very wealthy bourgeoisie, called in France *la haute* or *la grande bourgeoisie,* and the solid middle bourgeoisie, called *la bonne bourgeoisie* (Proust's own family seems to have belonged to both categories)—appear more stable in *A la recherche du temps perdu* than the aristocracy. Proust as the novelist concerned with the drama of social change focuses much of his attention on the Faubourg Saint-Germain, on the Guermantes family and their extraordinary power to attract. The party at the princesse de Guermantes' exemplifies their prestige, a prestige maintained by the guests they receive, and enhanced by the desire of the uninvited guests to be welcomed one day into the sacred precincts. But within the Guermantes circle, there are already fluctuations; loss of prestige and careenings downward, in the salons of Mme de Villeparisis, Mme de Saint-Euverte, and Mme de Gallardon, who represents a younger branch of the Guermantes. The bourgeois salons we already know in the novel, Mme Verdurin's and Mme Swann's, are not too typical because they are strongly characterized by ambition and snobbism. But Proust studies them carefully because they are going to change, in the second part of *Sodome et Gomorrhe* and later, and rise in the social hierarchy.

Sexual anomaly, after its clear depiction in the prelude, is fused and confused with social traits and attitudes at the princesse de Guermantes' party. The fragments of analyses that such a scene permits are never pleas in favor of inversion, but do recast to some degree the scientific explanations of the prelude. Proust seems to believe that inversion is a kind of malady or contagion, a fashionable

practice in certain moments of civilization. There is a slight
tone which suggests Proust's disapproval of society for
creating, through its lack of tolerance, the clandestine
community of inverts who inhabit the large metropolitan
centers of the twentieth century.

But in Proust a morality, as a law or a belief or a judgment, is always subordinated to aesthetics. On this point
he is indeed the disciple of Baudelaire and Flaubert. These
three unmarried writers, all sufferers from nervous dis-
eases, and devoted to a very pronounced mother-cult,
worked laboriously and in solitude. Art for Flaubert was a
duty and a regimen of life. Art for Baudelaire and Proust
was morality itself and a justification for their lives.

Proust's theories concerning society and the individual
in society are not always arbitrarily clear. In the party
scene that opens the second half of *A la recherche du
temps perdu,* one finds, on several occasions, Proust's theory that our social personality is the creation of the
thoughts and convictions of other people. But a more
deterministic theory is also demonstrated in the same scene
as when Swann is described, not in terms of his social behavior, but primarily in terms of family and racial heredity.

The traditional habits make the nobles a privileged
group, elevated above all others. The duc de Guermantes
may have a mediocre intelligence, and the duchesse de
Guermantes may be callous and sadistic in her remarks,
but for Marcel they have a symbolic value. The soirée
scene intermingles two strange peoples, inverts and nobles:
one group concealing its identity and actually ostracized
from society; the other so special and so rare that it resembles a collection of specimens, as of a rare flower, destined
for extinction. The brief encounter of the two brothers,
the duc de Guermantes and M. de Charlus, sums up the
entire soirée. The nobleman and the invert are at the same
time quite unlike each other yet not very dissimilar at all.
Beside them is Marcel himself, who is, in a way, the strang-
est person present. He is not a snob, but he is curious about
snobbism; he is not an invert, but he is curious about inversion. Half protagonist, half narrator in this scene, he is

deeply obsessed by the as yet unexplored question: Can I become a creator? As the sexual obsession grows in Charlus' mind during the rest of the novel, so the artistic obsession grows in Marcel's.

The soirée scene also has a documentary value, as a picture of one phase of Paris life about 1900: an ambiance of wealth and refinement, of snobbism and an already somewhat dated elegance and ceremoniousness. It is the picture of a social world which is going to decline into stages of disenchantment and decadence, in the same way that the ego of the protagonist will be consumed by disenchantment and pessimism. The curse of Sodom and Gomorrah hovers over all: those who damn themselves willfully and those who damn themselves involuntarily by pride and servility.

## 11.  *Sodome et Gomorrhe.*
### B.  The drama of passion within society

Following the reception at the princesse de Guermantes',
there is a brief preparatory passage for Marcel's return to
Balbec (his second and last visit to the beach resort),
and before the narrative in *Sodome et Gomorrhe* is devoted
to a spring–summer visit in Balbec and the environs. The
figure of Marcel becomes more important in the narrative.
Now definitely the protagonist, he is extremely concerned
with his fluctuating erotic thoughts. He dreams of many
girls, but more persistently of Albertine and of her caresses
than any of the others. During the late evening of the
princesse's reception, when Marcel, by cajolery and insinu-
ation, persuades Albertine to come to him after she had
called to cancel her visit, he has all the premonitions of his
future suffering. He fully demonstrates in the telephone
conversation with Albertine, as he demonstrated in their
encounters in *A l'ombre des jeunes filles en fleurs*, the
traits of a petulant, selfish, scheming lover. In his self-
analysis, Marcel makes no attempt to ennoble himself.
Even during this initial stage of his love for Albertine, his
feelings are deep—deeper than he fully realizes—but his actions and his thoughts are petty and egotistical. Later in
*La Prisonnière* and especially in *La Fugitive*, Marcel's love
for Albertine is recaptured as the most fully developed
theme in *A la recherche du temps perdu*.

  *Sodome et Gomorrhe,* after the prelude with Charlus
and Jupien and the reception chez la princesse de Guermantes, is Balbec, seen now not as the romantic setting for

a youth's reverie, where Marcel was awed and even terrified by much that he saw, but seen as a kind of hell, a city of the plain. The revelation of Balbec as Sodom and Gomorrah is gradual.

However, in contrast to the preoccupation in the first part with inversion, Balbec is reintroduced by a remarkable prelude that has nothing to do with inversion. The prelude has a title: *Les Intermittences du Coeur*. This passage on "the intermittences of the heart" (a title Proust once thought of giving to the entire novel) contains an episode of involuntary memory which is as important for the second half of the novel, as the madeleine-tea episode is for the first half. It is one of Marcel's sobering and deeply felt experiences, and one not to be recaptured throughout the rest of *Sodome et Gomorrhe*. Its poignancy, despite its brevity, is strong enough to counteract the continual erotic preoccupations which occupy so much of this section of the novel.

It happens abruptly, unexpectedly, as such experiences do, soon after Marcel enters the hotel and speaks with the manager who commits a large number of malapropisms in his speech. Marcel acknowledges to himself the real reason for this return to Balbec: the hope of meeting Mme Putbus' maid (whose available charms had been praised by Robert de Saint-Loup). He knows that Mme Putbus was invited by Mme Verdurin, who had rented the château of La Raspelière from Mme de Cambremer. Marcel was first led to Balbec by the dazzling romantic connotations with Balbec which Legrandin had described for him in poetic language. He has come back, older and wiser, along the devious road of Eros, because a chambermaid he has never seen, may come to a castle occupied by the Verdurins whom he has only seen infrequently, the castle rented from Mme de Cambremer, sister of the same Legrandin, the unwitting herald of an innocent and unreal Balbec. The labyrinthine way of Proust's novel is of such intricacy that at times the reader requires, with Marcel, the respite of a single unified meaningful experience: at the Grand

Hôtel de Balbec he now undergoes exactly this kind of experience.

He bends down to take off his boots. On touching the first button of the first shoe, he is shaken by sobs, and tears stream from his eyes. He sees, bending over him, when once before he was tired at Balbec, the attentive sweet face of his grandmother. The past returns to him, involuntarily, and he experiences the full grief over his grandmother that he had not felt at the time of her death. He remembers all the details of her kindness, and he soon learns how she concealed her illness from him, how, when Saint-Loup photographed her, she used a wide-brimmed hat to shade the signs of suffering on her face. He remembers his grandmother of the Champs-Elysées, as well as of Balbec, his grandmother in the train who was upset when he drank some cognac, his grandmother of Combray. These associations crowd in his mind, more clearly delineated than before.

This experience of memory, this total recall brought about by a fortuitous sensation, is allied for Proust with "the intermittences of the heart." *Car aux troubles de la mémoire sont liées les intermittences du coeur* (II, p. 756). During the usual course of the hours and the days, the total soul of a human being is "fictional" because its contents, its memories, are inaccessible. However, what Proust calls the spirituality of the body is at every moment enclosed within it, perpetually within our possession. A fortuitous sensation may bring back a part of the past and reveal its meaning. This is what happens to Marcel when he begins to unbutton his shoe. He relives the past with his grandmother, and understands it fully for the first time, and is strengthened by this reanimation in him of the virtues of Combray. It is precisely these virtues and the stable unwavering love of his grandmother that comprise a marked contrast to the new Balbec.

The intermittences of the heart, with which the novel henceforth is going to be increasingly concerned, are what controls the accumulation of our memories. Proust believes that this accumulation is at all times present within us, but not always accessible to our conscious mind. As he lives in the present, Marcel is going to testify over and over again to the disappearance of strong sentiments in him, to the cessation of loves that at one time dominated his existence. Even those individuals whom he loved dearly, such as his grandmother, are destined to die a second time. There is first the physical death, and then there is the death in the conscious mind of the one who lives. But the experience of deep love or strong sentiment never dies in the subconscious memory of a man. Although it is, of course, possible that no sensation in the present will ever bring back the love that once existed.

In the prelude scene to the new Balbec, we reach a high level of meditation on Marcel's meaning of the word *real*. It is true that he is held only briefly by this overwhelming experience of recall, and soon plunges into the "unreal" world of Balbec society. But the long narrative rests on these rare intuitions of time and the reality of the objective world. We have just learned once again, with Marcel, that things are not what they are. They are what we make them, they are the record of our subjective memory and totally present within us, although removed from the dangerous contingencies of the present. In other words, time is a form that beings and objects take within us. It is not, therefore, solely the chronological force that destroys sentiments and beings and things.

The lesson of Proust's idealism (for such is the only possible designation of his philosophy) is stated in *Combray* and *Un Amour de Swann* as well as in the episode when he bends down to unbutton his boots, but it is always being more fully justified and explicated, until it dominates all the themes and all the elements of the narrative in the final scene of the novel.

When Marcel enters the life of Balbec, colored now by the sulphurous screen of Sodom and Gomorrah, and speaks to us about so many personages, we realize that in reality he is speaking about himself; that is, about what these beings are for him. This is, of course, the law of idealism. Marcel's world is his idea of the world. Everything is constantly being transformed by his mind and his sensibility. Earlier in the novel, Elstir transformed a wall into the sea, and Swann transformed the face of a girl into a painting by Giotto. Now, Marcel, as protagonist and narrator, will be the only central absolute. Every object he describes, every being he talks with and analyzes, everyⁱbeing he loves, is relative and contingent and, in the last analysis, unreal. No matter what the situation is, no matter who the characters are, Marcel will be asking only one question, although it will never be phrased quite so specifically: Of what possible worth is anything that is not eternal? So far in the novel, the experiences of the madeleine cake, the steeples of Martinville, the trees of Balbec, and the unbuttoning of the shoes have been moments when the inner world of Marcel was exteriorized by his involuntary memory. Only those images of the past have been real. And we now move back into the unreal world of the present: the vanity of social life and the vanity of passions.

The foregoing remarks are not intended to portray Marcel Proust as a philosopher. He is a novelist, a "creative" writer in the highest sense, whose genius is his power of observation, when he is not writing, and his power of transfiguration, of poetic transposition, when he does write. Whether it be the scene at the Opéra, at the beginning of *Le Côté de Guermantes,* where the princesse de Guermantes and the duchesse de Guermantes are described as "white deities" (*blanches déités*), or the recruitment of Mme Verdurin's salon at La Raspelière in *Sodome et Gomorrhe,* the great spectacle scenes of the novel are not spectacles in the usual sense. They are examples of Proust's vision, of his understanding and poetic fervor. Everything is used by Proust as a means of understanding what is human. His novel is a compendium of many contrasting details, such as those to which we are now coming: the appearance of the dowager Mme de Cambremer, and the elevator boy (*le lift*) at the hotel, who is concerned with the tip Marcel will give him. Each character is integrated within a caste: Françoise in the servant hierarchy, as carefully as Oriane, duchesse de Guermantes is integrated in the aristocracy. The caste itself, its laws and habits, interests Proust profoundly; so do the vices and weaknesses of the representative of each caste he studies: Jupien, whose servility and pandering are integral parts of his character, and Charles Swann, member of the Jockey Club, in the highest rank of the French bourgeoisie.

Proust is not indulgent in his analysis of human nature. No moralist of his stature ever has been. At this central point in the novel, when Balbec is about to appear to Marcel in quite a different light from on his first visit when his grandmother accompanied him and when he was pampered by her and by Mme de Villeparisis, the subject of the novel is fairly clear. It is not (despite the claims made by various interpreters of Proust) the study of French society. Neither is it the analysis of love and passion in their various manifestations. The real subject of *A la recherche du temps perdu* transcends both of these subjects: it is the struggle of the human spirit with time. Marcel is faced with the impossibility of finding an absolute in daily life, in his observations of nature and art, and in his relationships with human beings. (The religious solution is not even posed by him, because he is not a believer.) The detailed answer to this struggle between the human spirit and time, will be reserved for the end of the novel, in *Le Temps retrouvé*, but we can already sense its early formulation. The answer to the struggle will be the creation of the novel itself.

The memory of the artist which permits him to reconstruct the past, is the one remedy against the disappearance of human happiness, against the changes of fortune each life knows, against oblivion that threatens even the greatest love in a single existence. But Proust spends more time, since he is a novelist, with the actual world, with places and characters and the multitudinous details needed to project the places and characters, than with the philosophical explanation of his world.

Only momentarily does Marcel's long delayed grief over his grandmother isolate him from Balbec. He is soon again caught up by the life of the hotel, where the servants (*chasseurs* and *liftiers*) are often compared to the chorus of boys in *Athalie* or the chorus of girls in *Esther*. His desire for Albertine, and for her friends, once again declares itself on a day when spring is in the air, and the flowering apple trees resemble peasants standing along a French highway . . . *ces pommiers étaient là en pleine campagne, comme des paysans sur une grande route de France* (II, p. 781).

But Marcel's resumption of his return to happiness is marred by a chance remark made to him by Dr. Cottard, the still faithful habitué of Mme Verdurin's clan. At the Casino of Incarville, Albertine and Andrée are dancing together and Cottard imputes to them a lesbian relationship, betrayed in the closeness of their bodies as they dance. This suspicion concerning Albertine is new to Marcel. It sinks deeply within his consciousness and never leaves him through the rest of the narrative. The suspicion, which will never be either verified or effaced, actually helps to crystallize his love for Albertine, and becomes one of the major ingredients of Marcel's passion and suffering. In this way the theme of inversion mingles with normal love, or rather the suspicion of inversion mingles with the faint beginnings of Marcel's love for Albertine. Blatant inversion dominates the passages concerning Bloch's sister and her actress friend, concerning M. Nissim Bernard who takes his lunch at the hotel every day in order to observe a young servant, and concerning, in particular, Charlus' meeting with the violinist Morel at the station of Doncières and their subsequent appearances together at the salon of Mme Verdurin.

Marcel's mother at Balbec is self-effacing. We seldom see her except for a few occasions when Marcel notices how her mourning has caused her to resemble her mother. Her thoughts and actions, her references to Mme de Sévigné are all part of the closeness she has established with her deceased mother.

An important change has taken place in Marcel. He is no longer intimidated by the hotel at Balbec, by the manager, by the people he meets. Now a privileged guest, he is much sought after. In this aspect of Marcel's ever-growing popularity, we sense the character of Proust in his real life. But in the novel there is very little explanation of why Marcel triumphs in this way. We sense only indirectly the charm and intelligence that would open all doors to him. Even the lavishness of Marcel's tips would not account fully for the special place he occupies with servants. Céleste Albaret, Proust's housekeeper for ten years, appears under her real name at the Hôtel de Balbec, as a maid whom Marcel befriends and who pampers him and speaks to him affectionately and humorously as if he were a child. One day Céleste turns the pages of a new book of poems and asks Marcel if they are not conundrums rather than poems. The book is *Eloges* of Saint-Léger Léger, who will sign his future work Saint-John Perse. *"Mais êtes-vous bien sûr que ce sont des vers, est-ce que ce ne serait pas plutôt des devinettes?"* (II, p. 849.)

We watch the result of Marcel's series of social triumphs in all classes, but we do not see exactly how he brings these about. The similar triumphs in the life of Proust have been analyzed in so many different ways by so many different friends and admirers that no one explanation is satisfactory. Thus one of the major psychological mysteries in *A la recherche du temps perdu*—the mystery of Marcel's personality, destined to remain a mystery—is related to a comparable mystery in the character of Albertine who though lengthily analyzed is still ultimately unknowable.

Now when she is with Marcel, she is attentive and tender, essentially passive and compliant, eager to please; but still she gives no real indication of love. One senses that she lies constantly, and that she wants very much to remain on intimate relations with Marcel. One already wonders whether venality sufficiently explains Albertine's behavior: and nothing is totally clear in Albertine's actions, her desires, her sentiments, or her death.

Mme Verdurin's salon, transported to La Raspelière, where her Wednesday gatherings will continue during the summer season, is the real site of *Sodome et Gomorrhe*. The salon has reached a point in its evolution where it is now conceivable that one day it may attain the highest social level. Many of the old habitués are still with Mme Verdurin: Brichot and his patiently explained etymologies; Saniette, who continues to be tormented by M. Verdurin; the sculptor Ski whom Mme Verdurin finds typical of the greatest kind of artist; Dr. Cottard and his wife. There is a new member, princesse Sherbatoff, who, though she adds the prestige of her rank, adds little else. The tyranny and the domination of "la Patronne" are stronger than ever. She controls the arrivals of her guests by sending carriages to meet the train. Her snobbism in music and art is still pronounced. Everything is easily sacrificed to sustaining the salon: the death of her favorite pianist Dechambre is forgotten in her acquisition of the violinist Morel.

Just as she once favored and protected the liaison of Swann and Odette, because it furthered the success of her salon, so now at La Raspelière she encourages and shelters two other liaisons for the same reason: Marcel and Albertine, on the one hand, and Charlus and Morel, on the other. Mme Verdurin does not hesitate to play the role of *entremetteuse*, of procuress. This sinister aspect of the salon is constantly offset by a humor which often verges on the grotesque. The rivalry between Mme Verdurin and M. de Charlus is a complex Proustian drama of comedy and grotesquerie where the sexes seem to be reversed, with Mme Verdurin playing the virile role. The comic effect is reached by classical devices: misunderstanding, ignorance, crossed purposes. On two successive pages the rivalry is particularly sharp and Charlus outdistances his rival who is unaware of exactly who the baron is. First, Mme Verdurin asks Charlus to recommend an old impoverished noble to serve as her concierge. Charlus replies that he could do this, but visitors would not wish to go beyond the concierge's office. Marcel calls this exchange the first "skirmish" between the two. *Ce fut entre eux la première escarmouche* (II, p. 967). Immediately after this, Mme Verdurin asks Charlus if he has ever met the duc de Guermantes. Charlus replies at first enigmatically and then,

with a benign smile, says that the duc is his brother . . .
*Mais puisque c'est mon frère* . . . (II, p. 968).

The Verdurin salon, transplanted from Paris to Balbec,
is essentially the same that we saw in *Du Côté de chez
Swann,* but it has changed. Nothing, no theme or character, is ever static or total in Proust. The tyranny of Mme
Verdurin is more obvious, her vulgarity, stronger, and
her willingness to condone any kind of liaison among her
guests, provided their presence can thus be assured,
more determined. At one point she even suggests to Marcel
that he and Albertine come to live with her!

Charlus' inversion is now more patent in the Verdurin
salon. Farther away from his real world, he is now more
careless. He betrays himself in every way: by speech, gestures, laughter, the choice of a beverage! But all of this is
accepted by Mme Verdurin, and M. Verdurin in a long
speech to Charlus divides the world into two groups, normal and abnormal, and places in the abnormal category
his wife and Charlus! As the traits of the invert in Charlus
become clearer, the traits of the megalomaniac also develop. There are moments when Charlus' feelings of greatness and power approach the stage of delirium or lunacy.
Gradually the reader is able to piece together the pattern
of Charlus' complicated life, and to see his relentless and
often devious efforts to enslave this or that person to his
desires. Even Aimé, the maître d'hôtel, had been solicited
earlier when he worked at the restaurant of Rivebelle (*A
l'ombre des jeunes filles en fleurs*) where he once refused
to carry out a commission of the baron's. Much of the
narrative of the novel is the elucidation of past incidents
which had remained shrouded in mystery. No detail is
merely a detail for Proust the novelist: it is also incipient
drama.

Marcel, as he continues to watch all this and to par-
ticipate in it to some extent, becomes more aware of his
own personal drama, his growing preoccupation with Albertine. He is beginning to realize the existence of two
Albertines: one growing in him, formed by his thoughts
and dreams; and the other outside, strange and always

unfathomable. This is the initial stage of the most fully developed drama in *A la recherche du temps perdu*. Marcel's behavior with Albertine is far from exemplary. In its deepest implications, it is not very different from Morel's behavior with Charlus. Perhaps Morel is harder, more Machiavellian. But Marcel's deceit, his trickiness, his determination to catch Albertine in lies, are aspects, at this stage, not of love, but of a fundamental distrust of human nature.

The interweaving of these two liaisons, both under the aegis of Mme Verdurin momentarily, represents initially the futility and the tragedy of the story of the cities of the plain in Genesis. The normal couple, Marcel-Albertine, testifies already to the defect of an excessive subjectivism in love, to the unknowable elements in the beloved and the fairly clear situation of unreciprocated love; the abnormal couple, Charlus-Morel, testifies to the more obvious (if not greater) degree of venality, of actual prostitution. As Charlus' attention and gifts increase, Morel's hardness of character and will to exploit grow. In Marcel himself we see the reflection of both Charlus and Morel: Charlus' effort to buy and subjugate the one he loves, and Morel's attempt to exploit the love of his patron and benefactor (if that love really exists) and to make himself the more desired by pretending indifference.

Marcel learns to understand himself by observing others and imagining himself in their place. Even in his analysis of Morel, perhaps the most venal of all the characters in the book, he is ultimately generous, understanding, and uncritical. This may be due to the fact that there is much of Morel in Marcel. One short summary sentence about Morel sheds light on Proust's psychology of personality, and applies as accurately to Marcel as to Morel. In it Marcel claims that the character of Morel is not uniformly bad, but is made up of contradictions. The image he then uses in order to describe the composite character of the young man, is that of a mediaeval book, with misconceptions, traditional absurdities, and obscenities. *Il ressemblait à un vieux livre du Moyen Age, plein d'erreurs, de tradi-*

*tions absurdes, d'obscénités, il était extraordinairement composite* (II, p. 1032).

Much attention has been paid to the final scenes of Charlus' degradation and moral collapse in *Le Temps retrouvé*, but the elements of willful evil and corruption are all present in the passage when Morel says to Charlus that he would enjoy seducing a young virgin and then abandoning her. Charlus' encouragement of such an exploit reveals to what extremes his conscience will allow him to go. When Morel designates Jupien's daughter (in reality Jupien's niece) as the intended victim, Charlus does, in his loyalty to Jupien, withdraw his approval.

The baron freely discusses inversion with, for example, Cottard and Brichot, but often in literary terms. Charlus is an avid reader of Balzac, as Proust was, and refers in specific scenes to two books in particular where the overtones of inversion are fairly strong: Carlos Herrera passing before Rastignac's castle in *Les Illusions perdues*, and the death scene of Lucien de Rubempré in *Splendeurs et Misères*. At intervals throughout the narrative the friendship between Swann and Charlus, and especially the resemblance of their voices, are stressed, briefly but pointedly.

Whereas the long passages in *Sodome et Gomorrhe* concerning the Charlus-Morel relationship are primarily discussions (Marcel even believes that Charlus' love for Morel may be platonic at this point), the scenes between Albertine and Marcel are active and frankly sensual. Marcel woos the girl with presents: hats and veils, and the frequent use of an automobile and chauffeur. Her jealousy is more pronounced as his attempts to bribe her become more extravagant. (The parallelism between Charlus and Marcel gives a beautiful effect of counterpoint to the days and nights at Balbec, when neither the older man nor the younger knows what his beloved is doing or thinking.) Marcel alternates between deciding to marry Albertine and deciding to break off with her. Once, in speaking of Albertine, he uses the word "prisoner," which will be the title of the next part of the novel, but he holds her prisoner now only by looking at her when Saint-Loup is present . . .

*je tenais Albertine prisonnière sous mon regard* (II, p. 1101).

At the moment when Marcel is on the point of breaking with Albertine, a seemingly insignificant event occurs which, in Proustian terms, affects Marcel traumatically, and catapults him into a desperate love and its anguish. In this event, Gomorrah, the city associated with lesbianism, joins with the Sodom of Charlus. When Marcel names Vinteuil as the composer he has referred to, during a train ride conversation with Albertine, she tells him that she knows Vinteuil's daughter and her friend intimately. With this revelation, spoken in a small railroad station far from Combray, and long after the death of Vinteuil, the image of desecration the boy Marcel had seen at Montjouvain fills his mind and initiates a suffering he has not felt before. Marcel sees himself as a spy hiding behind the bushes at Montjouvain and observing only a tantalizing fragment of a scene which had horrified him. This is an unknown land, a new phase of suffering which has just opened up for him. *C'était une* terra incognita *terrible où je venais d'atterrir, une phase nouvelle de souffrances insoupçonnées qui s'ouvrait* (II, p. 1115).

The brief episode at the beginning of *Du Côté de chez Swann* suddenly returns with new meaning that is not lost sight of during the rest of the novel. Marcel's immediate actions are dictated by this revelation which would have meant nothing if he had not witnessed the Montjouvain scene as a youth. He tries to protect Albertine from the predisposition to vice. He takes her to Paris with him, and he tells his mother that he must marry the girl. The last two pages of *Sodome et Gomorrhe* present a collage, a recapitulation of Marcel's itinerary and initiation up to this point. He looks out the window of his hotel room and sees the beach of Balbec, the sea, and the sun rising. His mother is with him, and also his grandmother, because his mother is thinking of her. Inside, he sees the familiar hotel room, and he also sees the room at Montjouvain where Albertine has taken the place of Mlle Vinteuil's friend. He hears the voluptuous laughter of the two girls as well as the muffled words exchanged on similar occasions between himself and Albertine.

The horrible image of Montjouvain is not effaced by the beautiful images of Albertine at Balbec and the moments of happiness Marcel has known with her. As he makes the formal announcement of marriage to his mother—the final words of the volume: *il faut absolument que j'épouse Albertine* (II, p. 1131)—he is fully aware of the sadness this marriage will bring her. And he knows that she will not reveal the sadness in her words or facial expression, just as she did not reveal her feelings at Combray, on the night when, disappointed by his behavior, she had stayed with him in his room. Like a palimpsest, these last two pages of *Sodome et Gomorrhe,* show theme behind theme, as specific moments of the past are joined with present anguish: Marcel's childhood, dominated by the solicitude of his mother and grandmother; the virtues of Combray violated by the traumatic scene at Montjouvain; the sea at Balbec, where Marcel's moments of happiness with Albertine are now annulled by the peril of her immorality.

After being essentially the observer in *Le Côté de Guermantes,* Marcel occupies the primary role through most of *Sodome et Gomorrhe.* Next in importance is M. de Charlus, whom we see most vividly in his strange relationship with Charles Morel. And behind Charlus is Mme Verdurin, whose salon at Balbec is the setting for the amorous adventures of both Marcel and Charlus. The tyrannical patronage of Mme Verdurin is the social force that brings about these recapitulations of thwarted and unreciprocated love, and the reader can easily and imaginatively move back from Swann's love to the two angels who visited Sodom, to the disobedience of the men of that city and the curse that was placed upon them. Temporarily in the novel the Verdurin salon at Balbec is the city of the plain (until the city of Paris later takes over the role) but there are so many recapitulations at Balbec, where Vinteuil is remembered by the faithful of the clan, as well as Elstir and Bergotte, that the moral theme is constantly being replaced by those of aesthetics and snobbism. The baron de Charlus is the one representative of the Guermantes in this part of the novel. His berouged face, his hunger for power, and his obsession with Morel mark an intermediary stage in his story, a point halfway between the proud enigmatic noble of *A l'ombre des jeunes filles en fleurs* and the crushed figure of *Le Temps retrouvé.*

The mysterious and perhaps inexplicable reasons for Swann's choice of Odette are the same for Charlus' choice of Morel, and Marcel's choice of Albertine. Odette, Morel, and Albertine are deliberately left vague and unknowable; they are phantom characters moving back and forth in salons and boudoirs, bearers of an invisible vice which the man who loves them (Swann, Charlus, Marcel) knows exists, and which will always be the obstacle to his happiness in love.

Behind the preoccupation with love and inversion, is the ever-present and ever-changing social manifestation of love, which Proust calls snobbism. Swann's love, like Charlus' and Marcel's, is never analyzed without its social concomitant in the snobbism of the aristocracy, the bourgeoisie, and the servant class. This snobbism, to which Proust returns over and over again, as to a study of predilection, is somewhat more accessible, somewhat more decipherable, than the study of love. But at times it equals love in its mysteriousness and complexity. Snobbism in *A la recherche du temps perdu* is ubiquitous, and its ramifications are so far-reaching that it seems even to annex to itself the experience of love. We can see it in the witticisms of Oriane and their effect on those around her. It is graphically portrayed in the attempts of Mme Verdurin to storm the fortress of the Faubourg Saint-Germain. It exists in varying ways and degrees in Odette, in Gilberte, in Rachel, and in Bloch. Originally the word "snob" in England designated a commoner's attempt to imitate a noble. Its general use in France designates a stupid admiration for anything fashionable. But in Proust, it is infinitely more complex. It is a major element in human conduct, and Proust's concern with it places his work in the same tradition with Balzac's *Comédie Humaine. Sodome et Gomorrhe* is the most Balzacian of the seven parts of *A la recherche du temps perdu.*

The intricately woven texture of artificial—or artificially motivated—impulses and habits and manias is the background for the love stories in Proust so that snobbism, with its emphasis on comedy and vanity, when treated with the more tragic study of love and inversion, does not weary or harass the reader.

The hereditary politeness of the Guermantes and their effusive amiability (which we see in Basin de Guermantes, Mme de Villeparisis, Mme de Marsantes, and the two royal highnesses, the princesse de Luxembourg and the princesse de Parme) are constantly belied by questions of hierarchy and protocol (*préséances*) and by traits of self-centeredness and egoism. The princesse de Parme, whose name once fascinated Marcel with its associations of violets and Stendhal, is a small humble-looking lady, active in charity functions. But Proust portrays her fundamental character as haughty and distant. In this, Proust is a true novelist, avoiding such portrait studies as are found in the *Mémoires* of Saint-Simon. Minor and major characters alike are recognizable by their speech and behavior and manias: Norpois' solemn speech of clichés, Legrandin's flowery apostrophes, Françoise's proverbs, Mme de Cambremer's use of three adjectives.

*Sodome et Gomorrhe* introduces the two dramas of passion in the novel: Marcel's and Charlus', which are in reality two aspects of the same dilemma for Proust. At the same time *Sodome et Gomorrhe* provides the two great social scenes: at the princesse de Guermantes' and at Mme Verdurin's. Charlus, the eminent aristocrat, appears, as a powerful character chez la princesse and as a vulnerable weakling chez Mme Verdurin; but at both places he also reveals nothing in himself: his class giving him all—his identity, his name, and his heritage.

## 12. *La Prisonnière.*
## (*The Captive*)
### A. The heroism of the mind

Whenever the theme of the "room" (*la chambre*) becomes important, the reader may well feel as if the novel is beginning again. Its real beginning was in Marcel's room at Combray. His room at Balbec initiated the new phase of his life when he left his family circle for the first time. His room at Doncières had no connection with his family, although it was not far from Balbec where his grandmother was, and Robert de Saint-Loup played at Doncières almost the part of a watchful parent! On the opening page of *La Prisonnière*, Marcel is in bed, as he was on the opening page of *Du Côté de chez Swann*, and this time he is in his room in Paris, in the apartment rented by his family from the duchesse de Guermantes. His father is traveling and his mother is at Combray. Only Françoise and his prisoner Albertine are in the house with Marcel.

This cohabitation, attacked by Proust's critics as unlikely in terms of bourgeois mores, Marcel's mother herself criticizes in the narrative as unwise. Yet she is accustomed to indulging Marcel: he has, since his parents recognized his illness, broken the rules of normal behavior from the beginning of the story. His need to stay in a room alone, his asthma attacks, his insomnia, have affected the lives of his family and friends. Françoise, Robert and even his mother easily grant him his whim of keeping Albertine in a room not far from his own, and of supervising, as much as he can, all of her actions. She learns the ritual of Marcel's room: the time when she can enter it, and the care that must be taken not to make any noise.

Musing on love, Marcel tries to define it as the effect of strong emotion on the soul. *L'amour n'est peut-être que la propagation de ces remous qui, à la suite d'une émotion, émeuvent l'âme* (III, p. 20). In the place of what he once thought was love for Albertine is jealousy, the sentiment aroused by her announcing her friendship with Mlle Vinteuil. He had believed that by taking her to Paris with him, he would remove her from all temptation, but now he realizes that Gomorrah is everywhere. *Gomorrhe était dispersée aux quatre coins du monde* (III, p. 23). But jealousy is an intermittent malady, capricious in its attacks, and various in its manifestations.

Marcel calls on his neighbor the duchesse for information about the clothing he wishes to give Albertine. On such a practical matter he consults the woman whose name once was so mysterious for him. He asks about the red dress and red shoes she wore on the evening she went to dine at Mme de Saint-Euverte's, when, for him, she suggested a blood-red flower, or a flaming ruby. On certain days, as he leaves the duchesse, Marcel meets Charlus and Morel in the courtyard, entering Jupien's lodging to have tea with Jupien and his niece, now Morel's fiancée. By this projected marriage, Charlus hopes to keep Morel more securely within his control. The pattern, only briefly referred to, complements Marcel's relationship with Albertine.

The long analysis of Marcel's passion and jealousy dominates most of *La Prisonnière* and *La Fugitive*. Throughout these seven hundred pages Albertine grows into a strange creature, half phantom, half girl. Marcel has realized from the beginning that his thoughts about her do not correspond to any reality, but he is unable to resist creating in his mind a being who probably bears only a very slight resemblance to the young girl, Albertine Simonet, who occupies a room in his Paris apartment and who comes to him at designated moments and offers him a ritualistic pattern of kisses and caresses. On the evenings when Marcel knows Albertine will not leave the apartment, he enjoys a feeling of possession both ethereal and sensual. At Balbec this pleasure had been fleeting and fragmentary. In Paris, he has almost the illusion that it is a permanent domestic happiness.

His moments of greatest security occur as he sees Albertine asleep. Her body in its natural state of relaxation becomes like a plant . . . *en dormant, elle était devenue une plante* (III, p. 70). In her sleep Marcel possesses her more fully than when she is awake. Often Albertine's good night kiss brings him the kind of peacefulness that his mother's good night kiss at Combray had brought him when he was a boy. At such moments mother and mistress are the same for him. Their kiss is a viaticum, a magic sign that will give him sleep and rest.

But physical satisfaction, the sense of ownership, and the experience of domestic happiness are infrequent in comparison to the moments when Albertine's lies, Françoise's hostility toward her, and his attacks of jealousy become obstacles to Marcel's happiness. He yearns for release from this love, but the jealousy that has succeeded love possesses him and obsesses him. He questions Andrée, who usually accompanies Albertine whenever she leaves the house, but from the reports he learns nothing, or at least nothing that he can credit.

As Marcel questions Albertine, and as he later analyzes his feelings in the solitude of his room, he realizes he is beginning to resemble members of his family. There is no need for them to be in the apartment, because they are in him. In his speech, when he is tender with Albertine, he recognizes accents and phrases of his mother and grandmother. In his growing preoccupation with weather, which has its bearing on Albertine's program, he recognizes his father. Above all, he now sees in his present behavior more than traces of tante Léonie, with whom at one time he believed he had nothing in common, because of her excessive piety and her hypochondria. The tyranny he exerts from his bed, in which he reclines so much of the time, the fact that his room has become his universe, exactly duplicates Léonie's character and habits. The souls of others are in him, and he is able for the first time in the weeks of exaggerated self-analysis to recognize them and to acknowledge the likenesses.

These similarities of behavior have moral implications for Marcel. At the moments of sexual union, he sees in Albertine, in the submissiveness of her body, the archetypal Woman, and he knows that in this act, he is recapitulating the experience of all the races of men before him. *O grandes attitudes de l'Homme et de la Femme où cherchent à se joindre, dans l'innocence des premiers jours et avec l'humilité de l'argile, ce que la Création a séparé . . .* (III, p. 79). But such an exalted passage, with its reference to Plato and the Bible, where Albertine is compared to Eve in her sexual submission to the male, ends in disillusionment, when Marcel sees on Albertine's face signs of wickedness and deceit and venality. The familiar sameness of the room provides the tranquil setting for the ever-changing, ever-turbulent drama for the love, which Marcel no longer enjoys, and which has now turned to jealousy.

Nowhere else in literature is the subjectivism of love so relentlessly tracked down and exposed as in *La Prisonnière*. Whenever Albertine appears to Marcel as a being in herself, she is unknown and unknowable, secretive and untrustworthy, a spy and a stranger in the house where she is held prisoner. And whenever Albertine seems to Marcel obedient and loving, a slave to his whims and his will, she is merely a reflection of himself, created by his desires, a feminine Marcel who merges with him as if she were his shadow.

The widespread critical campaign in recent years to see Albertine as a boy is based not on the novel but on Proust's personal life. Alfred Agostinelli was no model for the literary character of Albertine Simonet. In the novel Albertine is ambiguous, but not because of her sexual characteristics. She is ambiguous because she serves, not so much as a character in herself, but as the occasion for the protagonist's self-analysis, for his suffering, for his search of the real.

*La Prisonnière* is the most unremittingly "Proustian" of

all the parts of *A la recherche du temps perdu*. In the literal sense, the captive is Albertine, but in a more symbolic sense, it is also Marcel's soul. The feminine *âme de Marcel* is *la prisonnière* in more than one way. His illness, his jealousy, his desire to write all confine Marcel to his room. He scans *Le Figaro* daily to see if his article has appeared in it, and his preoccupation with the meaning of art and the seclusion of the artist grows in the second half of *La Prisonnière*. Beyond these three very specific forces that cloister Marcel—illness, love, and artistic ambition— lies the intermittent tormenting desire to know another human being. This quest, the most harassing of them all, isolates Marcel from everyone and everything.

Marcel sees Albertine as an allegorical goddess of the sea, as a name for his desires, the mirror of time. She is as evanescent as she is real: Venus risen from the sea. When she leaves the room, she is Eurydice going to a distant land. Both temptress and woman, dragon and girl, she is Mélusine. He had once loved Gilberte and called her Mélusine, and the two names of Gilberte and Albertine contain the same resonance, the same central syllable. As she sleeps on his bed, he sees in her face races, atavisms, and vices. *Des races, des atavismes, des vices reposaient sur son visage* (III, p. 72). In Albertine he possesses not one girl, but an infinite number of girls. All the girls of Balbec, and many others, pass, with Albertine, along the vertiginous current of life which a man imprisoned in his room would feel more deeply than a man swept along in that same current.

Both as the girl Marcel bribes with gifts and attention and as an allegorical figure, Albertine reveals the complex sensibility of the protagonist, the weaknesses of his character, and the extraordinary awareness he shows of each aspect real and imaginary in the captive girl. Albertine is a multiple image, and Marcel, as artist and lover, creates many of the Albertines which torment him. He is himself different in this new relationship, and he ponders on the fragmentation of a single human being, on the impulse of the lover to merge totally with the beloved, and on the

daily reiterated defeats he experiences, as, after each new
apparition of Albertine, he realizes he does not know her.

Marcel's efforts to know the Guermantes, in previous
sections of the novel, are not unrelated to his yearning to
know Albertine. With the curious members of the Guermantes, Marcel, like a student of Saint-Simon, is concerned with genealogy, with the realities of encounters,
with social characteristics and social upheavals, with history and myth. He has reached a point in the narrative
when he is almost ready to acknowledge and describe the
finiteness of the Guermantes, and the change that is coming about in their fame and prestige. From his study of
the Guermantes family, in which Oriane recapitulates the
legend of Mélusine, Marcel learns that the greatest for-
tunes and the most firmly established thrones collapse.
From the captivity of Albertine he learns in his personal
life the bitter lesson of solitude, the futility of trying to
know anyone else, the hopelessness of love, the never-ending torment of doubt and suspicion. Life in its mobility
and flux forever jeopardizes the prestige of noble families:
the Lusignans came to an end with Mélusine, and the
Guermantes approach their end in Oriane. Likewise, in his
life story, Marcel's successive infatuations for Gilberte
Swann, the duchesse de Guermantes and Mlle de Stermaria, have flourished and died. They all served as preludes to his present love for Albertine. While Marcel hesitates between the two images opened to him: imprisoning
himself within love, even as he is imprisoned in his room,
or a dismissal of Albertine in order to cure himself of this
torment, he knows that no matter what he does willfully,
the real cure of his passion will come about almost accidentally, without premeditation, beyond planning. Passion created and passion cured occur with the same mysterious whimsicality that presides over a man's birth.

Gradually Marcel sees into the greatest source of his
anguish: he will never know whether Albertine loves him.
It is never stated in the text that Albertine loves him, because we never know her mind. We are only made to
believe, as readers of this story, that if Marcel ever reached

the certainty that Albertine loved him, he would then cease to love her.

Action, in the ordinary sense of a narrative, is greatly abbreviated in the first half of *La Prisonnière*. Consisting mainly of Albertine's plans for walks and visits to take her out of the apartment, it is restricted by Marcel's suspicion and morbid jealousy. He prevents Albertine from calling on Mme Verdurin, for example, and allows her to go instead to a play at the Trocadéro. But he learns that Mlle Léa, the actress friend of two girls at Balbec whom Albertine had once seen reflected in a mirror, has the lead in the play. He suspects the worst, and his anguish returns stronger than ever. Albertine's lies are matched by Marcel's own, as he tries to trick her and extract confessions from her.

The subsidiary themes also are greatly reduced in this section. There are frequent references to Françoise's speech and some evocative passages on the sounds in the streets of Paris that reach Marcel and remind him of the world outside of his room. The calls of various tradesmen: the porcelain repairer and the goatherd, for example, and the sound of the iron curtains being pushed up in the morning when the stores open give Marcel a momentary joy, a form of participation in a life almost forgotten.

But persistently his thoughts revolve around the one, dolorous theme of love and jealousy. The theme is never presented tragically, but as the analysis of a complex malady and as the search for knowledge, and somehow related to the theme of sleep and sequestration in a single room. The richness of sleep, with its dreams and nightmares, is constantly contrasted to the bleakness of consciousness with the cruel lucidity that comes with wakefulness. The magical solutions to problems that sleep can bring are contrasted with the insoluble problems that torment the awakened consciousness. The effort Marcel makes to construct a life with Albertine is related to his sequestration in a room and his giving up of all life outside. In this effort, a whole ritual of existence has been established, rites that are performed, finally, mechanically. Marcel sees a relationship between these very personal, very localized rites, and the great rites of races and epochs, in which History tries to discover some meaning for the actions by which it is bound and defined. The formulas of life with Albertine are rigid and monotonous and drab, but they signify something greater, even as great battles have consequences beyond their immediate significance. The world of sleep and the solitude of Marcel in his room transcend the anguish of Marcel awake when he listens, incredulous, to Albertine.

When alone, Marcel tries to understand the meaning of Albertine's meaningless speeches; he tries to assess the insinuations made months previously by Aimé and Françoise, who do not like Albertine. His conclusions, even if they vary slightly from day to day, are always relentlessly pessimistic. He compares the incurable malady, love, to rheumatism, which, despite moments of calm, remains incurable . . . *l'amour est un mal inguérissable* (III, p. 85). In one of the most startling definitions Proust gives of love, he calls it the emanation of the beloved to all the points of space and time that the beloved has filled and is to fill. *Il est l'extension de cet être à tous les points de l'espace et du temps que cet être a occupés et occupera* (III, p. 100). Such a definition is at the same time the description of love's demise. The lover cannot possibly hope to go where the beloved goes. Only his anguish follows her. The initial phase of love (as Proust has written on many occasions) is desire for the person seen. Later, the experience of love is sustained only by a state of anxiety, or jealousy, in some form or other. In other words, love exists for Proust only if the beloved remains somehow elusive. *On n'aime que ce qu'on ne possède pas tout entier* (III, p. 106).

The harshest consequence of this theory would be: love is possible only when unreciprocated. Much in *A la recherche du temps perdu,* and in *La Prisonnière* in particular, would justify this conclusion. But the psychological implication in such a statement is not as important as the platonic vision it reveals. Albertine's carnality, in its fluctuations and unpredictability, is not as important for Marcel as what she designates beyond herself: an eternal object of incorruptible love. That is what he is searching for. That is the permanent vision which is beyond the impermanent, the corruptible, the venal, the untrustworthy, however much beloved Albertine.

Despite the pessimistic absolutism of countless formulas concerning love, in *La Prisonnière* the Marcel-Albertine love story is never treated as tragedy. That would not be Proust's method. No event, no episode is ever stylized as fatalistically, inevitably tragic. Even at those moments when Marcel's suffering and despair are most acute, his own infidelities in thought, sometimes in action, interrupt the intensity of his feelings and radically diminish the tragic note. Moral suffering is as intermittent for Marcel as asthma. At one time it will be interrupted by the street cries of fish vendors and window repairers (*A la crevette! . . . voilà le vitrier! . . .*) and at other moments by his desire to see and speak with the girl who brings the milk (*la petite laitière.* III, pp. 126, 127, 141). Love may dominate all other feelings in Marcel and all other problems in his life, but it does not remain fixed. His mind oscillates between the negative and the positive poles in his doubt concerning the nature and the origin of what he feels. Even at those moments when the intensity of jealousy has, it seems to him, suspended time, he still knows that it has not stopped, and that it will, in the hours and days ahead, fulfill its function and cover in oblivion what was once real suffering and love.

The extreme pessimism in love, as shown in *La Prisonnière*, is as Racinian as it is Proustian. But both Racine and Proust in their treatments of love, the one in its absolutism and temporal intensity, and the other in its temporally extended treatment, do not fail to stress its greatness. To both, love may well be an illusion, but if so, it is an illusion that enriches and does not deprive.

The honesty of Proust's probing and self-examination throughout *La Prisonnière* and *La Fugitive*, reaches almost heroic proportions rare in literature. The more subjective, the more powerfully creative he becomes, the more varied and truthful. The reader easily forgets the lengthiness of this part of the novel, in the candid, incisive treatment of Marcel's mind turned on itself, exploring its own extremes of suffering and dishonesty. Though Marcel in *La Prisonnière* is closer to Marcel Proust than in any other part of the novel, he still remains—it must be reiterated— a fictional protagonist, not an autobiographical character.

What is the composition, the style of this implacably truthful art? Each remark is an antenna extended in the air of the closed room, catching all the inaudible remarks in the air, remarks another artist would not record. The profoundest, most precise knowledge of self is necessary before any such exact assessment of character can be made.

Once before, in *A la recherche du temps perdu*, such an analysis was attempted, under very similar circumstances. In the love story of Swann, the same discipline was applied, the same jealousy and suffering were transcribed, and the same disillusionment reached. Swann's love for Odette was the prelude to Marcel's love for Albertine. The circumstances and the characters, as well as the form of the love and jealousy, present so many parallels, that one tends to establish a close bond between the two heroes, Swann and Marcel. Swann's love is treated only slightly more objectively than Marcel's love. Swann's intelligence and sensibility are those of Marcel at an earlier age. Odette's mysterious life of a *cocotte* and Albertine's captivity in this strange unusual cohabitation which forces her to invent daily lies are the necessary stimulations to self-analysis.

There is no forced analysis in *Un Amour de Swann* and in *La Prisonnière*. The two heroes, who are in some inexplicable way the same hero, listen, in the solitude of their passion, to the returning past and to the resurrection of the thoughts and occurrences of their past, constructs of the present. They both realize that the world with which they are in closest contact is that subjacent world which is always close to us but rarely heard by us. Under such an experience as love, the vibrations in the air almost seem audible, and what is heard is not merely the childish, simple, prevaricating words of an Odette or an Albertine, but the complete inextricable sum of words heard and said, of actions and gestures observed and performed. The dense compactness of memory returns in order to aid in the understanding of the present, in order to prevent the yielding acknowledgment of what is false and illusory in the present. Swann and Marcel are heroes of their own minds.

For both of them, jealousy is an enemy to their peace of mind, an enemy fought against in a void. Jealousy is never subjected to a struggle with the established rules of an honorable duel. Marcel compares it to the most familiar of all dreams, where the goal is never reached by the sleeper, in which the experience of frustration is sustained and augmented until the moment of awakening. Jealousy is invincible. The fight waged against it is never completed. The sensitivity of the two successive protagonists, Swann and Marcel, contains a strong element of lethargy, an addiction to day-dreaming which explains to some extent the excessive prolongation of jealousy. Swann's jealous reaction to de Forcheville and Odette's possible lesbianism, is similar to Marcel's aroused feelings when the mere name of Léa is mentioned and he thinks of the casino at Balbec.

Marcel, like Swann before him, finds masochistic pleasure in trying to put together the inconsistent parts of a dream. Life indeed is not unlike a dream, and the experience of jealousy brings out the memory of a nightmare in the awakened mind. The image of Albertine which the name Léa recalls is only one of a series of Albertines. And Marcel knows deeply that each one of these Albertines is incomplete. "No being can give his soul to anyone else," (*Car aucun être ne veut livrer son âme.* III, p. 150) Marcel concludes, despairing. (Almost the same formulation of the dilemma is in Claudel's *Partage de Midi*, in the moving debate between Ysé and Mesa.) In an effort to pierce the mystery of this dilemma, Marcel wonders if the reason does not lie in the nature of woman. Antedating every experience of man's love for woman is the original sin of woman, which may be precisely the reason why man loves her. Is this the reason why man, when he begins to love a woman, begins to suffer? Such a theory is at least implied in the text. *Ce qui rend douloureuses de telles amours, c'est qu'il leur préexiste une espèce de péché originel de la femme* . . . (III, p. 151).

In every chapter of *A la recherche du temps perdu,* Marcel's mind is at a very specific point in its development. The end, the goal of his development is knowledge, the ascertaining of the real, the discovery of truth. The first two volumes, *Du Côté de chez Swann* and *A l'ombre des jeunes filles en fleurs,* correspond to the first stage of development when, in his mind, the protagonist forms an ideal picture of the world. The imagination of childhood and adolescence gives to places (Combray and Balbec) and to characters (Gilberte, Oriane, and Albertine) an absolute essence, which in reality they do not have. Subconsciously, Marcel projects his desires (love) and his aspirations (society and literature) into all of his experiences. Blinded by the ideological power of his creations, the exterior world, to him, is merely the point of departure for the creation in his mind of places and beings which bear real names and unreal essences.

The third and fourth volumes, *Le Côté de Guermantes* and *Sodome et Gomorrhe,* correspond exactly to the second age of a man's development. This age is the skepticism engendered by the protagonist's first real contacts with the imaginary worlds of Balbec and Paris, and the society of the Guermantes. Here everything is disconcerting for the idealist. (The disillusionment in Combray will come later.) The real contacts with places and beings are the shattering of illusions. The deepest experience in Marcel's life, his love for Albertine, reveals itself only very slowly. The Guermantes coterie and the cities of the plain will have to be encountered first, before Marcel is able to isolate himself from them in *La Prisonnière* and *La Fugitive,* for the longest and most overwhelming realization of truth in the novel. Volumes five and six correspond to a third age, with its references to the other two, just as if there had been premonitions of age three in the first ages of Marcel's development. In *La Prisonnière* and *La Fugitive* the struggle is on two levels: Marcel's effort to live with Albertine, and his attempt to reconcile himself with the world. On the first level, all effort is futile. As the real Albertine does not correspond to the Albertine of Marcel's imagination, he has only to wait for the fever of jealousy to abate. But on the higher level this conflict illustrates the struggle of Marcel trying to create some kind of harmony between his tormented and disappointed mind, and the reality of the world. Since the spirit of man is destined to live in the world, it has to create there some kind of dwelling, some sense of law whereby his inner life may be enriched by the world's reality.

Each of Marcel's amorous experiences recapitulates these three ages: (1) the age characterized by the imagination of a child who believes easily in the accomplishment of the impossible, and invests with a marvelous poetry the names of places and the names of people; (2) the age characterized by disillusion when real contact is established, the consequences of which may be resentment or suffering or a combination of both; (3) the age characterized by a philosophical understanding of what is behind this pattern of belief and disillusion, and by an effort to feel the essences of things and beings, and to move beyond the world of appearances and superficial disappointments.

The conclusion of this third age is developed in volume seven, *Le Temps retrouvé*, but the first phase of the conclusion comes in *La Prisonnière*, at a moment when Marcel, alone in his apartment, waits for Albertine to return with Françoise. He has just recalled moments of tenderness in their love, moments when Albertine had shown herself loving and responsive to his feelings, and also, for such is the ironic infidelity of Marcel, he has just imagined, as part of his ever-enlarging erotic dreams, girls of all kinds: *petites ouvrières, midinettes, cocottes*, walking in the *Bois*.

He sits down at the piano, and opening by chance Vinteuil's sonata, begins to play. This is the beginning of a scene of primary importance for the transition between

Marcel as lover and Marcel as artist. The demarcations will
become clearer in Proust's dense, slowly moving narrative:
there will be many obstacles and revisions before the sense
of an artistic vocation becomes real and imperative for the
protagonist. But the piano scene in his apartment which
occurs almost midway in *La Prisonnière* (III, pp. 158–62)
resolves into a series of rigorous arguments with himself in
the course of which he moves beyond his amorous torment
over Albertine and the erotic fantasies over the girls who
fill his imagination, and raises questions about aesthetics
and the life of the artist.

The music of Vinteuil which he plays transports him
back to Combray, not to Montjouvain (his mind is momentarily at rest concerning Albertine), but to the Guermantes' Way where he had first felt the desire to be an
artist. He acknowledges that his recent life, in society and
in the tyrannical experience of love, has caused him to
give up the vocation of writer. By doing this, has he given
up something "real"? This is the first leading question
of the argument: *En abandonnant . . . cette ambition,
avais-je renoncé à quelque chose de réel?* (III, p. 158.)
Placed so importantly, the word *réel* takes on its full Proustian significance. He explores the question by asking it
over again in longer terms: Is there a reality in art which
can give to a man's personality its true expression? Before
he answers this, he states the proposition that each artist
is different from all others and gives a sense of individuality
not apparent in life. At this point, in his thoughts, while
still playing Vinteuil, he thinks of Wagner and places the
score of *Tristan* over the sonata.

The Wagnerian themes, by evoking their artistic truth,
only assure him that Wagner is the great master of the
kind of artist he has in mind. Music helps him to descend
deeper within himself, more than his life with Albertine
has allowed. He compares the harmony of Wagner with
the color of Elstir, and his thoughts on Wagner lead him
to consider certain works of art of the nineteenth century
of gigantic proportions: Balzac's *Comédie Humaine*, Hugo's *La Légende des Siècles*, and Michelet's *La Bible de*

*l'Humanité*. He raises the question of how these writers discovered the unity of their work, the principle that united so many different parts. He knows that in the case of Wagner's tetralogy and Balzac's *Comédie Humaine,* it came to them after much of the work had been done, almost as an afterthought. The discovery of a unity and the assembling of the various parts under one title must have given joy to the artist. But Marcel, with obvious premonitions of his own work, is awed by Balzac's and Wagner's Vulcan-like skill, by their ability to forge originality through the mere expending of labor and industry . . . *j'étais troublé par cette habileté vulcanienne* (III, p. 161). His conclusion to these thoughts is disillusioned. If this is art, this Vulcan-like forging, then he does not regret having abandoned it for the life he has led. *Si l'art n'est que cela, il n'est pas plus réel que la vie, et je n'avais pas tant de regrets à avoir* (III, p. 162).

The poetry of disillusion is an important aspect of Proust's art. He decomposes this theme and develops it with rare skill. A phase of disillusion is necessary before Marcel is able to reach the final phase, of consolation, and of assurance. *La Prisonnière* brilliantly testifies to Proust's persistent preoccupation with explication. Constantly giving a picture of life, which is never enough, he is bent upon finding a meaning of life also. The pictures—the dark pictures—of life fill six volumes. The meaning of life is relegated to volume seven, *Le Temps retrouvé.* But in the pictures of darkness, as in Marcel's room in Paris where he waits for Albertine to visit him, there are a few flashes of light, a few luminous intuitions, and one of these is Vinteuil's sonata. It had first, long ago, refreshed Swann's spirit and led him to feel something of the impact of his love for Odette. And now the same sonata performs, more modestly for Marcel, a similar function in helping to lead him away from the unreal toward what he will one day acknowledge as the real.

## 13.  *La Prisonnière.*
### B.  The heroism of the artist

Throughout the second half of *La Prisonnière,* as the theme
of Marcel's relationship with Albertine is developed to its
conclusion in the volume, more and more, other matters
intervene: notably, the problem of art, announced by Marcel's playing of the Vinteuil sonata, and the dramatic rivalry between M. de Charlus and Mme Verdurin.

The shift in emphasis is signaled by the unpredictable
death of the writer Bergotte, quickly related in six pages
(III, 182–88). A brief prelude mentions the writer's long
illness and his seclusion from the world. Bergotte survived
his fame as a writer and had lived with some degree of
equanimity. The circumstances of his death are swift and
accidental. Proust reports them on two pages, in his own
style but with such brevity that their poignancy is all the
more moving.

Bergotte suffered from uremia. He was reading a note
about one of his favorite paintings, the *Vue de Delft* of
Vermeer, in which the critic claimed a small patch of yellow wall was in itself a masterpiece. Bergotte could not remember this detail. He ate some boiled potatoes and went
to the exhibit. In front of the painting he saw the precious
detail of yellow wall, and wished that he had been able to
write as well as the wall—with its several layers of carefully applied paint—had been painted. *C'est ainsi que
j'aurais dû écrire. . . . Mes derniers livres sont trop secs,
il aurait fallu passer plusieurs couches de couleur, rendre
ma phrase en elle-même précieuse, comme ce petit pan de*

*mur jaune* (III, p. 187). As he repeats to himself this last phrase, *petit pan de mur jaune*, he falls, first on to a circular divan, and then to the floor, dead. Proust's reaction to Bergotte's death is to ask: Has he died forever? *Mort à jamais? Qui peut le dire?* In four lines only, Bergotte's wake is described. No one is present. His books, behind glass, have been placed three by three. They seemed to be watching over Bergotte's body, like angels symbolizing his resurrection . . . *toute la nuit funèbre, aux vitrines éclairées, ses livres, disposés trois par trois, veillaient comme des anges aux ailes éployées et semblaient, pour celui qui n'était plus, le symbole de sa résurrection* (III, p. 188).

To the brief, almost cruel narrative of Bergotte's death, Proust appends an hypothesis concerning immortality. The books of the author are represented as his mourners. They are the only characters of his wake. The meaning is ambiguous. The resurrection alluded to is either aesthetic— the testament of Bergotte's written work, or metaphysical —the survival of Bergotte in the minds of all those who had read him.

Death is one of the most important preoccupations in *A la recherche du temps perdu*. Art is looked upon by Proust as a struggle against death, as the only force that can oppose death with any effectiveness. This is the final import of *Le Temps retrouvé*. There is no real trace in Proust, even in Bergotte's death scene, of a belief in the survival of the individual soul. In the novel there are two death scenes: the grandmother's and Bergotte's, and two other deaths of great importance but not directly described: Swann's and Albertine's. The grandmother's death, in its physiological phases and in the various reactions of the family, is related in great detail. Bergotte's death is narrated briefly, in keeping with the swift accidental character of the death; and sparsely, in the final solitude of an artist with no family around him, nothing save the books he has written himself. It is easy to see in Bergotte's death a prefiguration of Proust's own.

These six pages in *La Prisonnière* are no mere digression. They are firmly attached to several of the important themes in the novel. The name of Vermeer returns to play a part in Bergotte's death. His death might not have come about at that time, had he not wished to examine the patch of yellow wall in the *Vue de Delft*. Inextricably associated with Swann, who had for years planned to write a book on Vermeer, the Dutch painter is one of Bergotte's favorites: soon, still in *La Prisonnière*, Marcel himself, in instructing Albertine on art, will refer to the paintings of Vermeer. From the newspaper, Marcel learns of the death of this man whom he had once admired. Then, with a shock, he realizes that Albertine has lied to him: she had claimed to have met Bergotte alive on the street. In Marcel's desire to call on the Verdurins, he thinks not only of Albertine, but also nostalgically of Swann, because it had been at Mme Verdurin's that Swann saw Odette. An entire concatenation of events has been put into motion by Bergotte's death, but especially Marcel's clearer understanding of what Swann's death had meant to him.

The death, almost at the same time, of these two men, Bergotte and Swann, who had played significant parts in Marcel's life, brings to Marcel's mind more than a sense of loss: it inspires a meditation on art and on the artist. As a person, Swann had meant much more to Marcel than Bergotte had, and yet Swann had not "produced." The intellectual, he was endowed with a fine sensibility, a knowledge of art, impeccable taste. At the announcement of Swann's death, Marcel realizes that there are certain questions he will never discuss with anyone else: questions about Vermeer, for example, about Boucher, about Combray. The death of a consultant and older friend has left suspended certain aesthetic problems that will never be resolved for him. (The same very moving testimonial was made by the young man Paul Valéry on hearing, in 1898, of the death of Mallarmé.) Then, with the pride of the creative artist, Proust, within the context of his novel, says that the boy whom Swann must once have looked upon as a fool (*un petit imbécile*) is to make the revered Charles Swann into the hero of one of his novels, and because of this, the name of Swann will not be lost, but will be per-

petuated for years to come. Swann, who first served Marcel
as an example of the lover, serves him now as an example
of the aesthete, the connoisseur, the engaging friend.

Some of the thoughts on Swann occur to Marcel as he
makes his way to the Verdurins, for the concert organized
by M. de Charlus which is to form one of the most concentrated, dramatic, and revelatory chapters in *A la recherche du temps perdu.* In it we follow the evolution of
relationships: of Mme Verdurin and her clan, of Charlus
and Morel, of Charlus and Mme Verdurin, of Marcel and
art, of Mlle Vinteuil and her friend, of Vinteuil and his
daughter, of Charlus and his cousin, the Queen of Naples.
Proust's contrapuntal skill sustaining, by developing, so
many themes at the same time is here deployed at its most
remarkable level. No one theme is overdeveloped. The dis-
tasteful and the comic follow one another. The psychological notations give way to aesthetic analyses. The dramatic
moments of personal humiliation and triumph occur without the emphasis of prolonged analysis. The entire scene,
taking place in the new salon of Mme Verdurin, on the
Quai Conti, brilliant as high social comedy, is also a recapitulation of the entire novel thus far, a welcome interruption from the cloistered weeks of Albertine's captivity
and Marcel's ineffectual surveillance. The captive is not forgotten during Marcel's evening at the Verdurin-Charlus
concert, but his thoughts about her are seen in a new context. In the perspective of other loves, she is seen also in
her relationship to Marcel as a potential artist. The meditation on Vinteuil's septet, as Marcel listens to it, is a deepening understanding of art, an understanding which had
begun a few hours previously in his apartment when he
played the sonata, and which will be affirmed and solidly
established in the long conclusive development in *Le Temps
retrouvé.*

The structure of the scene is supported by the rivalry
between Mme Verdurin, the hostess who is ignored, and
M. de Charlus, the guest who has organized the evening
in order to promote the interests of Morel as star violinist.
The guests have been invited by Charlus, chosen by him

for their prestige, for the flattery they will bestow on his favorite. Their impoliteness to Mme Verdurin arouses in her an anger and a desire to bring about a break in the Charlus-Morel relationship. As Charlus' megalomania grows through the reception, M. and Mme Verdurin resort to calumny, to revelations made to Morel and warnings that the young man is endangering his life and career in his relationship with Charlus. After Charlus' total and insolent triumph as host and impresario, despite his effeminateness, now blatantly disclosed after being concealed for so long, he is publicly humiliated by Morel who has succumbed to the calumny of the Verdurins. Thus humiliated, he is dramatically rescued and restored by his cousin, the Queen of Naples. At the outset, she had been the one guest who had talked politely with Mme Verdurin. In terms of rank and blood, she is the noblest of them all. On her early departure, she left her fan behind, and she now returns for it just after Charlus has been dishonored. With great wisdom of the world, she is imbued with tolerance and family pride. Without knowing exactly what has happened, she senses the degradation of her cousin, offers him her arm and reminds him that once her arm was strong enough to hold off the rabble at Gaeta [Naples]. *Appuyez-vous sur mon bras. . . . Vous savez qu'autrefois à Gaète il a déjà tenu en respect la canaille* (III, p. 322). Despite the many major defects in Charlus' character, despite his abominable behavior during the evening, the reader is moved by this rescue. Proust's own personal tolerance and sympathy radiate in the novelist's triumph.

This strategic intervention of the Queen of Naples completely reverses the roles of Mme Verdurin and of Charlus from what they were at the start. La Patronne is humiliated at the very beginning. She witnesses a temporary disintegration of her clan, and is powerless to prevent the baron from relegating her to a position of obscurity in her own salon. He dominates the salon by welcoming the guests he has invited, and promotes Morel's prestige. But at the end, the tables are turned and swift vengeance effected. Mme Verdurin's one consolation has always been the undoing of someone else's happiness, particularly of someone unfaithful to her clan. Though she strikes at Charlus through his inversion, this in itself is of no importance to her, as the orthodoxy of the clan is far more important than any moral issue like homosexuality.

Then the music begins. Marcel does not recognize it as Vinteuil's music until some time later when he hears the familiar phrase from the sonata. The posthumous work of Vinteuil, it is a septet, richer and more brilliant than the earlier sonata. As he listens to the new work, he realizes that the first compositions of Vinteuil were timid essays by comparison with this complete, triumphant, elaborately orchestrated septet. And he associates, because his thoughts on love never leave him for long, his earlier infatuation with Vinteuil's earlier compositions, and his love for Albertine with this final work of the composer. The analogy between himself and Vinteuil, between love and art, becomes fixed in his mind, when he imagines Vinteuil inspired by his daughter asleep, as Marcel had felt happiness seeing Albertine sleep. Marcel feels Vinteuil's love and suffering (which resemble in many ways his love and jealous suffering for Albertine) transposed in his art.

Marcel particularly responds to the joy of artistic creation which he feels in the septet. The little phrase of the sonata, which had once meant so much to Swann, is now enriched and transformed, deepened by the knowledge and the transcendence of suffering. He calls it a supraterrestrial joy, the reward of Vinteuil's personal anguish as a man and a father.

Mlle Vinteuil and her friend, who had been expected at the concert, do not come. Marcel learns of the patient, difficult work of deciphering the composer's manuscripts which had been done by the daughter's friend. Her competence in music, her admiration for Vinteuil and her devotion to his work in accomplishing a laborious task, were instrumental in preserving this posthumous work for the world. The sacrilegious scene at Montjouvain which Marcel had observed as a boy through a window, is now explained and justified in a greater perspective. The profane pleasure which had shocked him, would not have been felt by Vinteuil's daughter and her friend had both of them not worshiped the man and the composer. Their sexual love had, through the years, been transformed into a noble pure friendship. The reality of Vinteuil's art had survived the years of suffering and degradation. For Marcel, the lesson is grave and crucial.

The playing of Vinteuil's septet throws light on the two ways of his childhood which he has followed—without always realizing it—ever since. Everything is related to everything else, but not always patently so. Combray was the point of departure; now Combray enters his mind more luminously than ever, as he listens to Vinteuil's septet in the new salon of Mme Verdurin. Guermantes' Way is here in the salon, in the person of Charlus, descendant of Gilbert le Mauvais whom Marcel used to see in the stained glass window of the church of Saint-Hilaire at Combray. And Swann's Way also is represented here, in the person of Charles Morel now playing the septet, because Morel is the son of the valet de chambre of oncle Adolphe, through whom Marcel had once seen the lady in pink who years later turned out to be Mme Swann. Moreover, Marcel realizes that this concert would not have taken place if Charlus had not seen Morel one day in the station at Doncières. This septet, the culminating composition in Vinteuil's career, would not have been made possible without the friendship between the composer's daughter and her friend. The drama of jealousy which still torments Marcel might not have started if Albertine had not mentioned that she had known Mlle Vinteuil and her friend, and if Marcel as a boy had not spied on the two younger women at Montjouvain.

*Conclusion* Time expands all the themes of the novel and builds them into one another until the various stories, each so fragmentary and incomplete in itself, begin to form a solid and tangible structure, with historic meaning. The evening in the new salon, Quai Conti, of Mme Verdurin, is a complicated narrative in itself, but now, for the novelist and for the reader it becomes far more: it becomes the past that survives in names and passions and art, the past that supports and creates the present. The present is a festival of time, a dramatic performance for the onlooker. Marcel knows and acknowledges that the particular festival he has just watched and participated in is made up of many impure elements which have been conjugated one with the other, in dazzling, logic-defying contradictions.

At the beginning of the evening, he witnessed the Verdurins' cruel indifference to the death of the princesse de Sherbatoff, once the most admired of the clan. The social importance of the evening makes the announcement irksome, something to be resented. And yet, at the end of the same evening, their kindness for Saniette, ill and poor, whom they plan to help in such a way that he will not know who his benefactors are, contradicts their former insensitivity. Charlus' vice, a constant theme throughout the narrative of the evening, and his overbearing megalomaniacal temperament are offset by his kindness to Jupien's niece whom he plans to adopt and to whom he will give one of his names, ("d'Oloron"). In Charlus' long discussion with Brichot on the subject of sexual inversion, we learn, among many startling revelations, that Théodore, probably the same grocer boy at Combray whose face resembled the angels of Saint-André-des-Champs, is famous for his female conquests and for his willing compliance with male patrons. . . . The list of contradictions is endless, and Marcel the narrator concludes, and with this conclusion the concert-reception comes to an end, that no fixed image can adequately describe a character or a society or a passion . . . *et je conclus à la difficulté de présenter une image fixe aussi bien d'un caractère que des sociétés et des passions* (III, p. 327).

The transition from the Verdurin salon to Marcel's apartment is swiftly made. Brichot drives him home. On getting out of the carriage, Marcel sees Albertine's room lighted and the barlike shutters, an obvious symbol of the captivity, not only of Albertine, but of his own captivity from which he has, up to now, been unable to escape. Brichot, the Sorbonne professor, whose erudition Charlus alternately

praised and mocked throughout the evening, stays in his
carriage: he does not see the lighted window. He does not
know that a young captive girl is waiting for Marcel.
When the carriage drives off, Marcel pauses on the side-
walk before resuming his life with Albertine, still not realizing that he is entering the grating final phase of their
cohabitation. The streaks of light in the window form a
mysterious incomprehensible design, a *grimoire*, as he calls
it, a magic sign book. Only he can give meaning to the
sign. Only he knows what is behind the golden bars of the
window. He knows it to be—and calls it—a treasure. The
page-long paragraph is virtually one prolonged metaphor,
identifying love as the golden treasure. He knows at this
moment the full meaning of the verb *rentrer*, of "coming
home," and finding there the warmth of love, so different
from the dark coldness of the Paris night, and the complex
relationships of all the people he has just seen in the Verdurin salon. The luminous bars he sees from below, and
enjoys seeing, are the self-imposed prison of love. His
servitude is greater at this moment, and more inflexible,
than the servitude he has imposed upon Albertine.

From this point on in *La Prisonnière*, to the final lines
of the volume in which Françoise tells Marcel that Albertine has left, the cohabitation with the captive occupies
the narrative. The quarrels are more frequent. Plagued by
constant jealousy, Marcel probes incessantly and Albertine
lies unfailingly. Under such relentless prodding, Albertine's
lies become increasingly complex and hopeless. She undergoes a change during the long siege, as hope of placat-
ing and satisfying her jailor vanishes. Long before it comes,
both are resigned to the break. Each in his own way is
looking for the suitable means to effect a separation. Marcel
does not conceal his tendency to inflict on the girl a form
of moral torture. He makes her understand what she is
giving up in a purely materialistic sense. Albertine's venality is no worse than Marcel's exploitation of her weakness.

There are moments of respite, of half-believed-in hope
for happiness. The habits of cohabitation acquired together, the remembered moments of happiness in the past,

the moments of instinctive and unanalyzed love all count in the delay they impose on the secret convictions that each holds of the failure of their love and their missed opportunity for happiness. The hard lesson that Marcel learns from his life with Albertine is in the very title of this section. Love creates a prison for the one who loves, a prison which lasts as long as the love does.

Just as love is a prison for Marcel, so Time is for Proust. By the use of analogy, the protagonist's suffering over love is made to represent Time as the far more universal imprisonment of human nature. Love, for Proust, is the growth and fearful concentration of one individual's desire. It is solitary and has in reality nothing to do with the object of the desire. Love is that solitude in which a human life is imprisoned. With Marcel, love is an experience lived within that prison and explored there. Time is made of similar bars, similar limitations which cloister an individual life. This is the terrifying unity of Proust's novel. The psychological nature of love is as fearful as the physical nature of Time. The Proustian conception of love is the key to *A la recherche du temps perdu* and the justification for treating it at such length in the novel.

An important respite in the long battle scene between Charlus and Mme Verdurin in *La Prisonnière*, Vinteuil's music also serves as a respite in the last chapter where Marcel and Albertine gradually move toward the end of their love. Indirectly, Vinteuil's music which Albertine plays (on the pianola) for Marcel, is connected with his jealousy. But it also provides for him at this point a vision concerning the reality of art. For Swann, the sonata was a sentimental symbol; for Marcel, it is much more an aesthetic revelation. To Swann the *petite phrase* signaled a memory of happiness; to Marcel it reveals a possible vocation in which the suffering of love can be transformed and transcended. Love for Marcel establishes an almost unbearable contact with his inner life, whereas the music of Vinteuil establishes a serene responsiveness with his inner life. Not only is music able to resurrect a fragment of Marcel's past, it also holds out to him a promise of something eternal which he is not as yet fully able to define. The art of Vinteuil, both the white sonata (*la blanche sonate*) and the ruddy septet (*le rougeoyant septuor*), exteriorizes the complexities of what we might call an individual soul. This is likewise true of the paintings of Elstir (whose name is often linked with Vinteuil's) in *La Prisonnière*. There is an inevitable monotony in the works of a given artist, and this is due to the sameness of the subject matter: that is, the individual himself. A similar monotony is perceptible in the loves of Marcel, and for the same reason. Marcel often refers to the joyous motif in the septet of Vinteuil, which he defines as the joy an artist feels in his power to communicate the incommunicable, to reveal an inner life which cannot be transcribed directly. And Marcel wonders if he too is capable of this kind of joy.

From the playing of the septet at Mme Verdurin's, through the scenes with Albertine until the coming of spring, the figure of Vinteuil becomes increasingly important for Marcel. Vinteuil—whose name suggests Vincent d'Indy, and whose sonata, according to lines written by Proust to Jacques Lacretelle, is based upon Saint-Saëns' sonata for piano and violin in B minor, and whose "little phrase" is a composite of many musical memories from Wagner, Franck, and Fauré—is the most humble of the creative artists in *A la recherche du temps perdu*. Elstir and Bergotte, during their lifetimes, both enjoy a marked degree of fame. But Vinteuil died unnoticed and practically unknown. Years after his death, the triumphant septet brings glory to his memory, and forces Marcel to concentrate his thoughts on the relationship between the personal life of the artist and the reality of his work.

The tragedy in Vinteuil's personal life was dramatically revealed to Marcel in Combray when he observed the scene of Montjouvain. Years later he still remembers the shocking profanation and sadism in this scene. That early trauma explains to a large degree his distress with Albertine. The couple, Vinteuil's daughter and her friend, are replaced in Marcel's imagination by Albertine and some other girl or woman. The beauty of Vinteuil's music and its relationship to human life are constantly obscuring the stark human tragedy of Vinteuil the man. On four different occasions in the narrative of the novel the compositions of Vinteuil are played and described: (1) the evening at the Verdurins when Swann hears the sonata, after he had once heard it a year previously without knowing the name of the composer; (2) at the soirée of Mme de Saint-Euverte's Swann hears the sonata again and it awakens in him his memory of Odette; (3) in the Swann apartment, Mme Swann plays the sonata for Marcel; (4) in Mme Verdurin's new salon, Quai Conti, Marcel hears the septet, in a large distinguished company of guests whom M. de Charlus has invited.

Vinteuil's music is an important element in the symmetry that exists between the destiny of Swann and that of Marcel. The sonata grew in importance for Swann as he attached it to his love for Odette de Crécy. When Mme Swann plays the sonata for Marcel, he feels only a very slight reaction, nothing comparable to what he knows to be its effect on Swann. But later, on hearing the septet at the Verdurins (*La Prisonnière*), a soirée exactly parallel to the Saint-Euverte soirée (*Du Côté de chez Swann*), the music becomes closely associated with Marcel's love for Albertine. Marcel is quite ready to believe that Vinteuil's septet was, in part, occasioned by the tragedy of his daughter's inversion. The motivation that compelled Vinteuil to write the septet is therefore similar to the motivation that compelled Marcel to come to hear it. Behind the composing of the work and its performance at the Verdurins', there are at least four couples involved in a tragic and impossible love: Mlle Vinteuil and her friend, Vinteuil and his daughter, Marcel and Albertine, Charlus and Morel. The prefiguration of these four groups is the Swann-Odette couple and the white sonata of Vinteuil, prefigures the rich, fully realized composition of the septet.

Tragedy or failure, or a combination of both, doom all these passions in *A la recherche du temps perdu*. We already know of Swann's jealous love which ended in indifference. We are in the midst of Marcel's fluctuating thoughts about breaking with Albertine. And we have just witnessed Morel's public denunciation of his benefactor Charlus. The only possible exception to this fatal list is the love between Mlle Vinteuil and her friend which appears to have turned into a purified friendship.

During the playing of the septet, Marcel listens to two opposing themes, on which he has had already many intimations. On the one hand, he hears the recreation of a work of music which fills him with an exceptional spiritual joy. The septet is fixed for all time, absolute in its form and beauty. But on the other hand, except for those moments of total immersion in the music, Marcel follows in his own mind and in the speech and gestures of the other characters, the flux and changeableness of everything opposed to the absolute, of everything relative: desire, ambition, rivalry, longing, jealousy, maliciousness, ignorance. In a spiritual sense, the evening at the Verdurins, with Albertine waiting for him in his Paris apartment, is important to Marcel, because he realizes, or is very close to realizing, the need to reconcile the absoluteness of art and the relativity of human feelings.

The artist is the reconciler of antinomies: Marcel remembers and uses this belief in the lessons on art he gives to Albertine. These lessons are among the happiest moments during his life with the girl. Each great composer, Marcel contends, creates a unique world as Vinteuil did. The uniqueness of this world is the evidence of genius. When Albertine asks whether this is true for literature, Marcel demonstrates the theory at greater length with examples from the novels of Thomas Hardy, Dostoievsky, and Stendhal.

Such moments of respite and instruction are at best intermittent. The theme of Venice begins to appear more and more frequently. Marcel thinks of Venice, which he does not yet know, as once he had thought of Balbec. The imagined Italian city signals a new phase. The pleasure he has in offering Albertine—and watching her wear—dresses from Fortuny does not offset the anguish he feels when he thinks of all her secrets he will never know. His restoration now of having wasted time reminds us of Swann's disillusion over Odette and his feeling of having wasted years over an unsuitable woman. One evening when Albertine's kisses seem to him indifferent, Marcel half senses that she is planning to leave. And this fear is confirmed when he hears her opening her window, a gesture he takes as a revolt against him as a lover more than against the rule imposed on the house by his asthma. But Albertine does not leave. The next day Marcel takes her to Versailles where he compares the blue of her coat to the blue sky, and remembers his grandmother's habit at Combray of watching the steeple of Saint-Hilaire and the blue sky above it. The sound of an airplane interrupts the meditation on the peacefulness of the color blue. It is a chilling moment of change in Marcel.

Once having decided to go to Venice, he now waits for the appropriate time to complete his break with Albertine. But it is Albertine who chooses the day and who leaves him. On the morning when Françoise tells Marcel that she has left, he remains outwardly calm but then breaks out in a sweat, just as he had done when Albertine first told him in the tramway she knew Mlle Vinteuil.

Marcel has already said in the narrative of his life with Albertine that love is space and time felt by the heart. *L'amour, c'est l'espace et le temps rendus sensibles au coeur* (III, p. 385). In one sense, all the years of his life have been translated into her and she has become in truth a great goddess of Time . . . *elle était plutôt comme une grande déesse du Temps* (III, p. 387).

*La Prisonnière* brilliantly testifies to the very solid architecture of *A la recherche du temps perdu*. Questions and themes in *Du Côté de chez Swann* are here answered and elaborated on. The introduction to Vinteuil's music is magnificently justified. With the roles of Charlus and Albertine in *La Prisonnière*, we watch the conjunction of the condemned cities of the plain. The scene of Montjouvain opens out into an inferno, and also, in the rescue of the septet from oblivion, into redemption. The anguish of the boy waiting for his mother's good night kiss deepens into the more tragic, more inescapable anguish of Marcel's waiting for the love that Albertine cannot offer him. The blue of the sky of Combray, a source of spiritual strength for his grandmother, now becomes the blue of a Fortuny gown, the blue of the sky at Versailles when Marcel determines to break with Albertine. The question of the writer's vocation that Marcel had first felt along the Guermantes' Way is now infinitely more acute and more pressing. Just as Vinteuil's brief sections of the sonata have now become the septet, a more intricate musical form, so Marcel's resolve to be a writer also develops from what was once a whimsical wish to firm determination.

## 14. *La Fugitive.*
### (*The Sweet Cheat Gone*)
### A.   The role of memory

Until its definitive publication in the Pléiade edition (volume III), this sixth part of Proust's novel was called *Albertine Disparue*. For this bare, simple title, Scott-Moncrieff invented one of his most elaborate translations: *The Sweet Cheat Gone*. The final title, *La Fugitive*, in its simplicity, is more suggestive. Albertine has escaped from Marcel's apartment, and he is going to try in every possible way to bring her back. During the opening pages, she is the fugitive from captivity: *la prisonnière* escaped. But even when Marcel learns of Albertine's death, she remains *la fugitive*, because in his mind she is not dead. He continues to explore her past with all the feeble and insecure means at his disposal, in order to calm his jealous suspicions over a girl now dead. *La Fugitive* applies both to the girl who has escaped life with Marcel and to the girl who has escaped life itself.

The entire volume of *La Fugitive* is a long meditation on three themes concerning Albertine: on her absence, then on her death, and finally on the slow process of forgetting her. The word *oubli*, one of the Proustian vocables of great importance, designating the long story of mental life and death, is the key word in *La Fugitive*. On few other parts of *A la recherche du temps perdu* does Proust expend such infinite patience, such honesty of search into his own feelings, such close analysis of those impulses of his heart he calls "intermittences." *La Fugitive* is a prolonged heroic

effort toward self-knowledge. During the first half of this
section, Marcel is alone. He receives briefly Robert de
Saint-Loup, Bloch, Aimé, and Andrée, but these visits are
interviews and commissions. He turns Saint-Loup to spying
on Albertine with her aunt Mme Bontemps in Touraine,
and after Albertine's death, Marcel turns Aimé, the maître
d'hôtel at Balbec, to finding all the various details about
Albertine's life at Balbec. For a long time, the past remains the present for Marcel, and the cause of his suffering.

If many of the questions and themes raised throughout
*Du Côté de chez Swann* find their answers and are pursued in *La Prisonnière*, the specific section entitled *Un
Amour de Swann* is an elaborate analysis of how Swann's
love for Odette came into being. It is the study of the phases
of a development, of a growth in feeling and intensity. *La
Fugitive*, and to a large degree *La Prisonnière* also, is the
even more elaborate story of the disintegration of a love.
In the case of Swann, only a very brief record is made of
the love's end. We are not given the analysis of this ending.
But Marcel's love for Albertine, almost from the very beginning, is depicted as the harassed sentiment he does not
dare trust. From the earliest stage of his love for Albertine,
he watches her and listens to her, without ever fully believing that he is watching or hearing the truth. The experience of love does not bring with it a knowledge of the
beloved, and this absence of knowledge, this impossibility
of ever knowing, prolongs love's unhappiness and suffering.
In the case of Albertine, love decays just as love grows. *La
Fugitive* is the fullest expression of this decomposition.

With no break in the narrative between *La Prisonnière*
and *La Fugitive*, Marcel's defeat in love is histrionically
emphasized by Françoise when she tells him of Albertine's
escape. The opening sentence of the new volume is Marcel's comment on this announcement: *Comme la souffrance
va plus loin en psychologie que la psychologie!* (III, p.
419.) This simple exclamation is both a commentary on
the news brought by Françoise and the sermon text for *La
Fugitive*. We learn about ourselves by suffering, far more
than we can learn in the acquisition of knowledge. Pain is

the great teacher. This insight will go far beyond the story of Albertine (Marcel will use it later to affirm for himself his ambition to become a writer) that reality in the world is seized by our feelings and senses, more than it is apprehended by concepts and abstractions and facts.

What has happened in terms of plot and story is totally banal: the protagonist Marcel has been deserted by the girl he loves. He refuses to believe that the escape is final. Marcel is a man of habits (*un homme d'habitudes*) and, despite all the distress it has brought, his cohabitation with Albertine created a pattern he does not wish to renounce until his love for the girl dies. His jealous love continues to live after the mistress has gone. Robert de Saint-Loup plays the role of the understanding friend which Marcel had once played for Robert at the time of his suffering over Rachel: but Robert's mission in Touraine is a failure. Marcel compares his suffering to that of Des Grieux in *Manon* and to Phèdre. But the love chronicle in *Manon Lescaut* has none of the intense depth of analysis in *La Fugitive;* Phèdre none of Marcel's "intermittences"; and Marcel none of Phèdre's moral anguish or fatalism.

At a moment of self-humiliation, Marcel wires Albertine to come back to him on her own conditions. But just after sending the wire, he receives one from Mme Bontemps reporting the death of Albertine in a riding accident. This event does not immediately alter Marcel's suffering. He has to live again the happy and unhappy moments of the past, he has to accede to his lingering jealousy by trying to reconstruct Albertine's secret past, and all he will find are facts or semblances of facts which he is unable to credit. The summer evenings in Paris die very slowly, and Marcel is harassed by memory.

The exaggerated comparison between himself and Racine's Phèdre underscores the differences between tragic love and Proustian love. A horse was important in the death of Hippolytus and Albertine, and that similarity, however far-fetched, is sounder than the Marcel-Phèdre analogy. In Racine the heroines are passionate, and there is not one real example of a passionate woman in Proust's novel. The lover in Proust is always the man: Swann, first, then Robert de Saint-Loup, Charlus, and Marcel. By comparison with these lovers we learn very little about the objects of their love: Odette, Rachel, Morel, and Albertine. And among these four, Morel, as a character, is perhaps the clearest. Moreover, the man's love in Proust, whether it be Marcel's or Charlus', is never fatalistic or predestined or inevitable, as in Racine. The love of Hermione and Bérénice and Phèdre is for a very specific individual (Pyrrhus, Titus, Hippolyte) whom we see as clearly as we see the suffering heroine. By comparison with this individualistic love, Proust's version is something else, a sentiment not so much for a specific individual, but for something this individual represents, something beyond the individual. Swann loves Odette because she reminds him of Zephora as painted by Botticelli. Marcel loves Albertine because she reminds him of *la bande des jeunes filles*, the picture of youthful vitality, of summer playfulness and sensual indulgence. What is Racinian in Proust is that a few lovers love the unattainable, to fall in love with the impossible idea of love. There are some characters in Proust who derive an immediate facile pleasure from sexual love: the duc de Guermantes, Bloch, Albertine—but there are no notations on that kind of pleasure. And then, there are those who love, and who suffer from love, from its ultimate elusiveness. Three characters in particular represent this suffering: Swann, Marcel, and Charlus. And the suffering is minutely described in the cases of Swann and Marcel. It is only implied, but strongly felt by the reader, in the case of Charlus.

The entire dramas of Swann and Marcel, which are in many ways the same drama, are played within the hero, in the silence of his being with no intrusions from the outside. The birth, duration, and death of love for Marcel take place within him, and finally have little to do with the one loved. This total subjectivity of love was analyzed early in the novel, in Marcel's own case, in the very precise, very intense way his attention was fixed on a name: Parme, for example, Balbec, Guermantes. Around each of these names he created a geographical or legendary reality, in much the same way he creates a personality around the names of Gilberte and the duchesse de Guermantes and Albertine. The same phenomenon takes place in each of these tales of love, a modification in Marcel's unconsciousness, an accident in the flow of life which arrests his attention and initiates a legend that becomes real.

Love is, then, the creation of a person distinct and apart from the one who bears the name in the world. Albertine lives first in Marcel's mind, and then, after her death, she continues to live in his memory. Never does she seem more alive for him. *Jamais elle n'y avait été plus vivante* (III, p. 478). This memory is made up of an infinite number of moments, and, what is most remarkable for Marcel in this daily resurgence of memory, is the fact that the memory of one moment is not modified by what took place after that moment in the course of his love for Albertine. His love resembles, therefore, a collection of moments, each one autonomous. His images of her multiply as he desperately tries to find consolation, but there is sorrow over the loss of each Albertine, and his grief is thereby multiplied. A thousand different memories rise up around him in the darkness of his room. If Françoise happens to disturb the heavy curtain at his window and a ray of sunlight enters, it brings with it a memory of happiness now painful.

Françoise, who hated Albertine when she was alive, is now compelled, by the strictness of the Combray code, to pity Marcel's grief and even to weep with him. She had resented Albertine just as she had once resented Eulalie in Combray who visited tante Léonie, but now she sees both of them, Albertine and Eulalie, in a new light.

Marcel realizes that soon the cold weather will come, and he knows that each season will bring its own set of memories, its own particular kind of suffering. Winter he associates with Gilberte in the Champs-Elysées, and a certain kind of sadness connected with their games, and also with evening visits from Albertine. In order to forget her, he would have to change the cycle of the seasons. Everything reminds him of her, everywhere he turns there is some sign, some recollection ready to fill his mind. He reproaches himself for acts of unkindness, and for not having seized happiness when it was within his grasp, for his stupidity at not having recognized happiness when he had it. Such self-accusations do not, however, prevent his continuing his investigations into Albertine's past. Aimé he knows to be the best type of emissary-investigator. He is from the working class (*gens du peuple*), motivated by self-interest and gain, but devoted to the one he serves and indifferent to any moral code. In other words, Aimé is the kind of accomplice whom Proust used in his own life on so many occasions.

But as soon as Aimé is dispatched to Balbec to look up certain details of Albertine's activity there, Marcel's almost hostile suspicions subside, and he is assuaged by memories of tenderness and sentimentality. The name of Gilberte often occurs to him at such moments, and he realizes the many resemblances between the two girls and the fact that he had fallen in love in the same way, with the same kind of girl. Love is an eternal repetition of the same story and the same circumstances. The beloved is innumerable yet unique.

The painful details of this exploration into the past, both investigation and involuntary memory, alternate with thoughts of an almost philosophical nature. Love for Proust is the desire of one man, Marcel in this case, and the history of such a love is the history of the multiple modifications of this feeling as it grows and diminishes and grows again. Just as the beloved incites desire, she diminishes herself as a personality. The restless erotic imagination of adolescence, described by Chateaubriand as *le mal du siècle*, comes often to mind as one reads these pages of *La Fugitive*. The romantic suffering and malaise of René in Chateaubriand precludes the existence of a woman. And Albertine becomes so vague in the Proustian analysis that one easily feels her presence is unnecessary.

Marcel has all the signs of a certain kind of artistic temperament (in reality Proust's temperament). It is the temperament of a man who daily asks himself the two most

humiliating questions any man can ask himself: Am I able
to love anyone? Is it possible that anyone will love me?
These two questions go together and they form, in the case
of such a writer as Proust, and of such a potential writer
as Marcel, the ransom of genius. Marcel's room in Paris,
after he has learned of Albertine's death, is turned into a
laboratory. Like Faust, he conjures up the visions of his
mind. If happiness came to him through Albertine, there
would be no story to relate, and his room in Paris would
not have been transformed into a prison-laboratory. Marcel
knows that art rises out of love threatened or condemned.
The very meaning of passion is of suffering and woe. Passion, according to Denis de Rougemont (*L'Amour et l'Oc-
cident*), is associated with death, or the wish for death. It
is that experience which brings its own destruction.

Marcel feels, during the course of his spiraling thoughts,
that he has committed a double assassination, that he is
responsible, by his conduct, first as a grandson and then as
a lover, for the death of his grandmother and for the death
of Albertine. Such a possible guilt is only one of a series of
enigmas which he knows will never be solved. The characteristics of his memory, in its fluidity, its imperceptible
emanations, prevent his concentrating for long on any
one enigma. As changeable as his memory, he relives his
past and sees the transformations of the faces he has
known, faces under different kinds of daylight, under
storms and cool days of springtime and sun-drenched days
of summer. Only jealousy seems untouched by the passage
of time, because jealousy has no past and no future. It is
always present, the one sentiment in *La Fugitive* which
relates Marcel to the present. Albertine is dead, but he is
still jealous, and he compares himself to a man whose leg
has been amputated and who still feels pain in the missing
leg . . . *comme ceux amputés, le moindre changement de
temps renouvelait mes douleurs dans le membre qui n'existait plus* (III, p. 491). Marcel meditates especially on
the double unfolding of Albertine's life: on her life outside
of him, her private life of which only she was fully aware,
and her life within him, framed by his thoughts, his knowl-

edge, his jealousy, and his love. Beyond this theme of his meditation, but closely related to it, is the theme of the role of chance. It is the long series of *if's* in his life that account for his meeting Albertine, and for his jealousy over her. If Swann had not one day mentioned to him the Persian architecture of the church at Balbec, if the Hôtel de Balbec had not been built, if he had not dreamed romantically of the fog enclosing the coastline of Balbec . . . he would never have met Albertine. But now his experience of love is an integral part of his life and his temperament. Now, easily, he relates his anxious waiting for Albertine every night to the anxiety he knew as a child in Combray when he waited for his mother's good night kiss. All his mistresses, whether real as Albertine, or imaginary as Mlle de Stermaria, are the daughters of his anguish . . . *nos maîtresses sont filles de notre angoisse* (III, p. 505) —a metaphor both provocative and explicit. Marcel himself has engendered his own suffering, even as he engendered a unique Albertine. . . . These are the thoughts which swarm within him, and every echo from the outside, every echo of reality causes a slight deviation in his thoughts, a new emphasis, which becomes a new theme.

Proust follows Racine in his depiction of passion as deeply felt only when thwarted or forbidden. But we never have in Racine the indifferent slow beginning of love, as in Swann's love for Odette, and Marcel's for Albertine. We never have in Racine, the power of the lover to create the image of the beloved, to create the statue he will love. And finally, we never have in Racine the intellectual pleasure of love which is in Proust, and which is manifested in the attraction of the lover to someone in a milieu not his own, to a world that he can only imagine and explore.

The intellectual pleasure a Proust derives from friendship and love in worlds different from his own is the pleasure of expanding his own knowledge, his own personality, his own capacity for understanding. The milieu of the Verdurins for Swann, is comparable to the milieu of *les jeunes filles en fleurs* for Marcel, and to Jupien's milieu for Charlus. In the normally accepted sense of love, each object of love in Proust is unworthy of the lover: Odette is unworthy of Swann, Rachel of Saint-Loup, Morel of Charlus, Albertine of Marcel. In each of these four cases, where the pattern of social dichotomy is very marked, love is solitary, a sentiment forced back into the one who loves and never deeply felt by the object of the love. Love in Proust creates terrifying limits for itself, boundaries which are those of solitude in which the life of the lover is imprisoned. No human experience has such immobilizing unity as the experience of love in Proust, and the reader must accept the laws of this unity, if he is to feel this experience.

At one point in the text, Marcel compares his introspection to the turning of the leaves in the book of his memory, defined as a collection of testimonials . . . *feuilletant notre mémoire comme un recueil de témoignages* (III, p. 510). The metaphor beautifully describes the endless repetitions of memory which Marcel cannot escape in his rehearsals of the past, in his many returns to an episode or a detail in order to understand its possible meanings. He moves back and forth between the present and the past in what often seems to be the same voyage. So great is his desire to know (especially to know whether Albertine had had lesbian relationships) that he forces belief on what he knows cannot be believed with any real assurance of truth. At one moment, he even approaches belief in the immortality of the soul. He looks up at the sky and his thoughts mount there as if they were prayers . . . *je commençai à croire possible l'immortalité de l'âme* (III, p. 511).

When a letter from Aimé, who writes from Balbec where he has talked with people who had known Albertine, confirms his suspicions of her lesbianism, Marcel's suffering deepens considerably. The assurance (which he will soon doubt) that Albertine practiced this vice turns Balbec into a kind of hell for Marcel. His suffering, for which at the moment he sees no antidote, causes him to feel stranded in life, on a limitless shore, where he will never meet Albertine no matter which direction he takes. This emptiness of space resembles the hallucinations of a nightmare where movement is thwarted and useless.

The long meditation in *La Fugitive* and its introduction
in *La Prisonnière* form together one of the most distinc-
tively Proustian developments in *A la recherche du temps
perdu,* one on which theories of Henri Bergson on time and
memory seem to be applied. Proust formally disclaimed any
influence of Bergson on his work when he pointed out that
the dominant theme in his novel is the distinction he emphasizes between voluntary and involuntary memory. This
distinction, Proust says, is not found in the philosophy of
Bergson: it is even contradicted by it. The reasons for this
denial are hard to ascertain, and they may quite easily be
Proust's desire, natural in most writers, to seem original.
Yet, one can say, at least, the writing of Proust, especially
in *La Fugitive,* is an illustration, either conscious or subconscious, of Bergson's preoccupations and theories.

The conception of time, as treated by the typical romantic artist, emphasized an awareness of the passing of
time, its flight, the brevity of happiness, and the fixed
chronology of events in the life of a man. The major romantic poems: *Le Lac* of Lamartine, *Tristesse d'Olympio*
of Hugo and *Le Souvenir* of Musset, all establish a clear
distinction between the present and the past, between the
happiness of the past and the desolation of the present.
Bergson repudiates such a distinction. The mind of man, by
the uninterrupted flow of memory, is constantly making the
past present. In fact, Bergson seems to deny the usual concept of present time, by claiming we are always living the
past, always making the past present. The clear chart of
romantic sentimentality, by which the past event is beautiful and sacred, and the present sad and tortured, the art
of Proust totally blurs and often drastically reverses. Only
one kind of time counts for both Bergson and Proust, and
that is what may be called inner time or time of a man's
inner life, not controlled by chronological time of calendar
dates and the hours of a clock.

As time passes, in its ordinary sense, it brings with it, in
the life of each individual, events of insignificance as well
as of momentous import. As events in themselves they are
not as important as the effect they have on an individual's

personality. With each moment of time our personality is
changed or altered to some degree. We are not one ego,
but a multiplicity of egos. No experience can be fixed as
we are living it, no event immobilized, no sentiment prolonged. Everything changes every minute. But when the
past returns to fulfill itself in the present, to compose the
present, as it does in Marcel's meditation on Albertine after
her death, then an event or a person may be seen as something whole and unchanging. More subtle and more disastrous than those destructions caused by earthquakes and
bombs are the gradual transformations which time in its
passing brings to individuals and things. Marcel has already
experienced—and been shocked by—such transformations in
himself. His changed attitude, for example, with respect to
Swann, and his love for Gilberte represent major transformations in Marcel's personality.

Time therefore is not always a succession of events,
which prescribes an orderly development of personality.
Proust often uses the tide metaphor of ebbing and flowing,
*le flux et reflux,* to describe the pattern of Marcel's thoughts
and to account for the contradictions in his impulses and
sentiments. If at one moment he calls to mind the image
of Albertine dead, in the next minute he is convinced that
the dead girl is still living. A gesture, a word, a remembered walk, are sufficient to bring back a fragment of the
past and to substitute it for the present. Long after Albertine's death, Marcel continues to suffer an extreme form of
jealousy over her putative vice. He is amphibious—another
image drawn from the sea, as Albertine herself had seemed
to come originally from the sea at Balbec—living simultaneously in the fluid element of the past and in the reality
of the present. The death of his love is infinitely slow. Particularly in his dreams, the past returns to Marcel as if it
were beginning all over again. In musical terminology, it
is a *da capo,* the rebeginning of a melody, *ces* da capo *du
rêve qui tournent d'un seul coup plusieurs pages de la
mémoire* (III, p. 538). In Marcel's awakened state, a
thought will become so obscured by the crisscrossing of
memories, that it ends by losing all significance for him. In

this long-drawn-out mental experience following Albertine's death, everything is subjected to the fecundating power of recall, everything becomes a possible peril to the protagonist's peace of mind. As Time is elastic, passion dilates it.

La Fugitive is a meditation on time and the survival of memory. The experience itself, as it is related, is its own exegesis. It is a progressive revelation on the life of time in the mind, on its indivisibility, and on the uninterrupted activity of the subconscious. Aspects of Bergson's philosophy and Freud's psychology are here, but translated by Proust's art and sensibility. No precise debt can be ascribed to Bergson or Freud, because Proust is not a disciple, and his art exemplifies, as well as theories associated in our day with Bergson and Freud, traditional moralists and psychologists of French literature, a Montaigne, for example, and a La Rochefoucauld, who centuries before Proust had analyzed the ruses of man's conscience, and the repressions of man's subconscious. However, the conscious and the subconscious experiences of La Fugitive testify to the most significant beliefs of modern literature and art. In addition to the explicit theories concerning time and psychology, which inevitably bring Bergson and Freud to mind, is the implicit theory in Proust, one especially apparent throughout La Fugitive, that an artist is not to be judged by the nobility, the dignity, or the high morality of his subject matter. He is to be judged, rather, by the profundity of his vision, by the depth of his understanding. In this respect especially, Proust takes his place beside James Joyce and Franz Kafka. The feeblest and the most frequent complaint levelled against these three novelists, Proust, Joyce and Kafka, the greatest novelists of the century, the triumvirate who have reshaped the form of the novel and given to it new directions and potentialities, is the immorality of their themes and their delineation of frightening states of consciousness. Accusing a work of immorality is always the first form of denunciation. It is the most puerile, and the one inevitably most futile. (If the reader has persevered this far in A la recherche du temps perdu, it is likely that all possible moral judgment on Proust the man has disappeared in the reader's mind.)

Marcel is beginning to feel fatigue from the long meditation, and a sense that his memory in its ceaseless movement is destroying itself. He has already used such a phrase as "the ending of my love": *mon amour finissant* (III, p. 554), and the key word "oblivion" (*oubli*) which will take on its full meaning in the second half of *La Fugitive*. Spring comes once again to replace the cold drabness of winter. Now, in the early profusion of spring, the single figure of Albertine is being replaced by a group of girls . . . *Paris m'apparaissait innombrablement fleuri de toutes les fillettes* (III, p. 555).

We have reached a point in the narrative when Marcel's love for Albertine begins to die, with outlines of a rebirth of love. Gilberte was first a part of a group of girls in the Champs-Elysées before she became the object of Marcel's love. Albertine was at first indistinguishable from a large group of girls on the beach at Balbec, before she too emerged as a distinct individual. And now Marcel thinks of a new situation, actually a recurrence of a familiar situation. For him, love has been, and still is, while he remains in his apartment, a kind of malady which exerts its power over his whole organism. Imagination, memory, and sensibility are all interrelated in maintaining this special fever of illness. Even when his perception tells him that, for example, Albertine is dead, his imagination will contradict the perception and overcome it. The only way Marcel had been able to hold Albertine in a physical sense, to make of her a presence in his life, had been to make her a captive. His jealousy had demanded this act and this situation, as jealousy for Swann was solved by his marriage with Odette. But Marcel's love grew only as the beloved eluded him. The imprisoned girl, the love object, becomes a fugitive, and as she succeeds in remaining elusive, she insures the continuation of the love.

To isolate any one theme in the profusion of themes in *La Fugitive* is to risk destroying the pattern of Proust's art. The novel has to be read in the context of the whole book.

No one episode alone is self-sufficient or satisfactory. By moving ahead in the narrative of Proust, one is always at the same time moving backward, to a new, almost miraculous understanding of the past. In many ways, the story of Albertine is a gloss on the story of Gilberte and the story of Odette.

There was first the highly poetic phase of imagination, of wonderment and reverie when Marcel had yet to meet Albertine. This phase of love was developed ecstatically in Marcel's early love for Gilberte. And then there was the phase of jealousy, sustaining and deepening the feeling of love, and which had previously been analyzed in Swann's jealousy over Odette. The third phase, which begins now, is characterized by suffering and oblivion, and this too we have followed, although more briefly, in Marcel's love for Gilberte. Suffering in love is always accompanied in Proust with lucidity and understanding, the understanding which seems to make the suffering bearable and prepares the way for the resumption of love.

## 15. *La Fugitive.*
### B.  The role of time

It is unusual for Proust to indicate clearly, as he does in
the next hundred pages of *La Fugitive,* actual stages of a
psychological development. As the memory of Albertine
moves in Marcel's mind toward oblivion, Marcel analyzes
three moments or distinct phases, each one characterized
by exterior events which help to distract his mind and to
create him anew. The first stage is dominated by Gilberte's
return into the life of the protagonist, the second by conversations with Andrée who brings back his past with Albertine, and the third by a visit to Venice. By the end of
this third chapter, Marcel is very much back in the social
world of Paris and all traces of his suffering over Albertine
have disappeared.

   In fact, the first phase is so dominated by a new infatuation, which begins on a walk in the Bois de Boulogne on
a beautiful All Saints' Day, that Albertine recedes momentarily from his preoccupations. A vague erotic excitement
stirs in Marcel as he watches a group of three girls, two
brunettes and a blond. On a later occasion when he sees
them again, the blond girl looks at him in such a peculiar
way that he is attracted to her. This is a familiar pattern,
although more rapidly formed than in earlier episodes. In
order to discover the identity of the blond girl, he under-
takes a detective-like investigation, with the help of tele-
grams sent to Robert de Saint-Loup. This again recalls
recent investigations into Albertine's life.

   When the girl's identity is determined, the important

story of Swann is resumed, for the girl is Gilberte, now
Mlle de Forcheville. At Swann's death, Odette was grief-
stricken and went into prolonged mourning. She of course
inherited Swann's large fortune. Soon after, by her uncle's
death, Gilberte becomes one of the wealthiest heiresses of
France. Odette remarries de Forcheville who adopts Gilberte and gives her his name. But before this adoption,
Swann's most cherished desire is realized—after his death—
namely the presentation of his daughter to his great friend
Oriane de Guermantes. The few lines describing the luncheon at the Guermantes when Gilberte meets the duc and
the duchesse are charged: what is said and implied about
Swann is pointed and cruel. Gilberte timidly refers to her
father, and Oriane and Basin both acknowledge that they
knew him, and in fact remember him well. But Oriane's
reception is cool: her references to Swann suggest nothing
of the intimacy she shared with him for over twenty-five
years.

In a comparatively short time Oriane has an apparent
change of heart. It is a painful epilogue to the episode of
the duchesse's red slippers in Le Côté de Guermantes.
Wealth, social ambition, her mother's new marriage, even
Oriane's example, brings about a similar—and even more
serious—betrayal, in Gilberte, who, by not speaking of her
father and disowning in her mind her Jewishness, denies
him. This example of Gilberte's snobbism is one of the most
painful in A la recherche du temps perdu, and it serves,
brilliantly in terms of La Fugitive, to parallel the oubli of
Albertine which gradually takes place in Marcel's heart.

Whereas the first half of La Fugitive essentially concerns Marcel's solitude, the second half deals largely with
his re-entry into the world and society. The change that
has come about in Gilberte's fortune and character is so
drastic that there is little reference to the young girl Gilberte and the Swann milieu where Marcel first knew her.
But there is the familiar activity of walking in a garden,
this time the Bois de Boulogne, and amorous exaltation in
watching young women. There is the return of Marcel's
possible literary vocation when the article he had sent long

before to *Le Figaro* does appear in a prominent place in the newspaper, and he receives two letters about the article, one from an unknown person, and the other from Mme Goupil of Combray, a woman he had hardly known but who was a neighbor during the last years of tante Léonie's life and of whom we have read in *Du Côté de chez Swann*. This first stage toward indifference is completed only when Marcel attaches himself to several themes of his past and to the new forms they take in the present.

Marcel's dreams of literary fame, stimulated by the *Figaro* article, and the traits analyzed in Gilberte's character, preside over the two combined revelations of *oubli*: the betrayal to Swann's memory of both Oriane and Gilberte, and Marcel's own infidelity to the memory of Albertine. As Gilberte visits the Guermantes, they find in her more brilliant social graces than they remember in Swann: *elle a un brio que Swann n'avait pas* (III, p. 582). Other changes in fashion and sentiment accompany these major changes in fidelity. Two drawings of Elstir, chosen for Oriane by Swann, now hang in the salon and attract attention because Elstir has become famous. Gilberte is not told that these drawings in the Guermantes' home were acquired largely because of Swann's impeccable taste.

In signing her name, Gilberte uses only the initials of her first name: G. S. Forcheville. This is a further denigration of Swann, and Marcel prophesies that the S is destined to disappear completely. To Gilberte's popularity at the Guermantes and her faithlessness, Marcel opposes, with sad irony, Swann's love for his daughter and his hope that her love for him would insure the survival of his memory.

About this time, Marcel begins to tell people that a dear friend of his has died. He is able to refer to this loss because he no longer feels it. His memories of Albertine now are fragmentary. He is able to feel, to measure the process of *oubli* in himself, and to sense the second stage of indifference has begun. It coincides with a visit from Andrée in the course of which Andrée discloses to him that Albertine practiced an extreme form of lesbian eroticism. Though Marcel can never be sure whether Andrée tells the truth, he realizes that his love for Albertine has diminished so much that now he no longer looks for reasons to establish her innocence.

At this point in *La Fugitive*, Proust illustrates what he has called *les intermittences du coeur*. It is the law of change that affects the accumulation of memories in the mind. The memories themselves do not change, but the manner in which they affect us does. On these pages we see Marcel, as we see him almost always throughout the novel, attentive to the slightest variation within him, to the modifications of his heart his memories make. He follows step by step in himself one of the common laws of human psychology, the law of change by which the most violent sentiments totally disappear, and the most cherished sentiments die. At this juncture, when Marcel returns to the world, and the Guermantes, the images of the past he wants to recall do not always rise to his consciousness. This is what Proust seems to mean by the intermittences of the heart, the intermittences of a man's sensibility. We would like to impose on our memory a static and systematic regime which might be called upon willfully when needed. But this is not the case, and Marcel feels a certain degree of dismay at not being able to recall facts of his inner life. At those moments in his past when he was in love with Gilberte, with Oriane, and with Albertine, he was able to prolong the worry, the agitation, and the desolation associated with these loves. At such times suffering became almost an indulgence for Marcel. But afterward, more oblivious, when suffering can no longer be aroused, he cannot summon at will the causes for suffering. He is merely waiting for another experience, another love which will form in much the same way as the earlier loves. In *A l'ombre des jeunes filles en fleurs*, Marcel had already analyzed the gradual disappearance of images and memories connected with Gilberte. This analysis is resumed in the case of Albertine and explored in far greater detail than with Gilberte. The diminution of Marcel's love for Oriane was the most briefly narrated because his feelings for her never reached an intense stage of suffering.

In the cases of all three, the actual women—coquettish Gilberte, snobbish Oriane, vulgar Albertine—had very little to do with the mysterious figures of beauty and seduction into which Marcel's imagination had transformed them. The action of the novel is, in part, the gradual recognition of these defects in the consciousness of the protagonist. This realization is aided by the effect of time as it reveals what the imagination has masked or changed.

Thus in the second phase Marcel makes progress in his capacity to understand and judge his past, to analyze the causes of his emotions and thereby to begin the process of sublimating them. These fresh attacks of lucidity do not in any way endanger or destroy the sensibility of the protagonist. On the contrary, they bring about a new perceptiveness in Marcel, a new emotional vigor. At every moment during the slow death of a major emotional experience, such as the gradual disappearance of Marcel's suffering over Albertine, a gain is being made for the preparation of some new unknown and unannounced experience. In these three stages of indifference, Marcel's attention is very much held by Gilberte in the first, by Andrée in the second, and by Venice in the third. As the suffering subsides, a return of the past as the appearance of Gilberte, and a new experience as a first visit to Venice, become events perceived at a high poetic level. His past image of Gilberte is modified by the new way in which he sees Gilberte, and his visit to Venice with his mother is a personal experience raised to an aesthetic level. At almost every point, with greater appreciation of the difficulty of ascertaining the truth about any being or situation (. . . *je me disais combien il est difficile de savoir la vérité dans la vie.* III, p. 620), Marcel, in an attempt to mitigate the futility of these desperate discoveries, tends to dwell on the exterior beauty of some aspect of nature or civilization. Not only are the passages on Venice among the most beautiful in Proust, but they serve also to depict Marcel's increasing indifference and to prepare for the themes and developments which will occupy the last volume of *A la recherche du temps perdu.*

Clearly, the third stage, the visit to Venice and its rich
complex beauty, will be used in other ways as well. At this
stage, Marcel's memory of Albertine is dim and his suffering over her virtually non-existent. Balbec, the site associated with Albertine, is also remote from Marcel's thoughts:
Venice brings back the earlier, more peaceful memories of
Combray. The contrast—between the black marble, the
slate roof of Saint-Hilaire which the boy Marcel saw from
his window at ten in the morning when the shutters were
opened, and the golden angel on the campanile of Saint
Mark's which he now sees at the same time in the morning
from his room in Venice—is striking. His mother's presence
in Venice is a constant reminder of Combray. Marcel is
attentive to her love, her thoughtfulness, her efforts to mask
the grief she still feels over the death of her mother. He
contrasts the humble shops of Combray or the church
square with the Venetian palaces of porphyry and jasper,
the streets of Combray with the sapphire water of the
Venetian canals. The Venetian girls he watches and follows remind him, not so much of the group at Balbec, but
of a girl of Méséglise and the girl selling milk at the railroad station when he was on his way for the first time to
Balbec.

At Balbec, Marcel found a new world (Mme de Villeparisis, Albertine, and Elstir) as well as a familiar one
(Françoise and his grandmother). In Venice in the build-
ings and the gondolas, he also discovers a new world, but
in the memories it calls up, he finds a familiar world as
well. His mother meets Mme Sazerat by chance and invites
her to a restaurant. There Marcel hears two waiters speaking in a somewhat derogatory way of an old couple. Marcel
sees the old lady first and recognizes the marquise de Villeparisis, despite an eczema covering her face and her ad-
vanced age, hunchback, and fatigue. The old gentleman
who soon joins her is M. de Norpois, her lover from long
ago, whose voice, though weakened by age, is now even
more eloquent and ornate than the speech which Marcel
recorded in former years.

The slow pace of Proust's narrative at this point gives

to the Venetian episode of Mme de Villeparisis and M. de Norpois a rich sentimental flavor. So many events and years have intervened since we saw them last that they return now as remembered figures, in a new setting. The physical change in their appearance is dramatically portrayed and will serve, in the general architecture of the novel, as an important prelude to the matinée Guermantes in *Le Temps retrouvé.*

Mme Sazerat, when she hears that Mme de Villeparisis is in the restaurant, asks Marcel to point her out. When she was a young girl, her father ruined himself because of his love for Mme de Villeparisis, considered then the most beautiful woman in Paris. Though she has suffered from poverty all her life as a result of her father's infatuation, she is proud he had loved her. Marcel points Mme de Villeparisis out, but Mme Sazerat mistakes another woman for her because she is now hunchbacked, red-faced, and frightfully ugly (*une petite bossue, rougeaude, affreuse.* III, p. 634). Marcel's reply that she is the woman (*C'est elle!*) is the dramatic reaction to the change brought about by the destructive powers of time.

And yet in the same passage, the ceaseless fight waged against time by a human being is illustrated in Norpois' speech: his volubility maintains a steady commentary on food and politics, the intrigues of history and contemporary political figures. More than ever, M. de Norpois appears in the role of teacher, and Mme de Villeparisis seems to have assumed the role once occupied by young Marcel when M. de Norpois was his parents' dinner guest.

A telegram comes to Marcel mysteriously signed Albertine and speaks of marriage and the desire to see him. He tries to return the telegram, but ends by stuffing it in his pocket. Unable to summon Albertine back in his mind because her memory has died in him, he realizes how completely indifferent to her he has become. The telegram (to be explained later) confirms Marcel in his belief that he has ceased loving Albertine (*J'avais définitivement cessé d'aimer Albertine.* III, p. 644) and that the love has now been consigned to oblivion (*la loi générale de l'oubli.* III,

p. 644). As he ponders over this mysterious law, he arrives
at the humility which comes with a love of life, and he
realizes that love of life is the oldest of our love affairs—
it survives all our specific loves (*Notre amour de la vie
n'est qu'une vieille liaison* . . . III, p. 645).

Marcel's exploration of Venice is partially guided by his
study of Ruskin, and also by memories of his discussions
on aesthetics with Swann. When he examines Giotto's angels on the chapel's ceiling, he compares them to strange
birds or to young pupils of Garros, the famous French
aviator. The Renaissance and the twentieth century are
constantly being fused and contrasted in Venice, during the
night walks, particularly, along the narrow streets (*calli*)
when Marcel finds himself often preoccupied by the familiar *agitation* of erotic desire. The word *agitation*, first
used with Swann for the traumatic moment when he could
not find Odette at the Verdurins, is used to describe Marcel's feelings on several occasions. He decides to stay on
alone in Venice after his mother leaves, and the reason
seems to be hope for some amorous adventure. But the
mother's role in Venice is extremely important. Marcel's
attachment to her is such that he is overcome with sadness
when alone he listens to the sentimental singing of *O sole
mio*. The beauty of Venice fades for him, and his erotic
desires diminish, as his feelings of guilt grow and torment
him to such a degree that he rushes off to the station just
in time to join his mother for the return to Paris.

As the train moves through the Italian landscape, the
familiar life which awaits both of the travelers in Paris, is
immediately evoked by three letters which the mother and
son read and comment on. The first, from Gilberte to Marcel, announces her marriage to Robert de Saint-Loup. This
letter clarifies the mystery of the telegram which was signed
not Albertine, as Marcel had first believed, but Gilberte.
Gilberte's somewhat affected handwriting had sufficiently
altered the letters to make the names almost identical. The
physical identity of the two names in the letters *-lbert* emphasizes the resemblance of the two loves which has now
reached a similar stage, the same level of detachment in

Marcel's memory. But time will continue to bring its unsuspected modifications in Gilberte, and precisely because
of this announced marriage.

The two other letters, addressed to Marcel's mother, are
opened by her. The first, from Robert de Saint-Loup, repeats the announcement of his marriage with Gilberte de
Forcheville, and the second, even more extraordinary, announces the marriage of young Cambremer, nephew of
Legrandin, with Mlle d'Oloron, niece of Jupien who had
been adopted by Charlus. The reactions of Marcel and his
mother to these two marriages are quite different, and the
pages which analyze their reactions introduce one of the
major themes of *Le Temps retrouvé:* the prodigious social
changes that take place in France. The reasons for these
social changes are complex and are not the same for each
generation. Marcel's mother represents one fairly stable
level of French society, and her reflections are closely allied
with what *her* mother would have said. Indeed, the grandmother's memory is very much present during the analysis
of the letters.

Marcel and his mother are taken totally off guard by the
contents of the letters because they contradict the norms
of society, the laws governing the distinctions between
French social classes. The older witness to a world that
normally does not allow such alliances, the mother reacts
with uncomprehending astonishment. Marcel's reaction is
far more complex, and he dwells largely on his sadness
upon hearing the news. He knows far more about Gilberte
and Robert, and about young Cambremer and Jupien's
niece, than his mother does. Yet he would be unable to
explain to her all he knows. Actually it would take all that
we have read thus far in the novel to understand something
of the complicated social relationships, psychological dramas, and moral infringements which the two marriages
involve. In each marriage, two totally different worlds are
joined: in the first, Swann's world, or the rich bourgeoisie,
with the Guermantes' world, or the highest of French aristocracy; in the second, Jupien's world, the servant class,
with Mme de Cambremer's world, the provincial nobility.

The sadness Marcel feels does not come from snobbism or desire to see the strict social hierarchies maintained. His reaction is related to his memories of Combray and of his childhood, with its two ways: Swann's and Guermantes'. With the marriage of Swann's daughter and Oriane's nephew, the two distinct worlds of Marcel's childhood are fused, and the separate identity of each is lost.

Marcel reviews in his mind, without always being able to articulate them to his mother, the dramas and dilemmas, social and sexual, which have led up to these conjunctions, and thereby recapitulates the novel. As the protagonist he reviews the past and as the narrator he discloses fragments of the future.

In the analysis of the Cambremer-d'Oloron marriage, we learn of the role played by the princesse de Parme, who liked Legrandin and wished to help introduce Mme de Cambremer (mother of the groom and Legrandin's sister) to the highest level of society. It was she who approached Charlus for the hand of Mlle d'Oloron. Charlus, amused by the idea, is hopeful that young Cambremer is an invert like Legrandin. In a way, Legrandin's two vices, snobbism and homosexuality, are hereby rewarded, strengthened, made, at least, compatible. Jupien's niece, the seamstress, whose high moral qualities everyone admires, would not have been adopted by Charlus, if he had not loved Morel and befriended Jupien. A quick glance into the immediate future brings to a sad end the story of Jupien's niece (who is called his daughter in a few passages in the novel). She dies of typhoid fever a few weeks after her wedding. The letter announcing her death (*la lettre de faire-part*) was addressed to almost all the greatest families of Europe. Within a very brief space of time a total transformation in social status had been brought about by what some will call history, or by what others will call the secret dramas of passion. The death of a plebeian girl causes the princely families of Europe to go into mourning . . . *la mort de la petite roturière met en deuil toutes les familles princières de l'Europe* (III, p. 671). The princely power of Charlus and the semi-concealed power of his perversion over him are, in some ways, largely responsible for this transformation.

The background of Gilberte's marriage with Robert, though not so astounding, is infinitely more complex. In the making of this marriage, Robert's mother, Mme de Marsantes, whose excessive kindness and humility cause her to promote this union, plays an active role. Throughout all of this final passage in *La Fugitive*, four mothers play important parts. Mme de Marsantes, who had once forced her son to break with his mistress Rachel, has now brought about the marriage with Gilberte, and will in the future reconcile Robert and Gilberte when their marriage is endangered. Gilberte's mother, Odette, now Mme de Forcheville, had not at first approved of the marriage of her daughter, and would have preferred a prince as a son-in-law. But we learn that after the marriage, when Odette's income is diminished, Robert becomes her protector and gives her the money (Gilberte's money) which she needs. Odette continues therefore the pattern of her life, that of a kept woman, her keeper now her son-in-law! In return for this favor, Odette aids Robert in his extramarital alliances, especially in his infatuation for Morel.

The thoughts of Marcel's mother, and her constant references to her own mother, during the long train ride, initiate the entire passage. Her viewpoint on these marriages, reinforced by what her mother would have said, is the point of departure for Marcel's own interpretation. The opposing theories are neatly demonstrated in the first reactions to the marriage of Mlle d'Oloron. Marcel's mother calls it the reward of virtue, the ending of a novel by George Sand. *C'est la récompense de la vertu. C'est un mariage à la fin d'un roman de Mme Sand* (III, p. 658). Marcel's response is not stated orally, but he says to himself: it is the reward of vice, a marriage at the end of a Balzac novel. *C'est le prix du vice, c'est un mariage à la fin d'un roman de Balzac* (III, p. 658).

A striking change has taken place in Gilberte, reinforced by the many changes in her name. Already the change from Gilberte Swann to Gilberte de Forcheville signaled

the change from the young girl Marcel played with in the
Champs-Elysées, to the snobbish young lady ashamed of
her father. By her marriage Gilberte becomes the marquise de Saint-Loup, and she will later, before the end of
the novel, become duchesse de Guermantes and bear the
very title of her father's friend Oriane, to whom he had
longed to present his daughter. But Gilberte will find the
society she had wanted to enter uninteresting, and gradually give it up. Neither will her marriage with Robert give
her personal pleasure. In public, Robert behaves in an exemplary way toward Gilberte at first, but even this changes
in time.

The change in Robert de Saint-Loup is, for Marcel, more
tragic than that in Gilberte. Marcel had once believed that
friendship lasted longer than love, but his disappointments
in Robert are overwhelming. In time, Robert's inversion becomes more and more flagrant, although Marcel would
never have believed it when he first knew him at Balbec
as the handsome, gracious, golden-crested bird of the Guermantes family, though Robert's suffering over Rachel, Marcel remembers, contradicted this happy impression. Marcel
recalls the attentiveness and constant kindness bestowed on
him by Robert in Balbec, Doncières, and Paris. But now
his marriage for money, his infidelities, his luxurious way
of life, squandering Gilberte's money on Morel and others,
have brought about deep moral changes in Robert which
finally even Marcel has to acknowledge. He even extracts
money from Gilberte to pay Odette in order to protect his
own love affairs.

The reasons for Marcel's sadness at this point in the story
are many. His thoughts during the train ride with his
mother constantly include references to the future in order
to round out themes and episodes related to the marriage
announcements. He calls his sadness the mournful moving
from one house to another . . . *la tristesse, morne comme
un déménagement* (III, p. 664). His love for Albertine, his
friendship for Robert, his love for Gilberte, had once
seemed to him imperishable, but now even these sentiments
fade. Whether a love affair, social position, or power, each

is submitted to the same principle of change and dissolution. Marcel now believes that the creation of the world did not take place at any beginning. It happens every day. *La création du monde n'a pas eu lieu au début, elle a lieu tous les jours* (III, p. 669).

A brilliant analogy between families and nations ends the passage. The mutations of property (Robert de Saint-Loup, after his marriage, will live at Tansonville, which was Swann's property) correspond to the ever changing frontiers between countries. One Muse takes over from all the more notable muses of art and philosophy: the Muse of History. *La Fugitive* ends with a meditation on History, and emphasizes the way in which it has affected Marcel's fervent friendship for Robert de Saint-Loup. He weeps when he contrasts the charming outgoing manners of the Robert he had known at Balbec and Doncières with the new Robert whose cold evasive manners he interprets as stemming from a friend's need to conceal his own sexual inversion. Marcel meditates on the curious physical and temperamental resemblances between Rachel and Charles Morel.

The slow meditative passage on such revelations are followed in the next volume by a rapid series of changes in personalities, personal relationships, and social situations. Once these changes are perceived (as in *La Fugitive*), they suddenly appear everywhere in unexpected frequency (as in *Le Temps retrouvé*). We have learned that the most inviolable situations may change. *La Fugitive* has prepared, first with the very slow change in Marcel as his love for Albertine turns to indifference, and second with the swift laconic announcement of the two marriages, the gigantic irreversible movement of change to be narrated in *Le Temps retrouvé*. It is not fair to say (as has been claimed too often) that Proust records only degradations in the unfolding of history. There are rehabilitations also, in the cases of the Verdurins, Odette, Oriane, and Robert, and there are stable continuing values, in Françoise, Marcel, and Marcel's mother.

The external changes are reflected in changes taking

place inside Marcel, in the evolution of his thought and his character. At this point in *A la recherche du temps perdu*, it is possible to see that Marcel has passed through two very important phases of personal development, and is already engaged in a third.

The world of the child, the first phase (reminiscent of Auguste Comte's theory of the cyclical development of the world's age), is supernatural in the sense that the parents are absolute laws and the child obedient to, and dependent on, them. Marcel's love for his mother never dies. The very early mention of Geneviève de Brabant in the opening page of *Du Côté de chez Swann* is the story of the devoted mother and the protected son. Marcel as a child willingly submits to parental authority and love. Until *Le Temps retrouvé*, the family is the great stabilizing force in Marcel's life. The one break in this solid structure is the boy's illness, an illness which gives him certain privileges with his parents, but which also prolongs his childhood well into adulthood. In Venice, the episode in *La Fugitive*, the role of the mother is again pre-eminent, and the capricious child repents his capriciousness, and joins his mother before she leaves the city.

The second phase occupies the largest part of *A la recherche du temps perdu*. The supernatural or magical belief in absolute laws, which the child feels, is lost when he enters the world and encounters a multiplicity of laws, no one of which seems absolute. Marcel's two major adventures outside of his family are his participation in the salons, with society, and his amorous adventures. He tries to find the absolute laws governing these two kinds of experience, but at the end of *La Fugitive*, he acknowledges failure. Nothing mystical or foreordained governs the laws of social situations and of love. Marcel studies ambition in Bergotte, snobbism in Legrandin, and passion in Mlle Vinteuil, and concludes that never can we know enough about anyone else to claim an understanding of a human being or a social situation.

Marcel is now on the verge of the third phase. Here he questions: What is reality? What do we know? He is faced, already in the passage on the Muse of History, with the impossibility of arriving at absolute laws. No one person can be known sufficiently well enough to recognize in him the laws of change. We are merely the result of change. Marcel is about to reach in the narrative the moment when, in the evolution of his life, the artist and the moralist fuse, and he will give to the harassing problem of reality an appropriately Proustian answer.

### 16. *Le Temps retrouvé.*
### (*The Past Recaptured*)
### A. The triumph of Swann's Way

Marcel's sadness at the end of *La Fugitive* continues
throughout the opening of *Le Temps retrouvé*, where he
is at Combray, with Gilberte, living in her father's house at
Tansonville. Combray, at the beginning of *Du Côté de chez
Swann*, was an enchanted world for young Marcel, but
he now sees it in a different light. The Vivonne is a narrow ugly stream. The two walks, Guermantes' Way and
Swann's Way, no longer delight him. Gilberte has changed.
He has changed. In their conversation he learns, but too
late, that she had loved him when he was a boy suffering
for love of her. She tells him of the childish erotic games
she and other girls played with Théodore in the donjon of
Roussainville. For the moment, Marcel's melancholy seems
incurable. Nothing remains of his earlier feelings, and he
meditates on the theme that everything perishes in this
world, all traces of beauty, such as the Vivonne, and all
traces of sorrow, such as his agonized love for Gilberte.
From the window of his room at Tansonville, he can see the
steeple of the church of Combray. It is farther away than
it was from his room at tante Léonie's, and he sees in this
the experience he is undergoing: the effect on him of the
distance of space and the distance of years.

Gilberte had first appeared to him in front of a hedge of
pink hawthorns, as Albertine had first appeared on the
beach as if just come from the sea. He thinks now of the
chance events which seem to have directed his life: the

late afternoon, for example, when he saw Gilberte walking
with a young man, an event which, more than anything
else had caused him to break with her. The disappointment
with Combray he now feels is largely the absence in him
of love. He now lives close to Gilberte and is constantly
in her company: he has not forgotten that she was the first
woman he loved, the first enigma, his first romantic creation. He knows now that when he had first perceived her
on the path (*le raidillon*) at Tansonville, he saw her as the
prefiguration of the entire group of girls he watched on
the beach at Balbec. When he wrestled with her behind
the laurel bushes of the Champs-Elysées, she was in a way
the angel and he Jacob, because he had been wounded on
that occasion and never able to recover his first innocence.
As Gilberte, now married to his best friend, assumes in
Marcel's life the familiar role of friend and confidante—
each is a confidant for the other in the Combray conversations—it becomes clear that Gilberte is the symbol of love,
that, incarnated in Albertine, she was also the source of his
prolonged failure with her. Each apparition of a woman
in his life is the same; despite the varying (and yet not
very divergent) psychological and moral considerations,
Gilberte is the beginning and the end of the same myth,
and Gilberte's daughter (whom we will meet at the matinée Guermantes after the war) will also assume Gilberte's
role and represent to him all of his youth.

During the opening pages of *Le Temps retrouvé*, the
mythical aspect of Gilberte is stronger than the real Gilberte unhappily married to Robert. But Marcel is more objective in his discussion of Robert, and in his disappointment over him. No character in Proust moves further away
from our first idealistic picture we have of him than Saint-
Loup. No character, not even Charlus, with whom he is
constantly compared in this last volume, contains within
his personality greater extremes of vice and virtue. Subter-
fuge, lies dominate Robert's life with Gilberte. In his private life, his inversion obsesses him (he loses his Croix de
Guerre in Jupien's house of male prostitution). But Robert
the soldier and patriot survives all this. His knowledge of

military strategy, his bravery and his love for France are exemplified in his last conversations with Marcel, in the letter to Marcel in which he gives to the word *poilu* a deeply spiritual meaning, and in the sacrifice of his death.

Marcel describes Robert's death with complete simplicity. He stays in his room for several days on hearing the news of Robert's death at the front. He thinks of his first meetings with Robert at Balbec and the color of his friend's eyes, as green as the sea—the color of Albertine's eyes, whom he had also met first at the sea. Their lives, Albertine's and Robert's, had scarcely touched. Yet now both are dead. They had been, in their relationship with Marcel, apprehensive of his health, and attentive to his needs. Marcel's sadness is far deeper over Robert's death than it had been over Albertine's. Robert continues to live in Marcel's grief, and unexpectedly, in the sincere grief of his aunt, Oriane. Robert's last appearances in the novel, in the Paris salons on his leaves from the front, resemble his first appearances at Balbec. Through the years he had not altered physically, despite his sinister, disguised moral degradation. He still resembles a golden bird, the lithe movements of his body reminiscent of his mother. His erect head always gives the impression that he is inspecting what he looks at. Ornithology continues to dominate the descriptions of Robert up to the very end. His blond hair is compared to a bird's aigrette. As he walks back and forth, he is both a lord in a salon and a bird in a cage. He represents a zoological worldliness, yet his manners, ever so slightly, but noticeably, begin to resemble those of his uncle Charlus. For those who can see it, the hereditary vice of the Guermantes is evident in Robert de Saint-Loup.

In a passage from the Goncourt Journal (actually a pastiche of Proust), Marcel reads of the Verdurin circle. This reading serves two purposes. It is a transition between his visit to Tansonville with Gilberte and his return to Paris during the war when we meet almost all of the characters still alive. It also serves to raise once again the question of Marcel's becoming a writer. In comparing his own powers of observation to those of the Goncourt brothers, he concludes that he is vastly inferior, with no real disposition, and no real talent for writing. This is the last time Marcel renounces literature. In the second half of *Le Temps retrouvé*, the illumination will come with such forcefulness that he will not resist the conviction that he does have the vocation and the vision necessary for the making of a writer.

Paris in wartime occupies a long chapter which serves as a set piece where we see again the characters and the changes that have come about in their lives and their relationships, where we follow some of the dramatic sociological transformations with which *A la recherche du temps perdu* is concerned.

The war itself is never related in *Le Temps retrouvé*, but it is the background now for all the themes which have been firmly established in the structure of the work. Only such an upheaval as war, particularly of the proportions of the 1914–18 war, can bring about what Proust has been gradually and minutely describing from the very first volume of his novel: namely, the victory of Swann's Way over Guermantes' Way. In its broadest terms, it would be then the victory of the bourgeoisie over the aristocracy. "Victory" is too militaristic, too absolute a term to use here, but even in a purely military sense, it would be, for such a writer as Proust, a relative term. Time allows no such thing as a victory. As Proust's creations speak of the war, and as we see the various ways in which the war affects their lives, we are convinced of the separateness of each individual, of the extreme relativism of such terms as defeat and victory, and of all the possible and improbable changes that transpire in any one life and character. Indeed, almost every reference to facts and to characters in the chapter on Paris in wartime indicates change, a change which is the result of simple and inevitable evolutionary processes as well as of unpredictable, cataclysmic reverses of fortune.

By 1916, the two reigning queens of Paris are Mme Verdurin and Mme Bontemps. They exploit the war for all the wrong reasons, for social prestige, for the exercise of power, for the exercise of tyranny. The small clan of the Verdurins, partially observed through Swann's eyes in the

first volume of the novel, has now a terrifying solidity, a
nightmarish power. While this is not deliberate parody,
it is that kind of harsh reality which resembles parody in
its unlikeliness and grotesqueness. The rising power of Mme
Verdurin, who reads of the sinking of the *Lusitania* as she
dips her *croissant* into her *café au lait,* signals the end of
the Faubourg Saint-Germain. But if we have read Proust
attentively thus far, we are certain that the reality of Mme
Verdurin's new world and new prestige, built upon the
destruction of a world war, is as symbolic as every other
world described by Proust. Combray and the Faubourg
Saint-Germain were Marcel's two great illusions in *Du Côté
de chez Swann* and *Le Côté de Guermantes.* In *Le Temps
retrouvé,* in the opening passage and in the chapter on
Paris in wartime, these two major illusions of his life die.
They disappear as completely as the world of passion has
disappeared for him, and as the world of his parents. Only
one world remains for him to try: the world of art, and that
test is held in reserve, in the carefully paced economy of
the novel, for the last episode of the matinée Guermantes.

   The war, the history of France, the basic changes that
French society undergoes, the changes in taste and fashion
are all recorded in the evolution of the major and minor
characters of the novel. Morel, once Charlus' protégé, insolent and venal, becomes a deserter in 1914, but is deco-
rated at the end of the war and emerges a respectable and
respected gentleman, who, as a journalist, writes articles
vilifying M. de Charlus. Bloch, whose Jewish traits Proust
analyzes in minute detail, represents throughout most of
the novel pretentiousness, vulgarity, and ludicrous behavior
in social scenes, such as the evening *chez* Mme de Villeparisis. A coward at the beginning of the war, he is transformed by the war. When he appears at the matinée Guermantes, even his appearance has changed.

   Of all the characters in *A la recherche du temps perdu,*
after Marcel himself, Françoise and Charlus are the most
elaborately analyzed: they appear in *Le Temps retrouvé,*
both strangely changed and the same. The two worlds they
represent, at the two extremes of society, are, in the social

sense, divergent, and in the basically human sense, similar.
The aging servant who reflects the solid moral viewpoint
of France, has surprising traits of cruelty and immorality,
of narrowness and ignorance. The aging baron demonstrates
at almost every point in the novel, and even during the
final scenes when his degradation is seemingly total, a lofty,
intelligent and philosophical view of society, a vast culture,
a generosity of spirit, a sense of justice and objectivity in
questions concerning the war, and the history of France
and Germany. Proust presents these two characters as distinct personalities, who are, at the same time, a synthesis
of a race, a nation, and of mankind.

We never know the heart of Françoise. We never know
exactly what she thinks concerning any character or any
event. Her feelings control her convictions, and they are
motivated by an inextricable alliance of tradition, rote, and
of momentary fashion. The reasons for her dislike of Albertine were too complex for her to know, and yet not too
complex for Marcel to discover. During the first half of Le
Temps retrouvé, Françoise seems, despite the rigor of her
professed moral view, to have accepted the irregular sexual
life of Charlus, Robert, and Legrandin, and sides with these
men rather than with their favorites. This may well signal
a change in Françoise, brought about by time, but one cannot be too sure. She resists time better than anyone else in
the novel. In fact, she remains almost as impenetrable as
time itself. She is more the force of time than a character
affected by it.

Her speech is timeless for Marcel; in it he hears locutions
and proverbs that go far back into the history of France.
There is a moment when the language of Françoise's
daughter seems to affect the pure speech of the old servant, and Marcel observes this slight change with the sadness of a witness watching the past disappear. In its own
way, the world of servants is as elaborate, or as hierarchi-
cally organized, as the Guermantes world. Françoise is as
adamant, as clearly drawn, as histrionically presented as
the most overpowering member of the Guermantes family.
We never see Françoise in any one fully developed episode

as we so often see M. de Charlus. She comes and goes as the one always behind the scenes, an invisible witness, who records in her mind what she sees and who comments on it to herself. When she speaks to Léonie, at the beginning of the novel, or to Marcel, at the end, we can be sure she is not speaking her full thoughts.

She appeared first, wearing the pleated bonnet (*tuyaux de son bonnet*), in Léonie's house at Combray, almost a figure from a niche, a statue of the past. (Mme de Guermantes also seemed at Combray to come down from the stained glass of Saint-Hilaire.) The savor of a distant past was in her speech, and the tyranny with which she reigned over her part of the house is reminiscent of the servants in Molière. Cruel to animals and other servants, she is kind to Léonie. She is an excellent nursemaid and expert cook. She comes to understand Marcel's ways, and protects his life, in very much the same way Céleste Albaret protected Proust's life during his last years. She survives with Marcel, as if she represented all the traditions of his life and his world, and outlives the family affection of her master and his loves.

The histrionic richness of Charlus' character gives him the dominant role in scene after scene in *A la recherche du temps perdu*. The several models for this personage have been pointed out by scholars, and yet he is a man whose nature in the novel is far more dramatic and complex than the nature of any of his possible models. His character, or rather the mystery of his character, is developed slowly throughout the novel, in a series of stages. No one scene reveals all the facets of his personality, nor all his vices and virtues. He is depicted successively as a monster, fallen angel, penetrating critic, aristocrat, and reprobate. In his first scenes he is mysterious and unpredictable. The entomological scene at the beginning of *Sodome et Gomorrhe* clarifies for Marcel the character of Charlus. The subsequent scenes are increasingly tragic revelations of Charlus in his quest for power and satisfaction. The decline of his worldly influence begins with the Verdurin concert in *La Prisonnière*. In *La Fugitive*, he is an isolated, tragic

figure, ostracized by the members of his family and by
the social worlds where once he was a triumphant figure.

When Marcel is on his way to the matinée Guermantes,
years after the war, he sees Charlus for the last time. His
hair and beard are white now and he is half paralyzed.
Jupien is with him and is caring for him. For Marcel,
Charlus has the fallen majesty of a Lear, and he watches
him bow to Mme de Saint-Euverte, whom Charlus once
would have scorned, but who has now unexpectedly become prominent. Yet Charlus bows to her as ceremoniously
and humbly as if she were the queen of France.

There are two detailed episodes (in the early chapters
of *Le Temps retrouvé*, entitled "M. de Charlus pendant
la guerre") which illustrate two of the major aspects of his
character: his intelligence and his homosexuality. Early
one evening in Paris, Marcel encounters Charlus trailing
two Zouave soldiers. The baron interrupts his pursuit and
talks with Marcel at length and brilliantly about the events
of the day: a lofty monologue on the war, on Germany,
on history, on the relationship of this actual epoch of history to the past, on dilettantism, on M. de Norpois' articles
and mistakes in them. The monologue, occupying more
than forty pages broken up by Marcel's comments and
thoughts, is an elaborate intellectual appraisal of the moment in history colored by Charlus' defeatism and by his
attachment to Germany. He points out, intermittently, an
analogy between the behavior of individuals and the mas-
sive efforts of nations in wartime. Charlus deplores the useless destruction of the past (we learn, for example, that
the church at Combray was destroyed by the French and
the English because it was used as an observation post by
the Germans) and the toll of human life. He contrasts the
real motives behind the actions of people in wartime with
their professed motives.

The second episode is a Grand Guignol performance:
abject and comic at the same time, where, in a brothel
run by Jupien, Charlus is chained and beaten by boys
Jupien claims to be apaches and butcher boys. It is a com-
plementary scene to the prelude of *Sodome et Gomorrhe*.

The analogy of the bee and the orchid for the activities of Charlus and Jupien softened the disgusting aspect of the courtyard scene, and the almost comic vacuous innocence of the boys in the brothel scene offsets the sordidness of Charlus' masochism. The ritualistic quality of the scene, dictated by Charlus' imagination as he tries to re-enact the florid dreams of his eroticism, is countered by the nonchalant attitude of the young men.

The grandiose proportions of Charlus' fantasies contrast with the subjugation of his nature to a tyrannical vice. Many scandalous or suspected cases of perversion have been cited as models for Charlus: Montesquiou in particular, Oscar Wilde, Serge Diaghilev, Vautrin, in the novels of Balzac, and Proust himself. The officiating Jupien and his establishment are close indeed to what is known of Albert Le Cuziat and his house. But Proust never depicts reality exactly as it is. Discrepancies constantly confound the scholar who endeavors to attach any pure fact to Proust's novel. Before the scene in Jupien's hotel, Charlus, talking with Marcel as they walk along the street, compares the fate of Paris to Pompeii and the biblical cities of the plain. The meaning of Charlus' vice outlives the specific vice itself. The novelist is always seeking the reality behind the anecdote, the meaning behind the colorful or sordid detail. The fact that Mme Verdurin continues through wartime to receive her friends and maintain her clan, and that Charlus continues to track down and enjoy his pleasure, is far more significant for Proust than the actions themselves, whether the Verdurins' monotonous speech or the half-ludicrous, half-abject scene of Charlus chained to a bed.

In the violent, almost repugnant scenes of *Le Temps retrouvé* in which both Mme Verdurin and Charlus are unmasked more pitilessly than in previous chapters, Proust shows himself, as in countless other scenes, the master portrayer of the disorder of human life. Ferociously he explores all the worlds of sensation as they proliferate under any given stimulus. Man's subconscious and his sensory perceptions are the two principal concerns in Proust's art. Each

thought in the subconscious is able to engender so many
worlds not controlled by the chronology of time or by
the imposed logic of man's reason, that Proust's analysis
never gives an impression of exhaustive objective truth.
His great passages, concerned, as they almost always are,
with man's consciousness caught unaware, are attempts,
often desperate, to seize upon the reality behind the proliferating thought.

It is doubtful that Proust would ever scandalize a new
reader today. He has so dominated, with Joyce and Kafka,
the art of fiction since his death, that the contemporary
reader is prepared, before opening *A la recherche du temps
perdu,* to accept human reality as something impenetrable,
ineluctable, unfathomable. Whenever Charlus, for example, is in the forefront, the analysis of his appearance and
of his action and the recording of his speech are never in
themselves the goal of Proust. The reader never actually
makes very much progress in his basic knowledge of
Charlus. What we know about him, we know very early in
the novel, far earlier than Marcel knows. More than an
analysis of Charlus, Proust has attempted to give us,
through Charlus, a feeling for the inexhaustible complexity
of life. He shows us, and notably in the case of Charlus,
the way in which a life is lived, and also how it is relived,
in the endless repetitions of desires and manias; and how
this complexity involves infinitely more than the bare banal
anecdotes. If an anecdote is the starting point, it becomes
the center of what might be called a vertigo. The vertigo
inevitably comes about in Proust's art because of the desperate and incessant attempts to know. A single detail, as
it grows in importance in the mind of the narrator, always
has at first some relationship with life, and yet, in its isolation, it seems whimsical, pointless.

For all of these reasons there is no common measure between the life of Proust and *A la recherche du temps
perdu.* Proust's very conception of the novel would deny
such a supposed parallel. The striking disparity between
Proust's (far from distinguished) correspondence and his
novel, is a further substantiation. One of the major revela-

tions which life brings to Marcel and which he records frequently in the narrative is the abyss which often exists between a man's thought and his words. In the middle of Charlus' long monologue in *Le Temps retrouvé*, this principle occurs to Marcel as he listens to Charlus' discourse on patriotism: *nos pensées ne s'accordent pas toujours avec nos paroles* (III, p. 774). He is reminded of the scene he observed from the stairway window when he saw Charlus and Jupien in the courtyard below. He thinks also of certain judgments voiced by Françoise and Albertine which were at odds with their real thoughts.

Charlus' monologue, involving so many themes and topics, and revealing him as a highly intelligent observer and commentator, is followed by Jupien's hotel scene which, though it occupies fewer pages than the monologue, is more memorable for its surprising revelations. The hotel is run by Jupien for Charlus' pleasure, a pleasure difficult to associate with the man who spoke so movingly to Marcel in the streets of Paris. We follow first the agility of a man's mind, and we are then introduced to the dismal monotony of his pleasure and vice. From the picture of Paris at night, with airplanes and search lights in the sky, we move into an internal scene of total pandemonium where eminent men from various professions seek sexual pleasure with young men who disguise themselves to sustain the illusion of fantasy. In each room of the hotel some variation of sexual fantasy is performed. After the rites, the boys and the clients meet downstairs and comment in the most natural way on what has just passed. The "postmortems," as it were, are motivated by men who wish to prolong their fantasies, and by the boys who wish to earn extra money.

Marcel observes this extraordinary hotel, this true wasteland of passion, and makes no comment on what he sees and learns, because there is no comment to make: the scene explains itself. It is its own commentary, as empty as any daily function of man performed mechanically. . . . When Marcel tells Jupien he has had the impression of watching a tale from *The Arabian Nights,* Jupien replies that if he ever wishes to observe a scene, not of forty, but of ten thieves, he has merely to check on whether Jupien's window is lighted. The window is the "open Sesame" which will literally open the door on a scene as absurd as the bombing of Paris which is taking place at that very moment.

Jupien's hotel scene in *Le Temps retrouvé* illustrates explicitly what was shockingly and surprisingly disclosed in the courtyard scene at the opening of *Sodome et Gomorrhe*. But it is also far more than that. It explains Proust's belief in the reality of what seems unreal, and in the inevitable monotony of the real. Whatever the scene in Proust—a salon reception, a Zeppelin raid over Paris, the hawthorn hedges in May at Combray, Jupien's brothel—its significance is not in its traditional beauty, but in what it reveals of the real and the unreal, the realistic and the imaginary, the conscious and the subconscious. Proust agrees with Flaubert that there is no such thing as a beautiful subject for art. When Flaubert said that Yvetot is equivalent to Constantinople (*Yvetot vaut Constantinople*), he stated an aesthetic principle which accounts for such a scene as Jupien's hotel. As Elstir fused in his paintings land images with sea images, to such an extent that one stood for the other, so Marcel, observing the behavior of Jupien's clients, sees the fantasy of a man's mind transformed into a realistic performance. Proust is saying that a sexual performance is nothing in itself. It is a rite which has to be enacted at regular intervals because it stands for, and symbolizes, man's craving for unity and perpetuation.

The social documentation, particularly this episode in Jupien's hotel, has been called by some critics a history of 1900–14. But this definition is far from sound. There are too many omissions in terms of history, and too many emphases of a certain type of sensibility, for *A la recherche du temps perdu* to be properly considered social documentation. The work remains steadfastly a novel. Such a scene as Jupien's, although more surprising in the revelation of its mores than other scenes, proceeds in accord with

Proust's method of analogy and contrast, and the development of motifs.

The epilogue continues the effect of the main scene on Marcel. He sees the fire started by a bomb dropped from an airplane, and he thinks of the volcanic eruption that destroyed Pompeii, and of just such a scene as he has observed in Jupien's hotel, fixed and held in lava for centuries to come. During air raid alarms, people take shelter in the darkened Métro, and there, despite the imminence of death and destruction, such a man as Charlus continues his advances, his lascivious promiscuity, under cover of darkness. Marcel thinks of the catacombs, and of the strange rites which took place there . . . *des rites secrets dans les ténèbres des catacombes* (III, p. 835). Whatever the catastrophe—an air raid, a fire, a tidal wave (*mascaret*)—man's desires are not distracted.

In this epilogue to the brothel scene, an epilogue to the major part of the novel and to the entire work as well, Marcel ponders the mystery, the contradictions in the personalities of Jupien and Charlus. He reaches the same conclusions: that life is dichotomous, illogical, contrary. Jupien's intelligence and sensibility have not deterred him from managing such a hotel as the one in which Robert de Saint-Loup dropped his Croix de Guerre. Charlus' vast knowledge and wit have not impeded his form of sexual insanity, of which he now seems to be the prey. Is love the cause of this? Are aberrations forms of love? Is love itself an aberration? Is it possible to see in M. de Charlus' strange ritual, in his being chained, a manifestation of his mediaeval temperament and imagination, a deep-felt need for virile solidity and attachment which others find in the normal experiences of love and marriage? Marcel tries to explain in terms of atavism and inherited ancestral traits the elaborate caricature of sexual gratification seen in the brothel.

This feudal torture, as a possible gloss on Charlus' aberration, brings thoughts of Robert de Saint-Loup back to Marcel's mind, and the passage comes to an end with a series of reminiscences concerning Robert and a noble interpretation of his death and his funeral. In his attitude toward the war, Robert had exemplified for Marcel the militarist and the patriot. And yet in the greater, all-embracing act of dying, he became a Guermantes, one of his race, symbolically visible in the church of Saint-Hilaire de Combray, where during the funeral mass a large red G stands out against the black drapes on the portal.

Proust's art is scrupulously composed with alternating emphases. During the first half of Le Temps retrouvé, which ends with a meditation on Robert, on the feudal allegiance apparent in his funeral, and on what he might have become had he lived, Marcel is unjudging and impartial, a little aloof from the action, but in the second half of the volume he resumes the protagonist's role. The focus of the picture of Paris during the war has been on the Guermantes, on Charlus and Robert in particular, but in the matinée scene where the new princesse de Guermantes is Mme Verdurin, the attention is centered on Swann. In describing the Guermantes, Marcel remains objective, but in his descriptions and reminiscences of Swann, he becomes more involved and more subjective. Swann is really Marcel's double. They are both tortured by jealousy in love and by aspirations to art. In many respects they have the same sensibility. Marcel's final approach to joy will come through Swann, through the apparition of Swann's granddaughter, and his sense of an authentic vocation. With the stories of Robert and Charlus, Marcel is held by bonds of sympathy and understanding, with affection for Robert and admiration for Charlus. But the daughter of Gilberte and Robert will personify the literary work to come in the final pages of A la recherche du temps perdu. As Marcel looks at Mlle de Saint-Loup, admiring her beauty and her youthfulness, and sensing in this descendant of Swann the piercing eyes of the duchesse de Guermantes and the curved nose of Robert de Saint-Loup, Marcel sees in her his own youth: elle ressemblait à ma Jeunesse (III, p. 1032).

Marcel is overjoyed at the intimation of creativity. And the first half of Le Temps retrouvé, where he observes and narrates a cyclical and ineluctable world serves as the preamble to this joy. There he studies the many ways in which a character is bound to his past and the past of his ancestors, chained, as Charlus is to the bed in the sordid scene of Jupien's hotel. Though the world around Charlus has changed, and his status with it, he is still stabilized by the enduring elements of his character. The duality of time is manifested in him: its processes have brought him prestige and position, white hair, paralysis of his body; and its ineluctability has given him strength, stability, and endurance.

## 17. *Le Temps retrouvé.*
### B. The aesthetics of the novel

Proust is essentially the author of one work, for which his early writings were mere exercises and preparatory drafts. At the age of twenty-five, he published a collection of stories, *Les Plaisirs et les Jours.* Between 1896 and 1904, he wrote a novel, *Jean Santeuil,* of a thousand pages, not published until 1952. During 1908 and 1909, he worked on an essay, *Contre Sainte-Beuve,* which grew to the proportions of a good-sized work, published in 1954. He began the writing of *A la recherche du temps perdu* in 1909 and continued work on it until his death in 1922.

This career, far more assiduous and more faithful than was once believed, was a long preparation, which culminated in the writing of the one work. In *La Prisonnière,* where Marcel listens to the playing of Vinteuil's septet, he realizes that all Vinteuil's earlier compositions had been timid essays, preparatory for the triumphant septet, the final work which uses the earlier compositions and their themes, develops them more fully, and represents the entire life of the composer. In the same way, the early writings of Marcel Proust all flow into the final work where they are deepened and transformed: the short stories and sketches of *Les Plaisirs et les Jours,* the novel *Jean Santeuil,* the critical work *Contre Sainte-Beuve.* The critic and the novelist are fully evident in *A la recherche du temps perdu,* but to them has been added the aesthetician, the artist who has come to a profound understanding of his method, his subject matter, and the philosophical meaning of his art.

Some critics have looked upon Proust's novel as primarily a love story, or a series of love stories, dominated by the very long episode of Marcel's love for Albertine. Others interpret it as a sociological novel, the history of the disintegration and disappearance of the French aristocracy. Proust himself defined his own novel by calling it the history of a vocation. As a boy, in his initiation to the Guermantes' Way at Combray, he examines his own literary aptitude. As a young man, while very much preoccupied with his jealousy over Albertine, he questions the reality of art and doubts intermittently whether the creation of art is to be preferred to the more direct involvement with living. At the end of the war, after his long absence from society, he returns to the new house of the prince and princesse de Guermantes, and has there such a compelling intimation on the reality of art and his particular talent as a writer that he leaves the gathering, determined to consecrate himself to art and adopt for himself the ways of living and creating he had observed in Bergotte, Vinteuil, and Elstir.

Among the manuscripts and notebooks recently discovered in the possession of Mme Mante-Proust, Proust's niece and heir, the collection of articles and essays, edited by M. Bernard de Fallois, under the title *Contre Sainte-Beuve*, serves as an admirable introduction to the aesthetics of Proust. Although the writing of this essay was begun in 1908, it is associated with conversations Proust had with his mother before her death in 1905. At the end of autumn 1908, Proust returned to Paris from a visit to Cabourg, in Normandy, where he had met the taxi driver Agostinelli, who served him first as a secretary and who was destined to play an important part in his personal life. He began the writing of an article for *Le Figaro* on Sainte-Beuve. Several months later, the article grew to three hundred pages. The title *Contre Sainte-Beuve* aptly represents Proust's hostility to the critical method of the critic. There are instances of personal memories in the essay, to be retranslated into the novel, portraits of friends and artists, notes on reading and art. Most of these pages, rewritten and transformed, will find their way ultimately into the novel.

In his many literary studies, Sainte-Beuve never separated the writer from his work. He believed that the literary art is explained by the man who did the writing, and he accumulated all the necessary factual information he could concerning the writer he was criticizing. He consulted correspondence, questioned friends and witnesses, read diaries and histories. Sainte-Beuve initiated the historical-biographical method which Taine was to refine by emphasizing *le milieu, le moment, la race* of whatever genius he was writing about.

A large part of Proust's novel is spent in denying the reliability and accuracy of such information. The self which a man shows in his daily habits, in his social intercourse, in his vices, is not for Proust the real self. It is a superficial self, a mask, formed by habit, by a routine of daily living, by the many constraints society imposes on all of us, by hypocrisy and cowardice and fear. Proust is concerned, as was Bergson, with the inner, real self, *le moi profond,* alive only in dreams and in very privileged states of consciousness.

Sainte-Beuve had scorned or neglected four nineteenth-century writers whom Proust was to place among the greatest of the creative spirits of France: Nerval, Baudelaire, Balzac, and Stendhal. Sainte-Beuve had personally known Henri Beyle (Stendhal) and had easy access to the kinds of information so important in the application of his critical method. Yet Sainte-Beuve judged all the novels of Stendhal as "frankly detestable." For Proust this was a blatant error in critical judgment, and for this and other reasons he castigated the biographical method of the critic.

It is not difficult to deduce from *Contre Sainte-Beuve* that Proust believes his real self to be diffused in the characters of his novel: in Swann and Bloch, in Elstir, Charlus, and Albertine, and recoverable there in a much more authentic sense than in his letters and in the mass of factual information we have concerning his life. He will claim that he is the real subject of his book, his essential rather than his autobiographical self. Such a novelist as Proust would like to compare himself to Orpheus, poet of mythology (it is noteworthy that in *Contre Sainte-Beuve*, Proust refers to himself as a poet), who is able to descend into hell in order to release Eurydice, the figure who represents for him lost beauty, felicity, and love. In the several magical passages when the past returns to Marcel in an overwhelmingly vivid way, bringing with it a sense of elation, he plays the role of Orpheus involuntarily, and the revelations made to him are of an esoteric and realistic nature. The source of these revelations is in himself, in the most profound reaches of the true self where the record and the occurrences of the past lie intact. The artist is the one who reaches this part of himself, even as Orpheus was able to reach the underworld.

Here again, the title of the novel, *A la recherche du temps perdu,* seems to indicate more than a search for lost time in any usual sense: it indicates a quest, a mission to recover something holy, something that, in the more simple terminology of Proust, is "real." The philosophers teach us —as does our daily life also, but without the ominous clarity of the philosophers—that the self is ceaselessly concerned with dying, that the self is absorbed with its future death. The novelist (especially Proust) has an opportunity, in the very practice of his art, to narrate, analyze, and project this absorption. Proust multiplies himself in his characters. He serves as a mirror as he reflects himself in Elstir and Léonie and Albertine. He lives his own death in the grandmother's, in Bergotte's and Swann's.

Although *Contre Sainte-Beuve* is principally a critical work, it contains many passages which appear to be first drafts of passages (and some of the most famous) in *A la recherche du temps perdu:* one on Venice, for example, which will appear in *La Fugitive;* the botanical passage on inversion which serves as prologue to *Sodome et Gomorrhe;* the grandmother's death scene in *Le Côté de Guermantes.* The close proximity between creative passages and critical theory in *Contre Sainte-Beuve* substantiates Proust's belief that every great creative artist bears in him a critic as well. The critic, perhaps somewhat disguised, is always present, always alert, in the creative artist.

If we accept Proust's own definition of his novel as the history of a vocation, we can read it as a work primarily orientated toward the discovery of an artist's vocation. *Ainsi toute ma vie jusqu'à ce jour aurait pu et n'aurait pas pu être résumée sous ce titre: Une vocation* (III, p. 899). Out of the vast repertory of characters in *A la recherche du temps perdu*, the creative artists, when they are functioning as artists, have the most stable personalities: Bergotte as the novelist, Vinteuil as the composer, and Elstir as the painter. However, the novices of art who, during the course of the narrative, approach the status and the vocation of artist, do not possess in the least the same stability of character: Swann, Bloch, Legrandin, Marcel himself. The artist has, in Proust's system of values, a fixed role in the universe, a fixed morality, which no other occupation provides, and which will not even be provided by having no occupation.

In each of the major instances, Proust depicts the artist as an isolated individual, isolated from the influence of other artists, and isolated in his personal life. No one of his artists appears as the leader of a group or a movement, or even as the disciple of a master or as the member of a school. Proust's own isolation during the years of his major artistic effort would seem to be the model for the creative artists in the novel. An ascetic life, of sacrifice, consecration, and concentration, is the basis for the vocation of an artist. The uniqueness of each artistic contribution supports Proust's belief in the necessary solitude of the artist, in his separation from disciples and masters and movements. The sole citizen of a unique country, the world he describes is so totally subjective that it cannot be rightfully attached to any preceding or subsequent art. Proust demands that the artist be faithful to art rather than to any given group of artists.

The life of a Proustian character is described episodically. We see him only at given moments in his lifetime,

and reacting to given circumstances. Proust does not provide a continuous development of any of his major characters. Among the creative artists, the character and the
life of Vinteuil, whom we see only briefly and intermittently, are given more specific treatment than those of Elstir
and Bergotte. He is shown as a self-sacrificing figure of
great pathos. The poverty of his life, his humility, his deep
love for a daughter who shows him no love and no respect,
are the elements of a tragic figure. The sacrifices he makes
for his daughter are related to those he makes for his music. The man and the artist seem to be one, and the posthumous glory, which crowns a life of failure, unites the
daughter and the work. The indecipherable manuscripts
are exhumed and copied and given to the world by the
composer's daughter and her friend who, in this act of
dedication, compensate to a degree for the suffering they
had inflicted on the man when he was alive.

Vinteuil's inner life, formed by his suffering and his
sensibility, is for Proust the subject matter of his art. Art
is the resurrection of the most obscure dramas of a man's
life, the resurrection of themes and visions, of sacrifices
and privations which cannot be articulated. That is why
the artist is defined by Proust as "the citizen of an unknown
country" (le citoyen d'une patrie inconnue. III, p. 257).
Each time a major artist comes into the world, the world
is re-created. Each major work of art will appear familiar
because it is formed out of the substance of a man: his
failures, his dreams, his suffering. But it is at the same
time totally unique, totally unlike every other work of art.
A work of art, if it has significance, is that which only one
artist could create.

Vinteuil is Proust in many ways: in his life in general,
his aloofness, his view of art as the summation of his life
as well as the communication and transcendence of his
life. Whatever joy Vinteuil knew as a man, it was certainly
the joy derived by creating an art into which he was able
to put so much of his feeling and suffering and understanding.

Proust in his treatment of the composer Vinteuil and of

the painter Elstir (whose work is more fully analyzed than
that of Vinteuil, although no element in it is used so persistently as the "little phrase" of the sonata) looks upon a
major work of art as a new beginning, as a form in itself
not dependent on previous forms or theories. The individuality and even the originality of the artist are emphasized in the novel as making a unique contribution, a
world in itself which, once again, explains the world.

Ingeniously the critics have traced elements in many
musical compositions that may well have inspired the
sonata of Vinteuil. Proust himself has listed some in a dedi-
catory note to Jacques de Lacretelle: Saint-Saëns, Wagner,
Franck, Fauré, and even indicated the specific works he
had in mind. The critics also have discovered many possible models for the paintings of Elstir partially described in
the novel: Renoir, Manet, Monet, Degas, Whistler. Yet in
terms of the novel itself, there is no need for concern with
the antecedents of Vinteuil or with those of Elstir. This
absence of antecedents is doubtless explained by Proust's
theory of art, so minutely explored and explained in *Le
Temps retrouvé*.

To indicate all that Proust owes to symbolism and impressionism would be equivalent to reviewing most of the
tenets and dogmas of those two schools. The influences
and the examples are there, on almost every page of the
novel. Proust's art, however, cannot be described or inter-
preted by reference to these influences. His art is the result of the way in which he used these influences, the way
in which he adapted them by his own sensibility to his
own purposes. This would be quite comparable to the
manner in which Elstir uses the impressionists (although
there is little reference to them) and the manner in which
Vinteuil uses Wagner and César Franck.

Impressionism denies the exterior form of objects, their
precise contours and shapes. It transcribes of objects only
what has remained in the memory of the artist. The form
of reality in a man's memory and his subconscious is different from reality as perceived by the senses. Proust's aesthetics start here, with this doctrine concerning the "inner"

nature of reality. Rodin, mentioned once in Proust's novel, used to say that the resemblance an artist should try to catch is the resemblance of the soul. This resemblance, perceived by the memory, is a resemblance in which all clear demarcations, contours, and forms are erased. Before Rodin and Proust, before the symbolists of 1880, Charles Baudelaire, in his brilliant article on *L'Art Mnémonique,* claimed that art is the work of memory. In *Du Côté de chez Swann* we read that reality is formed in the memory: *la réalité ne se forme que dans la mémoire* (I, p. 184). When we look at an object in nature, our first perception of that object is a correction of it, because it can only be a partial, an imperfect vision. Later, when that object is re-called, our memory adds elements to it, elements that we had literally not seen, or seen imperfectly, in our initial experience.

In the final chapter of the work, the matinée at the princesse de Guermantes, Marcel recovers his faith in art. A series of sensory experiences that occur in rapid succession, form together such a powerful revelation and give him such a profound happiness, that he accepts the idea of a literary vocation. With the end of the chapter, we are made to realize that he is going to begin the writing of the book we have just finished reading. The sensory experiences are a specific part of the novel's narrative, and they initiate, at the same time, considerations of an aesthetic order which illuminate both the narrative and the reasons why the narrative was written. The novel and the aesthetics of the novel are perfectly fused in these ultimate pages.

As he enters the courtyard of the prince de Guermantes, he steps back abruptly to avoid a car, and strikes his foot against some uneven flagstones (*les pavés assez mal équar-ris.* III, p. 866). A sudden wave of happiness engulfs him, the same happiness which had accompanied previous experiences with Vinteuil's music, the trees of Balbec, the steeples of Martinville, and the taste of the madeleine cake. In a few minutes he realizes that, thanks to the uneven flagstones part of the past is returning to him: it was in Venice that he had once stood on two uneven flagstones

of the baptistery of Saint Mark's. He imagines himself
bathed in cool azure light.

He goes into the residence of the Guermantes and waits
in the library until the music is over. He hears a servant
strike a spoon against a plate. This recalls the sound of a
hammer on a train wheel he had once heard at Combray.
The third experience, which follows fast on the first two,
is one which involves the sense of touch. After drinking
from a glass of orangeade, he wipes his mouth with a stiff
starched napkin. This sensation is similar to one he had on
his first night at Balbec when, after washing, he tried to
wipe his face with an overstarched towel. Another vision of
blue comes back to him, the sea at Balbec spread out like
the blue-green tail of a peacock.

Thus in the new hôtel des Guermantes, three experiences of his past, associated with Venice, Combray, and
Balbec, having no connection with one another, return to
him with an overpowering sense of joy. From the intensity
of these fortuitous experiences, Marcel is able to define the
function of the artist. He sees this function as the willful,
effective communication of such moments of ecstasy with
their intimations of the past. As he relives them, he moves
outside of time. He is not in the past—now over—or in the
present, because he is totally occupied by the past. The
duration of this felicity is brief in each case, but it provides him with a heightened consciousness of life.

This accumulation of involuntary memories which occur
to Marcel in the courtyard and the library of the Guermantes reveals much more than the past. It reveals to him
the pure essence of time, and the pure essence of eternity
which for him is the depth of time visible through and
beyond the appearances of each day in the present.

But there is no essence unless there is something to reveal it. The shock of these sensory experiences make Marcel realize that there is a work to be undertaken, for which
he is now ready. . . . *Je remarquais qu'il y aurait là, dans
l'oeuvre d'art que je me sentais prêt déjà . . . à entre-
prendre . . .* (III, p. 870).

Several thoughts about art and the artist come to him

with an undeniable persuasiveness. He realizes that ordinary perception is of no value in itself for an artist. Perception becomes useful only when selectively preserved by memory. Only when resurrected out of his memory will it appear in its intrinsic beauty, its full reality. This experience puts him into contact with a fragment of time in its pure state (*un peu de temps à l'état pur.* III, p. 872). As exhilaration briefly obliterates the immediate setting—the Guermantes' library, in this case—Marcel learns that the intelligence is merely the arranger of things, that creative thinking is far different from ordinary thinking and ordinary perception.

A work of art is the life of the artist. Marcel has just made the momentous discovery that a record of this life resides in the deepest part of himself: a record he calls *un livre intérieur* (III, p. 879). And he is the only one able to read this book, or to decipher it. Although Mallarmé is not named in this passage, one thinks instinctively of his *grimoire* (in the poem *Prose pour des Esseintes*), the conjuror's book of magical recipes, of apparitions that can rise out of a secret ordering of words. For ten pages in the text (pp. 880–90) the word "book," *Livre,* punctuated as if it were a proper noun as Mallarmé had once honored it, dominates the meditation. According to this conception of Proust, the material of the work of art is intact at all times. The labor of the artist is a painful deciphering, a difficult transcription into words of what has been recorded in his psyche. *Ce livre, le plus pénible de tous à déchiffrer* (III, p. 880).

Marcel learns, as a corollary of this principal lesson, that the artist is not free to choose the subject matter of his art. The art he creates is predestined by his life and his character. What is imperative in the case of the authentic artist is the need to pass beyond the superficial daily self, the self expressed to all who enter his life, and to discover the true self which subsumes the past. The experience Marcel undergoes in the Guermantes' library ends as he takes a volume down from the shelf, in an almost desultory manner. It is George Sand's novel, *François le Champi,*

bound in red, from which his mother had read to him on
that distant evening when his parents yielded to the will
of a sick, oversensitive child. With the familiar title, the
sentimental experience returns and with it the feelings
about the prestige of literature, the sense that a life of
letters was a privilege which had so deeply affected Marcel even as a youth.

During that distant hour of reading and maternal attentiveness, the boy Marcel did not realize all the elements it
contained. Not until his maturity, at the moment in the
Guermantes' library, with his hand touching the volume of
George Sand, is the fullness of that remote hour revealed.
He knows now that an hour is not merely a quantity of
time. In order to describe what an hour is, Proust creates
one of his finest metaphors: an hour, he says, is a vase
filled with perfumes, sounds, designs, and climates. *Une
heure n'est pas qu'une heure, c'est un vase rempli de
parfums, de sons, de projets et de climats* (III, p. 889).
This metaphor of a vase is evocative of an Aladdin's lamp
from which anything can emerge. It is a figure of speech
designating the recesses of memory which are not special
but which contain, like microfilm, all the recordings of
reality. Memory is spaceless: it is a realm over which time,
in its conventional form, has no dominion.

The work exists in order to reveal the secret of certain
moments of intense happiness. Such moments in Proust's
novel would be those associated with the steeples of Martinville, the taste of a madeleine, a flowering hawthorn
hedge, the two uneven flagstones. The work, then, is the
invention of a language capable of describing such moments. It represents, therefore, a break with the ordinary
daily world, with what is usually designated as reality.
In addition to defining his own aesthetics, Proust attacks
"realism" in literature and calls "reality" that experience
which is common to everyone's life. Art has perhaps very
little to do with the appearance of things. Real life, Proust
writes, is literature: *La vraie vie . . . c'est la littérature*
(III, p. 895).

The future book, the substance of art, is something

totally hidden from the words of daily speech and the occurrences of daily life with which much of our time is spent in disguising our real sentimental life, in misleading those who watch and listen to us, and in deceiving ourselves. Proust knows that the experiences which are in his memory and which form the chapters of his "inner book" are in nowise exceptional or extraordinary. They are the recognizable banal experiences of most men. The work that lies ahead for him, the writing of his book, will bring about the resurrection of suffering and jealousy and ambition. His life will be recast in Swann's love for Odette, in Marcel's love for Gilberte, in Saint-Loup's love for Rachel. His own preoccupations with social life will be relived in Legrandin and Bloch. His worry over a literary vocation will be re-enacted in the pages on Vinteuil and Elstir, in Bergotte's death scene, in the suffering of La Berma at the end of the novel.

Our habits of life from day to day are characterized by an ignorance of life, by the bluntness of our vision and sensibility, by our fragmentary knowledge and experience. To remedy this ignorance and incompleteness, we create illusion after illusion about our loves, our work, our social relations. Proust looks upon a great work of art precisely as that unity which destroys the illusions forming our faulty comprehension of life. Art is, for Proust, the solution of almost every human problem.

The penetration of his vision isolates the artist from the world, cuts him off from ordinary reality. Proust therefore calls the artist's work a closed world. Marcel has already said this in *Le Côté de Guermantes*, in the scene at Doncières when he thinks of the paintings of Elstir. The painter's work is a closed realm, with impassable barriers: *Son oeuvre était comme un royaume clos, aux frontières infranchissables* (II, p. 125). And even earlier in the novel, in *Du Côté de chez Swann*, Swann had expressed the same thought as he listened to Vinteuil's sonata and found it to be a world closed off from everything else (*ce monde fermé à tout le reste.* I, p. 352), comparable to the beginning of Creation.

The writings of Bergotte, the novelist in the novel, are not analyzed or characterized to any large degree. But some of the remarks about the man himself and his relationship to art and to life seem to have an important place in the scheme of Proustian aesthetics. There is not very much nobility about the man Bergotte. Limited in wit, in scholarship, in social relationships, he has one characteristic which enables him to become a successful writer. He has a mirrorlike "negative capability," in Keats' phrase, (*le génie consistant dans le pouvoir réfléchissant.* I, p. 555), which reflects all of his life and all the events which have taken place around his life. It is of no consequence that this life of the writer, as Proust says, is mediocre and commonplace. Proust, of course, will illustrate this principle in his own novel, where most of the scenes are filled with idlers, superficial and even vicious characters, with characters of impaired moral integrity. The milieu, the world described by the novelist, is not important. What is important is the reflective power of the novelist, his ultimate value as mirror. If this concept of the aesthetic system is valid, then considerations of the irrelevance or the undesirability of "immoral" passages have no basis. Morality would be faithfulness to a vision of human elements as they are seen, a point of view, rather than to the reality behind the actions and characters described.

Proust's power of reflection is visible from the very beginning of the book. His memories of childhood, where so much is reflected that we do not normally associate with a child, have an impact on the reader of original, fully realized poetry. Combray's reality and dreams are fused with the two familiar walks, the two ways of Marcel's childhood. Swann's Way (or Méséglise) is the walk beside the hawthorn of Tansonville, but it is also, without his fully realizing it at first, the way to his love for Gilberte, his friendship for Bloch, his admiration for Bergotte. Guermantes' Way leads past the Vivonne with its water lilies, but it also leads to Marcel's future friendship with Robert de Saint-Loup, to his perplexing encounters with the baron de Charlus, to his invitation to a soirée at the princesse de Guermantes.

After the two ways are described—literally and symbolically—in the first three books, the central drama, Marcel's love for Albertine, is prefigured in the fourth, and will
occupy a large part of volumes five and six. Not until the
seventh and final volume, do we fully realize that the love
story of Marcel and Albertine, and all the other related
and subsidiary stories of the novel, are pretexts for the
fundamental drama of the work, a drama which will give
to the protagonist his greatest sense of decisiveness and of
his destiny, and which will give to his novel, before it is
written, the fundamental principles of his art. It is his
search for what is real. This search begins, as it does with
everyone, with memories of childhood, with efforts—deliberate and fortuitous—to recall what was real in childhood. From that moment on, all that Marcel experiences
and observes: friendship, social ambition and curiosity,
love and the suffering of love, examples of virtue and
forms of vice, the beauty of nature and the beauty of art,
will be related, subtly at times and obviously at others, to
his search for what is real. From the richly orchestrated
final pages of the novel, we learn that this search is the
most abiding of all the protagonist's interests, loves, and
sufferings. We learn that it surpasses his attraction to the
duchesse de Guermantes whom he loved at a distance when
he was a boy. It goes beyond his fascination with Charlus'
enigmatic and tragic character. More deeply rooted than
his appreciation for the paintings of Elstir, it is stronger
than his love for Albertine, and outlives his friendship for
Robert de Saint-Loup, the yellow-crested bird in the Guermantes' garden.

There is no message in Proust's novel, no message in
the usual sense. He was opposed, on theoretical grounds, to
a moralizing novel. But this search for the real, which
grows into the dominant motif by the end of the novel, may
well remain with the reader long after the book has been
finished. And it may be that the search which we have
followed will pass over into our own search for what has
meaning and value in our own experience.

The great moments in novels have the power, as we

attempted to describe in the opening chapter of this study, to bring about two creations for the reader: first, the creation of a world not his own—Combray, Balbec, the Paris of Balzac, the English moorlands called Wuthering Heights, the Faubourg Saint-Germain, the Alexandria of Lawrence Durrell, Graham Greene's Brighton Rock; then there is a second creation, actually a re-creation, that of the reader's own world. The reading of a great novel should throw into a new and unexpected relief the reader's own world and endow it with a perspective and form and universality it did not possess before. The reader will understand more profoundly about himself and his world what he had understood imperfectly or obscurely heretofore.

The art of Marcel Proust, because of his aesthetics as well as of his temperament, slows down all action in his narrative. He forces the reader to concentrate for a long time on a fact or on an action, as it is dilated and enlarged and explored in every possible way. We are never allowed to forget that all the acts, all the happenings in the novel are conceived of in the past. The conception of the novel is retrospective. The human body is not as frequently described in its active state, engaged in action, as it is as the vehicle of sensations and memories. The important moments in the narrative become extended moments because they are communions, experiences of total concentration: when Marcel looks at a hawthorn hedge, or the way a French nobleman wears his monocle, or the way in which La Berma recites a *tirade* from *Phèdre*.

These prolonged communions explain why all elements in Proust's novel appear abnormally enlarged, distended, even distorted. These nearly monstrous effects occur in the novel, in somewhat the same way that monsters and chimeras appear in the ornamentation of the Gothic cathedrals. In the graphic art of a Breughel and a Goya, and in the literary art of a Balzac and a Proust, a character is so overdeveloped that it becomes its own caricature, as if the painter or novelist had indulged a sadistic impulse.

But Proust, despite the extended moments of communion never exhausts the mysteriousness of beings and objects.

An individual human life is so bound up with the lives of
the men of his time, and with the very existence of the
world, that there is no end to his mystery, no clue to his
absolute reality. Analogy is the only principle by which
we begin to understand the mystery of human life. At the
very beginning of the novel, on one of the early pages of
*Du Côté de chez Swann,* the narrator evoked a memory of
his childhood when, in tante Léonie's bedroom he prepared for her a cup of linden tea. He describes the dried
leaves and flowers which he places in boiling water and
meditates on the many dramatic changes they undergo.
The drying of the flowers and leaves, the little bag sold by
the pharmacist into which they are placed, the boiling
water into which an appropriate amount of leaves and
flowers is placed, the infusion and finally the taste on the
tongue of the drinker. It is a long distance covered, a long
story of metamorphosis (quite comparable to the evolution
and change in a human character) beginning with the real
tree growing on the street which leads to the railroad station at Combray (*de vrais tilleuls, comme ceux que je
voyais avenue de la Gare*), to the taste of the hot linden tea
which tante Léonie drinks in her bedroom. (I, p. 51.)

Marcel Proust's novel is made up of just such extensive
adventures in experience as that of the taste of linden tea.
A world can rise up from a simple object, a single sensation.
In the careful construction of his work, the entire novel is
the necessary, indispensable background for the final scene,
at the matinée of the princesse de Guermantes.

# III. CONCLUSION

## 18.  The esoteric in Proust: symbol and myth

Proust's novel is avowedly an assertion concerned with
himself and for himself, the record of his understanding of
self and of the world. He implies that to make and complete this record was necessary in order to achieve the
satisfaction of self-knowledge and accomplishment. In this,
it was Proust's hope, inherent in the art of every novelist,
to communicate with successive generations of readers.
Guided somewhat by the aesthetics of John Ruskin, Proust
believed in the inexhaustible fecundity of art. The interpretation of any work of art changes and increases with
each generation that considers it. Ruskin's study of the
cathedral of Amiens revealed new illuminations on the
intricacies of Gothic architecture and mediaeval symbolism. For Proust, as for Ruskin, a work of art first represents a triumph over time, in the sense that it is an object
removed from the vicissitudes of time (although Proust
acknowledges the destructive work of time even on art),
and then represents a very subtle utilization of time. The
purpose of this final chapter is to point out some of the
ways in which time has been utilized in clarifying the
meaning and the art of A la recherche du temps perdu,
the ways in which we now understand more deeply Proust's
novel.

Roman emperors collected in their villas, as did popes
in the Vatican, statues of ancient Greece. Art historians
and philosophers through the centuries have written on
the laws that govern and explain the beauty of Greek art.
Today, museums throughout the world house collections

of paintings which already represent an age, and which have, in the perspective of time, become more and more significant. Proust came at the end of a period in Europe, in France in particular, when art had been turned into a veritable religion. "Art for art's sake" (*l'art pour l'art*), a doctrine Flaubert promoted and developed, Proust inherited and in a sense sacrificed his life to, in his determination to transform it into art. His illness and forced claustration served him in this determination. During the last years of his life, he lived only for the construction of this work, and incorporated in it everything from his life, his reading, his thoughts. Time lost is time not caught and immortalized by art. When the artist succeeds, he creates an object outside ordinary time and space.

When Marcel eats the madeleine cake in *Du Côté de chez Swann,* when he wipes his mouth with the napkin in the library of the prince de Guermantes in *Le Temps retrouvé,* time is abolished, because two widely separated moments of his life are juxtaposed. This operation of a sensory experience is comparable to the function of a metaphor which brings together two objects that have no relationship in ordinary life: the waiters, for example, in the restaurant of Rivebelle, compared, in their agility and flight, to angels. Much of the aesthetics of Proust is founded on these two laws: the power of a sensory experience to bring back the past, and the function of a metaphor to explain the unknown by the known. Art is not, therefore, a distraction or a diversion. It is for Proust, as for Baudelaire, responsible for the clarification and application of the theory, an instrument of research, a way by which discoveries are made concerning the meaning of the world, of life, of the exterior life of man, and the inner reality of his subconscious. Saint-Simon, with whom Proust has been so often compared, is exclusively a chronicler. And La Rochefoucauld, another model, is exclusively a moralist. In comparison to these writers, Proust is the greater for the scope of his poetry, for the epic import of some of the great passages, and for the power of his thought in which another universe is seen, or half-seen, to exist behind the familiar lineaments of whatever world he describes. Whereas the chronicler Saint-Simon and the moralist La Rochefoucauld impose rigid limitations on their writing, Proust expands his search (his *recherche*) to include the search for the eternal in man.

Proust would be the first to acknowledge that such a search is never over, that it is always interrupted by death. In this sense his work is incomplete, although his novel was finished before his death. But if he had lived longer, he would have continued to correct and enlarge his manuscript. No work of art is ever complete except in a relative sense, and Proust's novel, as well as the cathedral of Amiens and a Beethoven quartet, testify both to the greatness of man's creative power and to his impotency in translating his vision and his understanding. It would almost seem that the artist is punished for looking back at the life lived and the world seen, as Orpheus was punished when he looked back at Eurydice.

In the final scene of the novel, with the concert over, Marcel is confronted by the spectacle of time, manifested in the physical changes it has wrought on the many people he has known. As he describes this spectacle—the final experience, the final action—he thinks constantly of the work he wants to compose. The spectacle of time he sees and the urgency he feels to begin work on the novel are fused with the conviction that every great work of art destroys a few more of the illusions that contribute to our ignorance of life. He knows that such a creation as he contemplates involves suffering and the resurrection of sorrows. He will have to relive his love for his grandmother and his love for Albertine, but in doing this, he will acquire a deeper understanding. Proust's philosophy, a form of idealism, requires a constant resurrection of the past and a will to pierce what is beyond the immediate range of vision. This is demonstrated in the love stories of Swann, Marcel and Charlus, where reality is always being obliterated by the *idea*.

The use of metaphor is prevalent throughout the novel, but Proust is seldom satisfied with the creation of a mere metaphor, a familiar image juxtaposed with an unfamiliar in order to explain it. In this use of images, he tries to move beyond the first immediate and simple explanation (the comparison of Charlus to a bee, for example, in the prelude scene of *Sodome et Gomorrhe*), to a more far-reaching philosophical or anthropological explanation (Charlus' inversion, explained by inherited ancestral traits). This is the practice of symbolism when metaphor is used to designate a significant experience. According to a major tenet of symbolism, not only nineteenth-century French *symbolisme*, but symbolism of all cultures and epochs, art is able to suggest the essence behind the object.

Proust uses literary symbolism to capture in words the purity of a soul which has become clouded and darkened by the daily contacts with matter and deceit and passion. When Marcel, in the Guermantes library, at the end of the novel, wipes his mouth with a napkin, the vision he has of Balbec is so sumptuous and magical that he thinks of *The Arabian Nights*. That moment of vision is Marcel's escape from the mundanity of the present, and the force behind the power of art, based on metaphor and symbolism, by which the present is transformed and explained.

Through the progress of the narrative, Marcel learns, for example, that the most beautiful expression of Swann's love for Odette is a little phrase in a sonata of Vinteuil. The musical phrase has the purity of meaning which the real experience can never have. Of all the arts, music is the only one that does not need to be translated into concepts. The dramatic art of La Berma, the literary art of Bergotte, and even the paintings of Elstir, do not have the purity of Vinteuil's little phrase. As Swann listens to that phrase, it reminds him of his own mortality, and recalls his love for Odette. Elstir teaches Marcel that a painting is not a reproduction of nature, but the impression nature leaves on the artist. Elstir suppresses all demarcations in his paintings in order to give the effect of unity, of a fusion between the various elements of a picture. In this gift of unity, the artist relies on his memory and painting, thereby, a remembered image far more real than the actual scene.

Proust realizes that music, through sound, and painting, through color and form, give a direct sensory expression which literature cannot give. And music is the purest of the three, because it does not depend upon a reproduction of familiar images. Literary art, in order to reach anything comparable to the sensory power of music and painting, has to utilize the symbols and myths of mankind which are bonds between man's daily life and the obscure regions of his soul. The literary artist for Proust is the man who establishes these correspondences. Baudelaire and Rimbaud, before Proust, had taught the doctrine of the interrelationship between our senses: of the power a sound has, for example, to suggest color. And Marcel, when he describes the resonance that certain names have for him, merely reiterates this familiar symbolist principle. In the library scene, as Marcel waits for the concert to end, he acknowledges that the eating of the madeleine in his own life, which had brought back to him all of Combray, is comparable to Chateaubriand's experience, related in *Mémoires d'outre-tombe*, where the singing of a thrush brings back the image of the Breton landscape of his childhood. In this passage (III, pp. 919–20), Marcel associates himself with Chateaubriand, Nerval, and Baudelaire, in his understanding and use of a metaphor. He sees in the greatness of a metaphor the power to give back to the human spirit its primitive strength by forcing it to resume contact with the world. The simple act of eating a madeleine gives Marcel the occasion for an extraordinary spiritual experience.

Myth is the narrative extension of symbol. The word *mythologique* is frequently used by Proust, but there are no explicit doctrinal passages in *A la recherche du temps perdu* on myth as there are on the metaphor. But the use, the application of myth is implied over and over again, and always in the explanation of character and experience as they reveal resemblances with mankind's most distant and most shadowy stories.

Mlle Brée, in her brilliant study of Proust, and Mrs.

Vance, in her very pertinent article (published in *The French Review*), have called attention to the bird imagery in Proust, to the Guermantes family being designated as a race of birds.

Certain of Oriane's facial features are described from the beginning of the novel in ornithological terms. The comparisons seem to be perfectly natural, and it is only through Proust's repetitive insistence, and the association of imagery in Oriane's characterization, that one realizes that the descriptive comparison has been raised to the level of myth.

Both consciously and unconsciously, Proust is always trying to discover the esoteric meaning in everything. His major effort to recover the past, to join with the past, is in reality a search for the myth of the past, that is, the myth of time with the infinite number of resonances which time reveals when recaptured. In the gratuitous resurrections of the past (more than in the conscious remembering of the past) and in the creations fashioned by dreams, man effects a stay against the disillusionments of his life. By discovering the essence which lies beneath the appearance, the type behind the individual, the law which invisibly controls and explains the phenomenon, man partakes of the permanent.

Though Marcel remains the protagonist throughout the novel, two characters in particular assume important central positions: Oriane, duchesse de Guermantes, and Charles Swann. Both characters assume almost mythic proportions. Oriane is representative of the Guermantes family. Swann, Oriane's best friend, is the leading figure of the other world of the bourgeoisie, faintly kinglike. His name recalls Jupiter's incarnation in a swan, and his illness recalls the myth of the Fisher King. He is perpetuated in his daughter Gilberte (who marries a Guermantes), and in his granddaughter, Mlle de Saint-Loup (whose features represent both worlds, the Guermantes' and Swann's).

Oriane appears with characteristically mythical traits in six scenes: two brief preparatory episodes; two major scenes; and two epilogue scenes.

(1) In *Du Côté de chez Swann,* the boy Marcel is told he will see the duchesse, whom he longs to see because of her mysterious prestige, in the church of Saint-Hilaire at the nuptial mass of Dr. Percepied's daughter. He describes her: a blond lady, with a huge nose, reddish complexion, blue piercing eyes, wearing a mauve scarf of shiny smooth silk. Marcel knows she is the descendant of Geneviève de Brabant, but he is disappointed in her appearance. His description of her—her hair, complexion, nose, eyes, and a smooth metallic-looking breast are birdlike and will always dominate future descriptions of Oriane. At one moment in the Combray church, her glance falls on Marcel—and he falls headlong in love with her (I, p. 174).

(2) At the beginning of *Le Côté de Guermantes,* when Marcel's family occupies a wing of the Guermantes' Paris house, he spies on Oriane and thinks of her at Combray where her presence was like a swan on the Vivonne (a god changed into a swan) or a weeping willow on the banks of the Vivonne (a nymph turned into a willow tree). The swan and the willow have to submit to the laws of nature, as the duchesse has to submit to laws governing the human race. When she is in front of her mirror, arranging her veil and dress, she prepares for the part of a woman, and forces herself to forget her mythological greatness (*dans l'oubli mythologique de sa grandeur native.* II, p. 29). Marcel reiterates this comparison of Oriane with the divine swan who forgets he is a god (*en cygne, sans se souvenir qu'il est un dieu.* II, p. 29).

(3) The first major scene is at the Opéra, the evening of a gala performance, where an aquariumlike atmosphere is described by Marcel as he watches La Berma in a scene from *Phèdre* and the loge (*baignoire*) of the princesse de Guermantes. After the *Phèdre* scene, with the beginning of the second part of the program, the duchesse de Guermantes appears in the loge of her cousin and comes to sit in the front row. Dressed in white muslin, she is more simply attired than the princesse. One aigrette is in her hair, and this especially gives her a birdlike appearance. Her nose is arched like the beak of a bird, and she holds a

fan of swan's feathers. Her corsage glitters with sequins
and fits closely over her breast. The dress of the princesse
is completely white and she gives the appearance of a bird
of paradise. But Oriane's dress, because of the corsage, is
more shimmering and variegated, and she resembles, for
Marcel, Juno's peacock. The two cousins, in their ornithological elegance, seem to Marcel like a pantheon who,
from their high loge, contemplate the spectacle of humans
below them in the orchestra (*l'assemblée des Dieux en
train de contempler le spectacle des hommes.* II, p. 58).
It is an apotheosis for Marcel, and he feels that the snow-
like beauty of the two women must be the manifestation
of their inner life. At one moment, although she hardly
knows him, Oriane makes a friendly gesture to Marcel. It
is the second recognition, which bewilders him, and he
uses almost the same terms he had previously, for the
smile in the Combray church scene, when he compares
her smile in the Opéra to a dazzling blue rainfall: *l'averse
étincelante et céleste de son sourire* (II, p. 58).

He falls more deeply in love with her than ever, and
we realize it is because of her mystery and inaccessibility.
He is entranced with the unknown, and, as he thinks of
Oriane, he never fails to note her characteristics: her nose
like a bird's beak, her red cheeks framed by the piercing
eyes of an Egyptian goddess . . . *un nez en bec d'oiseau
le long d'une joue rouge, barrée d'un oeil perçant, comme
quelque divinité égyptienne* (II, p. 62). When she appears
wrapped in furs, he thinks of a vulture whose thick plumage is comparable to a kind of fur . . . *certains vautours
dont le plumage épais, uni, fauve et doux, a l'air d'une
sorte de pelage* (II, p. 62). This naming of a special type
of bird, a vulture, marks the beginning of a change in the
attitude of the protagonist toward Oriane. Earlier, before
he had approached her, he thought of her as a *mésange*
(tomtit), but the evolution of her character moves toward
a fiercer type of bird, a bird of prey. She is beginning to
manifest the first signs of hardness and cruelty. Is she
capable of love or friendship? The answer by the end of
the novel is: she is not.

(4) The next to last chapter of *Le Côté de Guermantes* is the dinner party chez le duc and la duchesse de Guermantes where Marcel is received as a favored friend, and at which point his feelings for Oriane have changed from adoration to an almost objective curiosity. He is fascinated by her appearance, her wit, her role of hostess, and, implicitly, her role of mythical creature. Her physical traits are described as typical of the Guermantes: the very special pink-rose complexion which deepens at times to a violet hue, the gold hair that is soft and fine, the suppleness of her movements, as stylized as the flight of a swallow, the raucous voice (*une voix rauque*) which sixteenth-century genealogists traced to the fabulous origin (*l'origine fabuleuse.* II, p. 439). The mythological impregnation of a nymph by a divine Bird has been used to explain the origin of the Guermantes family (*pour origine la fécondation mythologique d'une nymphe par un divin Oiseau.* II, p. 439). The family, in its aristocratic bearing, has been preserved through the centuries by the administrations of some invisible genie. The harsher, more impregnable character of Oriane, gradually emerges. There is something virginal and warlike about her, something of the huntress Diana in the Guermantes' forests, as well as the invincible and eternal bird of prey.

(5) The final passage of *Le Côté de Guermantes,* briefer than the long dinner scene, is the deeply significant episode of the "red slippers of the duchesse," in which Oriane demonstrates the coldness of her character in her lack of feeling over Swann's pitiful announcement of his imminent death. She will not accept the veracity of this news because it conflicts with her dinner engagement. Her radiant appearance seems related to the mortal cruelty of her action: a red satin dress, hemmed with shining stones, a red tulle scarf, and, at the end of the scene, the red shoes her husband insists she wear. This dominant color, with its overtones in the rouge shades of her face, may well be the symbolic premonition of Swann's death, the death agony of the swan presided over by the vulture. As the duc waits for his wife to come downstairs, he speaks of the ancestors

of the Guermantes, the kings of the island of Cyprus, the Lusignans, and indicates that Oriane refuses to speak of them. One remembers that Mélusine, the fairy-dragon, is associated with the end of the Lusignan family. At the beginning of *Le Côté de Guermantes,* we learned that the Lusignans became extinct on the day the fairy Mélusine disappeared (*cette famille de Lusignan qui devait s'éteindre le jour où disparaîtrait la fée Mélusine.* II, p. 11). Oriane is quite literally the contemporary Mélusine, whose death will mean the extinction of the Guermantes.

Especially in the scene of the "red slippers," Oriane's magical fairylike qualities, for Marcel, completely disappear. Stripped of the miraculous attributes he had once given her, she now appears as a selfish and doubtless ruthless woman. Each salon scene is a kind of test for Marcel in which he has to adjust to some new revelation, some new disillusionment. *Les souliers rouges de la duchesse* represents one of his most disillusioning experiences. Oriane, by her speech and action, denies her friendship for Swann, just as later Gilberte is to deny her blood relationship with Swann. This man, with the most mythological name in the novel, exists as a mysterious bond between the duchesse, his best friend, the woman whose death (which does not occur in the narrative) will bring about the extinction of the Guermantes, and his daughter, Gilberte, whom he fervently wants to present to Oriane. His death occurs before this meeting comes about. When Gilberte marries Robert de Saint-Loup, she becomes heir to the title of duchesse de Guermantes. Mysteriously the cycle is completed. Oriane is the second Mélusine (but Mélusine was also used to describe the girl Gilberte as she leaned her head against her father's shoulder), and Oriane in her cruelty is the female swan who devours her prey. The relationship between Oriane and Swann is one of spirit and character and mythological alliance. Oriane's coldness and sterility are reflected in Swann's literary sterility. Swann's curved nose (*nez busqué*) is matched by Oriane's bird of prey's beak (*bec d'oiseau de proie*). If the color of their eyes is different, there is there too, a possible mythological explanation: Swann's eyes are green, the color of the green waters of the Vivonne in Combray; and Oriane's eyes are blue, the same blue in the stained glass windows of the church of Saint-Hilaire in Combray. These are the two ways, Swann's and Guermantes', and they are destined to merge, to fuse one with the other at the end of the cycle, with the appearance of Mlle de Saint-Loup, the daughter of a swan and of a Mélusine.

(6) In the *danse macabre* scene of *Le Temps retrouvé*, in the salon of the new princesse de Guermantes, Mme Verdurin, Oriane appears for the last time in the novel, in company with all the surviving characters, and once again her dress is minutely described. Her body gives the impression of emerging from "wings" of black lace. It is the final reference to a bird: *ce corps saumoné émergeant à peine de ses ailerons de dentelle noire* (III, p. 927). Because of the shining jewel effect of her dress, she is compared to a sacred fish (*vieux poisson sacré, chargé de pierreries.* III, p. 927) and still incarnates for Marcel the observer, the protective genie of the family. She greets Marcel as her oldest friend: *"Ah! quelle joie de vous voir, vous mon plus vieil ami"* (III, p. 927). During their conversation, Marcel refers to the red slippers. Flattered by his memory, she replies that she thought they were gold shoes. *Je croyais que c'était des souliers d'or* (III, p. 1011). In two other passages of the scene, Marcel contrasts the fabulous origins, the mythology of the Guermantes, with their banal social life of the twentieth century (*origines presque fabuleuses, charmante mythologie de relations devenues si banales ensuite.* III, p. 974). His life has been made more poetic by knowing the Guermantes who first represented for him a mysterious keen-eyed, roseate-colored, bird-beaked, unapproachable race—whom he could consult on the choice of a dress for Albertine—and who finally became his useful friends (*la race mystérieuse aux yeux perçants, au bec d'oiseau, la race rose, dorée, inapprochable . . . [les] plus serviables de mes amis.* III, p. 976).

At Marcel's first visit to Balbec (*A l'ombre des jeunes*

*filles en fleurs*), when first introduced to Mme de Ville-parisis, Robert de Saint-Loup and Charlus, he analyzes in one very succinct phrase the excitement and bewilderment he experiences at such encounters. He feels himself surrounded by monsters and gods. *Tout entouré de monstres et de dieux . . .* (I, p. 730). The divine and the monstrous are elements in the mythological Guermantes. Robert de Saint-Loup has the aquiline features of his aunt. He is a gold-crested bird, a sun god, swift in his walk, seemingly aloof and insensible. Marcel calls the iciness of Robert's manners the rites of exorcism. Once these rites are performed, the aloof god becomes a warm friend.

If the Guermantes are compared to birds, Swann, who bears the name of a bird, is never described as one. His nose is curved (*nez busqué*) but it is never called a bird's beak. His daughter Gilberte has her mother's nose, but Gilberte's daughter has the beak nose of her father, a Guermantes, possibly the same nose as her grandfather's. Proust's emphasis on archetypes is one of the major preoccupations in the novel. A character is best known through the analogies he bears with nature and myths. The exterior world exists for Proust, but it is unknowable in any direct way. He seems to believe that the inner life of man is knowable but it constantly escapes us because it is always in a state of flux. Only the world created by the artist has absolute stability.

The three trees of Hudimesnil, at Balbec, are partially explained by the myth of Daphne, the girl in mythology metamorphosed into a laurel tree. Albertine asleep is best described by the image of the sea. Oriane, duchesse de Guermantes, recapitulates what is known concerning her distant ancestor Geneviève de Brabant, and demonstrates in her birdlike traits characteristics of winged harpies and angels, of goddesses with claws and beaks. The new hotel of the prince de Guermantes in *Le Temps retrouvé* does not have the traditions Marcel would have associated with an ancient inherited palace dominated by a sorcerer or a fairy and whose door would open when a magic formula is pronounced. He thinks of this as he crosses Paris in order to attend the matinée Guermantes and he sees the streets he and Françoise used to walk along to the Champs-Elysées. The substance with which the past is formed is smooth, sweet and sad (*un passé glissant, triste et doux.* III, p. 858).

Some minutes later, in the new Guermantes palace where he has a series of magical revelations, he formulates a significant generality on the archetypal patterns of his experiences. It is a passage Proust added to the original manuscript. Each person who makes us suffer can be associated, he claims, with some divinity of whom he or she is a reflection. On considering this thought and this fragmentary reflection, we experience joy rather than the suffering we once felt. Quite obviously, Proust's definition of art is an "artifact" made mythological and endowed with the power to transform pain into joy. The people who make us suffer can therefore be used as ways by which we approach the idea of the divine, and even by which our life can be peopled with gods and goddesses.

Marcel's mother and grandmother are in reality the same figure of woman, intelligent, virtuous, loving. They form the maternal and understanding image of woman as man's helpmeet. The magic lantern the boy uses in Combray at the very beginning of the novel shows the terrifying pictures of the wicked Golo who had betrayed Geneviève de Brabant. This historical-mythical figure of the suffering mother is Oriane's ancestor. *La Légende Dorée* describes Geneviève de Brabant as pious, beautiful, and kind. When abandoned in the forest, she devotes her life to her son. Mélusine is another example of the suffering mother, and she also is used to designate Oriane, and explicitly so, since Mélusine and Oriane both terminate a cycle of time and bring to an end the history of a family.

The legend of Mélusine, developed in central France, especially in the province of Le Poitou, describes her as half woman and half fish. She builds castles and is able to fly. Most of these attributes are ascribed by Proust to Oriane, who is called at the end of the novel a sacred fish. When Raymond de Poitou, in the legend, married Mé-

lusine, whom he had discovered one day in the forest, she
builds for him the castle of Lusignan. She gives him children and great happiness in his conjugal life. But one night
he breaks his promise that he will not try to see her on
Saturday nights. He spies on her and sees that the lower
half of her body has been transformed into the tail of a
serpent or fish. When Mélusine realizes the betrayal, knowing that she has been seen by her husband, she flies out
the window and disappears forever.

In association with the mythical overtones in *A la
recherche du temps perdu,* there are traces of color symbolism which seem to adhere to the traditional mediaeval
symbolism of colors. In the cases of the two most mythical
characters, Oriane and Swann, and especially in their relationship with the protagonist Marcel, the use of color
designates a patent meaning.

Oriane's blue eyes, so often emphasized, would seem to
stand for more than a mere inherited Guermantes physical
trait. Blue is traditionally the color of the Virgin, of
woman, and the blue eyes of Oriane smiling on Marcel in
the Combray church and at the Opéra, inspire in him an
intense form of happiness. Blue is the color of the sky and
the sea, of the infinity of woman's love, and the bottomless
depth of the subconscious where the endless search for the
infinite is conducted. Oriane represents not only Marcel's
boyhood in its most idealistic form but her own ancestral
past as well. But Oriane combines the purity of woman's
beauty with the cruelty of sacrificial law. Both goddess
and devouring swan, after accepting the homage of her
best friend Charles Swann on the night when Swann announces his imminent death and she fails him as a friend,
she wears the color red, in her dress and shoes, the color of
blood sacrifice.

Christian symbolism in the Middle Ages traditionally
designated gold (yellow) as the color of the Father, red
for the Son, and green for the Holy Spirit. The red binding
of *François le Champi* is associated with the son Marcel

in the good night kiss scene of *Du Côté de chez Swann*. His mother's reading from that book calmed him after his long anguish. At the end of the novel, in *Le Temps retrouvé*, when, alone in the Guermantes' library, he takes down another red-bound volume of *François le Champi*, and can hear, as if resounding through the years, the bell announcing Swann's habitual visit to tante Léonie's house in Combray. Then, Swann was another father for the boy, a man who seemed to imprison his mother at the dinner party. As Marcel grows up, he acknowledges Swann's mystical paternity, and watches, in the episode of the "red slippers," Swann's symbolic death, the death of his "father," whom he will himself replace as Oriane's friend. The red binding of the volume of George Sand is allied to the myth of the suffering son, and the red slippers of the duchesse suggest the myth of the sacrificed father. The death of the old king means the birth of the new king. Marcel is Swann; Swann, Jupiter the highest god; and Marcel the new god, the creator.

Swann, as Marcel's mystical father is quite literally the medium introducing him to life and art for the protagonist. Marcel acknowledges (III, p. 915) that from Swann comes not only the subject matter of his book but the determination to write it. He instills in Marcel as a boy the desire to go to Balbec where Marcel meets three members of the Guermantes family: Mme de Villeparisis, Robert de Saint-Loup, and M. de Charlus. In Paris he meets Oriane, Swann's great friend, and later the princesse de Guermantes. And through Swann, he has known the last incarnation of the princesse, Mme Verdurin. Swann is the favorite of the duchesse, and Charlus the favorite of the princesse de Guermantes. On several occasions Charlus' voice reminds Marcel of Swann. Swann's Way leads to Guermantes' Way. Swann, a god for Marcel, fathered Gilberte, and thereby made his wife Odette, desired by so many men, a goddess. Gilberte and Robert de Saint-Loup beget a daughter, Mlle de Saint-Loup, in whom time is recaptured and the two Ways joined, when Marcel meets her in the final scene of the matinée.

There is not one universe for Marcel Proust, but hundreds, and their interrelationships can be expressed only in recurring symbols and fragments of myths. The nihilism in his novel is strong and relentlessly analyzed: there is no such thing as an absolute in the mystique of the family, or in the experience of love, or in the flux of social position. The law of transformation and change replaces the concept of an absolute. Odette is a glowing example. Her many names designate the phases of her life: the lady in pink, first, for oncle Adolphe; Miss Sacripant for the painter Elstir; Odette de Crécy in the Verdurin salon; Mme Swann; and finally, Mme de Forcheville. She is the courtesan who has known many men; the idol and goddess because Swann (Jupiter) marries her; and finally, when her daughter begets a daughter, she is the female force who serves in the fusing of the two ways, the two contradictory worlds of the protagonist, which end by becoming the same world.

Marcel loves or desires all of the leading female characters in the novel, and each one of them, in Proust's subtle, intricate, harmonious art, is significantly involved in one theme. Odette is most closely associated with the Bois de Boulogne (the carriage drives and the "smart" apartment, the life of the courtesan-goddess). Gilberte is inseparable from the hawthorns of Tansonville. Albertine appears always against the background of the sea at Balbec. The figures of Marcel's grandmother and mother rarely speak without some reference to the letters of Mme de Sévigné whose love for her child has been incorporated by them. The very episodic character of Mlle de Stermaria is always imagined by Marcel, when he thinks of her, as surrounded by northern fog. The strongest association with Oriane is the stained glass window of the church of Saint-Hilaire where Marcel first saw her seated in the chapel of Gilbert le Mauvais.

Every major scene in Proust is a recapitulation and summation as well as a slow moving ahead in time. Proust develops his themes and his scenes like a miser saving money: accumulating small details, counting and recounting old and new relationships. In the salon scene of *Le Côté de*

*Guermantes* and *Sodome et Gomorrhe,* he revealed the poisonous effect of calumny and the slow disintegration in the characters. In the final scene of *Le Temps retrouvé,* the transformation is startling and macabre. The salon is a cemetery. Most of those present have undergone such physical changes that they are identifiable only by their names. They are phantoms: and Marcel, without realizing it at first, has aged with them. He joins them, as he walks from group to group, remnants of the past. He is the key to the puzzle of the dramas and the stories which involve them all. And all the elements of life in the past return grotesque and out of focus. The ambitions and the hopes of the young now appear as disillusionment, bitterness, agony. He recovers an extraordinary richness of intonations and resonances, of echoes and sentences which bind him more closely than ever to the past. He recovers those major traits in his character which we have followed since his boyhood in Combray: the passionate attentiveness he lavishes on whatever is in his presence, his miraculous powers of observation. The artist now, he is about to begin the writing of his novel: he will not have to invent, but will discover in himself all the various tonalities of his poem: the shades of jealousy and the ecstatic cries.

Marcel's appearance at the matinée Guermantes, after his long absence from Paris, is not unlike Noah's emergence from the ark and his new vision of the world. But the freshness of the world Noah looked upon after his long claustration, does not resemble the labyrinthine world of Marcel's Paris where society drives toward self-annihilation. The poetry in Proust's writing is in his power to ennoble whatever is coarse, to see behind the vilest motives a yearning for the absolute. If time is the first sorcerer who transforms everything, the artist is the second, for in recording the transmutations of societies, coteries, and individuals, he shows man's obsession with the eternal and the absolute in the midst of a world seemingly without absolutes. In this sense, Proust becomes then the most significant heir of the Romantics for whom literature is an attempt to reach the absolute. In his descent through the various circles of hell, Marcel usurps many religious terms, (*hostie, présence réelle*) because his search for the past is both an obsession and a rite. In the dialogues he records and in the words he himself speaks in the novel, Marcel is forever attempting to explain the most inexplicable parts of a man's life: his silence, his solitude, the dark night of his soul.

In his seemingly excessive preoccupation with the world: the worldliness of social groups, time, love, snobbism, painting, music, the prestige of names, Proust never forgets the real subject of his novel: the literary vocation of his protagonist. This spiritual theme dominates all others and bears a relationship with all others. It is the framework of the novel and pervades the matinée scene at the end. Throughout the final pages, all the dramas announced and developed in the novel are transcended and fused into the one taking place in Marcel's mind. The struggle is that being waged by the aesthete in Marcel, the artist, the potential novelist, and the terrified human observer of the immense changes brought about by time. More discreet than other themes in the novel, but never absent for long from any of the volumes, the two themes—Marcel's literary vocation and his obsession with death—assume the greatest importance and form both symbolically and in fact the conclusion of *A la recherche du temps perdu*.

Each of these two major preoccupations: the artist facing the work to be accomplished, and the man tormented by the constant annihilation which time brings subsumes and transcends all the themes in the novel. Love, friendship, convictions, social life, politics, nationalism, the works and the lives of great artists: all of these represent a struggle—however vain—against time. Even great works of art, which are the most resistant to time, succumb momentarily to it. However, only the effort of the artist, at least for a period of time, perhaps for a long period, will triumph over time.

With this thought, the objective of Marcel becomes luminously clear. He will describe the universe as it is reflected and formed by one mind, his own. The novel will be Proust's picture, an almost Oriental picture of secret rooms and corridors and seraglios: Odette's apartment on the rue La Pérouse, Marcel's room in Paris where he calls at will for his prisoner Albertine, the large reception halls of the princesse de Guermantes and her gardens, (like Esther's gardens in the Bible), where the world performs its cruel rites of ostracism and calumny.

The tableau of change Marcel sees at the Guermantes matinée increases his pathological fear of death, the annihilation of objects and beings, the collapse of human happiness, and the fleeting appearance we make in the world. Time is monstrously evident on the changed features and diminished bodies of those present. The human soul—he has been led to this conviction over and over again—is a dark abyss peopled with monsters. The human mind is a gateway opened to all kinds of neuroses leading to madness. Marcel has felt the signs of this madness in himself, and now he realizes that this torment of thought, this obsession with the destructiveness of time and the passing of human happiness create perhaps the most tormented of men, closest to insanity, the great artists. But the creation of their work is their refuge in sanity.

If Marcel is able to bring to life the child he once was in Combray when his mother brought out the copy of *François le Champi* from the birthday package his grandmother prepared for him, he will indeed become the writer, the translator of the past. The true books are those written about the darkness and the silence of the past.

Life itself, as it is lived, fluctuates. But memory is stable. Marcel thinks of the time when Gilberte once appeared to him on the path bordered by a hawthorn hedge, when he had loved and desired her. But he knows now that there is a second Gilberte, born not from his desire but from his memory. In this one example of Gilberte (*cette seconde personne, celle née non du désir, mais du souvenir.* III, p. 990), we have the two themes of the conclusion: the fearful change that time brings to human experience, and the artist's capacity to defeat time in a work of art.

As Marcel continues to contemplate the spectacle of the

matinée, all the dramas he has known and observed, all
the patterns woven by life involving individuals and events
(and which resemble the *boeuf mode* which Françoise
used to prepare and which was so much appreciated by
M. de Norpois) fall into place under the idea of death.
Marcel now acknowledges that this idea of death has been
his constant companion throughout his life. But it has not
been his only companion. The nascent idea of the book he
has also kept in him for a long time, and he carries in him
the future book which alone will transcribe the poetry of
all that the passage of time makes incomprehensible.

# BIBLIOGRAPHY

## Proust's Works

*Les Plaisirs et les Jours.* Calmann-Lévy, 1896. Reprinted by Gallimard, 1924.

> *Pleasures and Days.* Translated by Louise Varèse, Gerard Hopkins, and Barbara Dupee. Edited and with an introduction by F. W. Dupee. Anchor Books, 1957.

*A la recherche du temps perdu.* La Pléiade, Gallimard, 1954. 3 volumes.

> *Remembrance of Things Past.* Translated by C. K. Scott-Moncrieff and Frederick A. Blossom. Random House, 1932. 2 volumes.

*Pastiches et mélanges.* Gallimard, 1919.

*Chroniques.* Gallimard, 1927.

*Jean Santeuil.* Gallimard, 1952. 3 volumes.

> *Jean Santeuil.* Translated by Gerard Hopkins. Simon & Schuster, 1956.

*Contre Sainte-Beuve.* Préface de Bernard de Fallois. Gallimard, 1954.

*The Maxims of Marcel Proust.* Translated by Justin O'Brien. Columbia University Press, 1948.

## Proust's Translations

Ruskin, John, *La Bible d'Amiens.* Mercure de France, 1926.
Ruskin, John, *Sésame et les Lys.* Mercure de France, no date.

# Proust's Correspondence

*Correspondance générale.* Plon, 1930–36. 6 volumes.

*Correspondance avec sa mère* (1887–1905). Plon, 1953.

*Correspondance de Marcel Proust avec Jacques Rivière.* Annotée par Philip Kolb. Plon, 1956.

*Correspondance avec Reynaldo Hahn.* Annotée par Philip Kolb. Gallimard, 1956.

> *Letters of Marcel Proust.* Translated by Mina Curtiss. Introduction by Harry Levin. Random House, 1949.

# Books on Proust

Abraham, Pierre, *Proust.* Rieder, 1930.

Ames, Van Meter, *Proust and Santayana.* Willett, Clark & Co., Chicago, 1937.

Autret, Jean, *L'Influence de Ruskin sur la vie, les idées et l'oeuvre de Marcel Proust.* Droz, Genève, 1955.

Beckett, Samuel, *Proust.* Chatto and Windus, London, 1931. Reprinted by Grove Press, New York, no date.

Bonnet, Henri, *Le Progrès Spirituel dans l'oeuvre de Marcel Proust.* 1. *Le Monde, l'Amour, et l'Amitié.* 2. *L'Eudémonisme esthétique de Proust.* Vrin, Paris, 1946 and 1949.

——, *Marcel Proust de 1907 à 1914.* Nizet, Paris, 1959.

Brée, Germaine, *Du Temps Perdu au Temps Retrouvé.* Belles Lettres, Paris, 1950.

> A stimulating, carefully organized study of the principal aspects of Proust's writing.

Cattaui, Georges, *Marcel Proust.* Julliard, Paris, 1952.

Cocking, John M., *Proust.* Yale University Press, 1956.

Coleman, Elliott, *The Golden Angel.* Coley Taylor, North Bennington, Vermont, 1954.

Dandieu, Arnaud, *Marcel Proust, sa révélation psychologique*. Firmin-Didot, Paris, 1930.

> One of the most convincing psychoanalytical studies on Proust.

Dreyfus, Robert, *Souvenirs sur Marcel Proust*. Grasset, Paris, 1926.

Fernandez, Ramon, *Proust*. Nouvelle Revue Critique, 1944.

> A high point in Proustian criticism.

Ferré, André, *Géographie de Marcel Proust*. Sagittaire, Paris, 1939.

Fiser, E., *Le Symbole Littéraire*. Corti, Paris, 1941.

> The fourth part of this volume is: "Le romancier du symbolisme: Marcel Proust."

Green, Frederick C., *The Mind of Proust*. Cambridge University Press, 1949.

> A study resolutely and heroically confined to the text of the novel.

Guichard, Léon, *Introduction à la lecture de Proust*. Nizet, Paris, 1956.

> A slightly revised edition of *Sept études sur Marcel Proust*, a book first published in Cairo in 1942.

Hindus, Milton, *The Proustian Vision*. Columbia University Press, 1954.

*Hommage à Marcel Proust*. Gallimard, Paris, 1927.

> A reprint of a special number of *La Nouvelle Revue Française* of January 1923, devoted to Proust. Three groups of essays: *Souvenirs, L'Oeuvre, Témoignages Etrangers.*

Kolb, Philip, *La Correspondance de Marcel Proust*. University of Illinois Press, 1949.

Larcher, P.-L., *Le Parfum de Combray*. Mercure de France, Paris, 1945.

> A brief pilgrimage to Illiers, written by the curator of tante Léonie's house.

Martin-Deslias, *Idéalisme de Marcel Proust*. Préface de André Maurois. Editions Nagel, Paris, 1952.

> A new edition of a book published in 1947, chez

Janny, in Montpellier. It was written during the war, on the islands of La Réunion and Madagascar. The author is a philosopher who relies exclusively on the text of Proust for his exposition of Proust's idealism.

Mauriac, François, *Du Côté de chez Proust*. La Table Ronde, Paris, 1947.

Maurois, André, *A la recherche de Marcel Proust*. Hachette, Paris, 1949.
This study, primarily a biography, is also an introduction to the writings of Proust.

———, *Le Monde de Marcel Proust*. Hachette, Paris, 1960.
Valuable for photographic documentation, the text is a reduction of Maurois' longer study, *A la recherche de Marcel Proust*.

Moss, Howard, *The Magic Lantern of Marcel Proust*. Macmillan, New York, 1962.

Mouton, Jean, *Le Style de Marcel Proust*. Corrêa, Paris, 1948.
A pioneer book in the linguistic study of Proust.

Nathan, Jacques, *La Morale de Proust*. Nizet, Paris, 1953.
A study of the relationship between the leading moral systems of Proust's time and the novel.

Painter, George D., *Proust. The Early Years*. Little, Brown & Co., Boston, 1959.
The first volume of what the author claims will be the definitive biography of Proust.

Pierre-Quint, Léon, *Marcel Proust: sa vie, son oeuvre*. Kra, 1928.
For many years, the basic book on Proust.

Piroué, Georges, *Proust et la musique du devenir*. Denoël, Paris, 1960.
A detailed study of music in the life and work of Proust.

Revel, Jean-François, *Sur Proust*. Julliard, Paris, 1960.

Shattuck, Roger, *Proust's Binoculars*. Random House, New York, 1963.

Strauss, Walter A., *Proust and Literature: The Novelist as Critic*. Harvard University Press, 1957.
> The best study of the literary influences on Proust.

*Univers de Proust*. Le Point, Souillac, Lot, 1959.
> Articles by Bernard de Fallois, André Ferré, Georges Cattaui and Robert Vigneron. Profusely illustrated.

Zéphir, Jacques, *La Personnalité Humaine dans l'oeuvre de Marcel Proust*. Lettres Modernes, Paris, 1959.

## Essays on Proust

Blanchot, Maurice, "L'Expérience de Proust," *Faux Pas*. Gallimard, Paris, 1943, pp. 57–62.

Butor, Michel, "Les 'Moments' de Marcel Proust," *Répertoire*. Editions de Minuit, Paris, 1960, pp. 163–72.

Chauffier, Louis-Martin, "Proust ou le double 'je' de quatre personnages," *Problèmes du Roman, Confluences*, (no date).
> A brilliant essay on the roles of Proust as protagonist, narrator, and author.

Du Bos, Charles, "Le Côté de Guermantes," *Approximations I*. Plon, Paris, 1922, pp. 58–116.

Galand, René, "Proust et Baudelaire." *PMLA*, December 1950.

Levin, Harry, "Proust, Gide, and the Sexes." *PMLA*, June 1950.

——, *The Gates of Horn: A Study of Five French Realists*. Oxford University Press, 1963.

O'Brien, Justin, "Albertine the Ambiguous." *PMLA*, December 1950.

Peyre, Henri M., *The Contemporary French Novel*. Oxford University Press, 1955, pp. 67–101.

Poulet, Georges, *Etudes sur le temps humain*. Edinburgh University Press, 1949, pp. 306–401.

Turnell, Martin, *The Novel in France*. Hamish Hamilton, London, 1950, pp. 317–406.

Vigneron, Robert, "Genèse de Swann." *Revue d'histoire de la philosophie.* 15 January 1937.

——, "Marcel Proust et Robert de Montesquiou." *Modern Philology.* November 1941.

——, "Marcel Proust ou l'angoisse créatrice." *Modern Philology.* May 1945.

# CHRONOLOGY

| | |
|---|---|
| 1871 | 10 July: Proust is born in Paris (Auteuil). |
| 1880 | First attack of asthma. |
| 1882–89 | Attends the lycée Condorcet in Paris. |
| 1889 | Military service in Orléans. |
| 1892 | First literary articles in *Le Banquet*. |
| 1896 | Publication of his first book *Les Plaisirs et les Jours*. |
| 1896–99 | Writes most of the unfinished novel *Jean Santeuil*. |
| 1899 | Discovers Ruskin whose work he starts to translate. |
| 1900 | Moves with family from 9, boulevard Malesherbes to 45, rue de Courcelles. |
| | Visits Venice. |
| 1903 | Death of his father. |
| 1904 | Publication of *La Bible d'Amiens*, his translation of Ruskin's study. |
| 1905 | Death of his mother. |
| 1906 | Moves to 102, boulevard Haussmann where he lives in a cork-lined room. |
| 1907 | Vacation in Cabourg. |
| | Meets Alfred Agostinelli. |

1908–09    Works on a critical study which will be pub-
           lished posthumously as *Contre Sainte-Beuve.*

1909       Begins work on *A la recherche du temps perdu.*

1913       Céleste Albaret becomes his housekeeper.

           8 November: publication of *Du Côté de chez
           Swann.*

1914       30 May: death of Agostinelli in airplane acci-
           dent.

1918       30 November: publication date of *A l'ombre
           des jeunes filles en fleurs.*

1919       June: moves to 8 bis, rue Laurent-Pichat.

           October: moves to 44, rue Hamelin.

           November: receives award of Goncourt prize for
           *A l'ombre des jeunes filles en fleurs.*

1920–21    Publication of *Le Côté de Guermantes.*

1922       April: publication of *Sodome et Gomorrhe.*

           18 November: death of Marcel Proust.

1923       Publication of *La Prisonnière.*

1925       Publication of *La Fugitive* (under title: *Alber-
           tine disparue*).

1927       Publication of *Le Temps retrouvé.*

1952       Publication of *Jean Santeuil.*

1954       Publication of *Contre Sainte-Beuve.*

# INDEX OF NAMES AND CHARACTERS